MASTERING M⚙BILE LEARNING

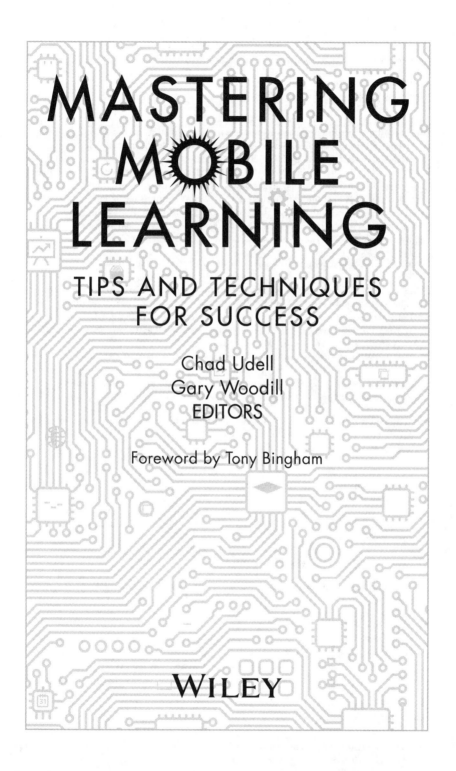

MASTERING MOBILE LEARNING

TIPS AND TECHNIQUES FOR SUCCESS

Chad Udell
Gary Woodill
EDITORS

Foreword by Tony Bingham

WILEY

For general information about our other products and services, please contact our
Customer Care Department within the United States at (800) 762-2974, outside the
United States at (317) 572-3993 or fax (317) 572-4002.

Wiley also publishes its books in a variety of electronic formats and by print-on-demand.
Some material included with standard print versions of this book may not be included in
e-books or in print-on-demand. If the version of this book that you purchased references
media such as a CD or DVD that was not included in your purchase, you may download
this material at http://booksupport.wiley.com. For more information about Wiley
products, visit www.wiley.com.

Library of Congress Cataloging-in-Publication Data

   Mastering mobile learning / editors, Chad Udell, Gary Woodill; foreword by
Tony Bingham.
       pages cm
   Includes index.
     ISBN 978-1-118-88491-1 (hardback); ISBN 978-1-118-88507-9 (pdf);
   ISBN 978-1-118-88502-4 (epub)
       1. Employees—Training of—Computer-assisted instruction.   2. Mobile communication
systems in education.   3. Information technology—Management.   I. Udell, Chad, 1976-
   II. Woodill, Gary.
HF5549.5.T7M357   2014
658.3'12402854678—dc23

                                                                            2014022658

Printed in the United States of America
HB Printing   10 9 8 7 6 5 4 3 2 1

CONTENTS

PART 2
STRATEGIC THINKING ABOUT MOBILE LEARNING 43

PART 3
THE VARIETIES OF MOBILE LEARNING EXPERIENCES 105

PART 4
DESIGN AND DEVELOPMENT PROCESSES FOR MOBILE LEARNING 185

PART 5
MANAGING AND DELIVERING MOBILE LEARNING PROJECTS 285

FOREWORD

Tony Bingham

If you've ever used your smart phone or mobile device to look something up, you've experienced mobile learning. Mobile devices are the consummate "just in time" learning tool, and they are remaking the learning profession.

I gave my first speech on mobile learning at the 2011 ASTD International Conference & Exposition. The topic of mobile learning was beginning to resonate in the training and development field as the proliferation of smart phones and the emergence of tablets caused all of us to realize the power these devices had for learning. ASTD has published three research reports on the topic since then, and a recurring theme in those reports is that organizations know mobile learning is an important component of a comprehensive learning strategy, but many either don't know where to start or don't believe they have the resources necessary to create and sustain a mobile learning strategy.

That is why I am so pleased that Chad Udell and Gary Woodill have collaborated to make this book, *Mastering Mobile Learning: Tips and Techniques for Success*, possible. In these pages, you will find great information not only on how to get started, but *why* to start—now.

Mobile learning isn't a fad. Smart phone sales continue to soar, and the reason is that people want their mobile phones for more than phone calls. A March 2013 report from IDC states:

> Driving volumes forward will be an increasing emphasis on smart phones, further penetration into emerging markets, and ongoing replacements on a worldwide basis. Looking ahead to 2017, IDC believes that total mobile phone shipments will reach 2,281.4 million units worldwide . . .

"The worldwide mobile phone market is poised for slow and certain growth, but the profile of the market is changing," says Ramon Llamas, research manager with IDC's Mobile Phones team. "Voice connectivity has always been the cornerstone of mobile telephony, but the proliferation of 3G and 4G takes the experience into data transmission and consumption. Consequently, we expect 3G mobile phones to make up a growing majority share of the overall market, while 4G mobile phones grow at a faster rate than the overall market."

In some countries, people have mobile phones, but not computers. Students in school today—the future workforce—use smart phones to access and share information every day. Mobile technology is transforming homework. A colleague recently told me that her high school student used Apple's Siri and YouTube videos accessed via his smart phone to complete a research paper. Do you think when he and his peers get into the workplace that they'll expect to have relevant learning content delivered to their mobile devices? Of course they will.

It is time for the learning profession to dive in, and Chad and Gary are pointing the way.

The book is laid out in five parts and provides the most comprehensive guidance on mobile learning adoption and implementation that I've seen. Chad and Gary have enlisted experts to help create this book, and you will benefit from their thoughtful contributions. From the honest assessment of what mobile learning is—and as importantly, what it is NOT (spoiler alert: it is *not* e-learning on a mobile device) in Part 1, to the last section, which provides an excellent assessment on one of the most-reported barriers of mobile learning adoption—how to keep up with the new developments in the space—Chad and Gary provide a roadmap that is useful for every learning professional.

One of my favorite sections is Part 2, "Strategic Thinking About Mobile Learning." Included are two chapters that both address the business case and the business drivers for mobile learning. Learning and development efforts achieve their best results when they are aligned with business goals and objectives. Understanding the business case for mobile learning—and being able to effectively advocate for its adoption—is a critical component in achieving more mlearning penetration in more organizations.

Mobile technology is changing the world and our experience of it. From an organizational perspective, mobile learning allows for a spectrum of possibilities that were not present before, and they continue to evolve. You, as learning professionals, impact organizations in ways other functional areas cannot, because you develop the talents of the people who do the work to achieve business goals. It makes sense that you should use the most effective tools and resources you can to do your best work. Mobile is one of those tools. Chad and Gary's book shows you how.

PREFACE

This book is a true collaborative effort on the part of many people at Float Mobile Learning. It is based on almost five years of blog posts, whitepapers, presentations, webinars, and newsletters from several members of the Float team, all on the topic of mobile learning. This aggregation of blog posts and other materials has been curated, merged, edited, extended, and updated to produce the chapters of this book. The book is for people wanting to learn more about the process of strategizing, designing, and implementing the emerging set of mobile learning technologies and the content and experiences that they make possible. The sequence of chapters in the book roughly follows a roadmap that we have developed for clients that outlines the entire process of implementing mobile learning, from initial stages of vision and planning, to choices about infrastructure, the design of content, and the management of the implementation of mobile learning systems.

One of the messages we want to relay is that, while mobile learning is doable, it is not simply a matter of using a mobile device to send training content to employees. It is more complicated than that, for many reasons. While it is new and still constantly changing, mobile learning is already happening and producing real benefits for those who have the vision and skills to carry it out. The material in this book is designed to make you better equipped to design and build mobile learning solutions in enterprise environments. After reading this book, we hope that you will appreciate the thought and planning that need to go into any mobile learning project and be able to master mobile learning yourself.

We want to thank many people for their contributions to this volume, starting with all the authors. As well, this project was only possible with the material support and encouragement of

Tom Marchal, president and CEO of Float Mobile Learning, and John Feser, COO of Float Mobile Learning. Thank you, Tom and John. Because of them, Float has a community of support in terms of colleagues who make our work better and easier every day.

At Wiley, Senior Editor Matthew Davis was the first person to appreciate the materials that the Float team had produced, and he ably facilitated the process that brought this book to fruition. Ryan Noll, senior editorial assistant, steered the book into production. Thank you to both of you, where Dawn Kilgore expertly moved it through the process. Thank you to all at Wiley involved with this project. And thanks to Matt Forcum for the amazing cartoons featured throughout the book.

Chad Udell would like to thank his wife, Renee Udell, for the care, love, and support she offers. Of course, he wants to thank his children, Sophia, Liam, and Carter, who never fail to entertain and amaze him. Chad also wants to thank his colleagues and friends at Bradley University, Jim Ferolo, and others, for their continued support and collaboration. Finally, Chad's parents, Bill and Jan, continue to give him inspiration and something to strive for. Thank you all so much.

Gary Woodill would like to thank his wife, Karen Anderson, for her loving support each day, and his colleagues at his consulting company, i5 Research—Sheilagh Marchand-Pegg, Matt Campbell, and Karen Balcomb—who have provided stellar backup over the past four years. A heartfelt thank you.

Gary and Chad would also like to thank Justin Brusino, community of practice manager, Learning Technologies, at ASTD, and Tony Bingham, ASTD's CEO, for their continued support for this project and for advancing mobile learning in the marketplace and raising awareness of its benefits to the diverse ASTD communities and members.

On behalf of Float, Chad and Gary would like to thank any and all of you who have continued to read our content, hear our message, and connect with us in the community. We know we have some of the very best clients in the world, and because of you, we've been lucky enough to amass this experience and expertise. Thank you very much.

INTRODUCTION

Chad Udell and Gary Woodill

The adoption of each new technology goes through a set of predictable stages. At first, the technology is just an idea percolating in the imaginations of a few visionaries, who see the possibilities, but are not in a position to deliver the technology. Then, one or two inventive individuals or companies builds an initial piece of equipment that incorporates some of these ideas, but is usually a much cruder version of the technology that comes later. As time goes on, more and more people develop expertise in the new technology and start to expand on it and share it.

Mobile learning has followed this pattern. From its first beginnings in the early 1990s, mobile learning has grown from a few experimental sites to a wave of new users in educational and training settings, with a growing body of knowledge on how to use this new learning technology in the most optimal way. The authors and editors of this book have developed a rich knowledge base about mobile learning from working with clients and the learning and development (L&D) industry over the past five years. We now want to share what we have learned with others in the industry, in order to help grow this new and exciting field.

The state of the mobile learning industry is rapidly changing around the world. The American Society for Training and Development's (ASTD) *2013 State of the Industry Report* confirmed that, as of 2012, mobile learning contributed only about 1.5 percent to the formal training hours offered by organizations, but that figure is misleading, as the report explains:

> The 2013 ASTD/i4cp study, *Going Mobile: Creating Practices That Transform Learning*, found one of the major challenges of implementing mobile learning is measuring its use and effectiveness. Forty-one percent of respondents in that study who use mobile learning admit that their organizations do not have metrics in place to assess the program's effectiveness. Over half of survey respondents say their organizations use mobile learning for just-in-time learning (65 percent), job aids (63 percent), and on-the-job support (52 percent). How much time an employee spends in an app, accessing this valuable information, may prove to be elusive as organizations are challenged to measure it.

This quote reinforces our strong view that mobile learning is mostly not about formal training. We also learn by looking things up when we need an answer, watching videos on our own time, and by chatting with others. All of these activities, and more, are available through the use of mobile devices. The problem is that these activities are often not thought of as learning, because they are not part of a formal curriculum developed by a training department. But, by using these activities, employees are still learning, often gaining knowledge that they can use immediately, retain, or come back to later.

The purpose of this book is to shift the thinking of learning leaders, instructional designers, and educational app developers working in large organizations to see learning differently when it comes to mobile. We want to show that appropriate and relevant learning can happen anywhere, any time, and any place, if you are equipped with a mobile device such as a smart phone or tablet computer. Beyond that, we want to help readers see the development of large-scale mobile learning as doable, using tips and techniques that we have learned and developed over the past few years.

We have organized the book as a means to success with mobile learning. It follows the same path as the roadmap that we use with our clients, and follows a broad sequence of five areas that you need to master if you are going to develop and deploy effective mobile learning in your organization.

The book is a compilation of the experiences of a group of authors, all associated with Float Mobile Learning, a learning technology company headquartered in Morton, Illinois, USA. Most of the essays in this book were originally written as blog posts over a four-year period, and are based on a wealth of actual experiences assisting clients to develop mobile learning in their own organizations.

The book is divided into five parts, each corresponding with a major phase of the development and delivery of mobile learning.

We think that it is important to understand mobile learning in some depth before launching into a specific project. As our colleague, John Feser, Float's COO, argues in Part 1, mobile learning, in his (and our) view, is not an extension of e-learning, but a set of disruptive shifts in how learning and development will be carried out in the near future. Executives must care about mobile learning, because the shifts identified by John will definitely impact the bottom line of companies. There are at least seven shifts in how learning will be carried out in enterprises, as outlined in Chapter 2 by Gary Woodill, Float's senior analyst.

So where to start? At Float we believe strongly that you need to start with a mobile learning strategy, says Scott McCormick, Float's director of client relations, in Part 2. That takes into account what Chad Udell, Float's managing director, calls the six Ps (Platforms, Policies, Procurement, Provisioning, Publishing, and Procedures). Scott, Chad, Gary, and John then present a group of chapters with details on different aspects of developing a mobile learning strategy.

In Part 3, the same group of authors writes about the varieties of activities and experiences that can fall under the category of mobile learning. Gary introduces the important concept of "affordances" to describe the different capabilities of mobile computing technologies and how these capabilities can be applied to carry out a specific training mission. It is important to understand the instructional design choices with mobile learning, before setting out to create mobile learning activities and experiences.

Part 4 is on the design and development possibilities of mobile learning, based on all we have learned over the past five years in this field. Because many companies want to start by converting existing print and electronic learning materials, Chad discusses the impact of ubiquity and mobility in designing for mobile learning and lists a number of considerations in designing mobile learning from existing content. A number of formats are available for developing mobile materials, as Heather Ford, Float's senior designer, indicates in her chapter on digital publications, and Daniel Pfeiffer, a programmer at Float, tells us about designing for multiple screen formats. In this section, Gary also talks about design for both assessments and social media, while Jim Ferolo, Float's director of user experience, writes about general mobile learning design principles, as well as the specific experience of designing a geolocation-based app. Part 4 also includes chapters on solving technical issues in mobile learning.

Then, in Part 5, Adam Bockler, social media and marketing manager at Float, looks at how mobile learning can be integrated with social media. Chad deals with the important issue of security in a mobile world in this section of the book, while Jim argues that training in mobile development is critical for success in the implementation of mobile learning. The book ends with Gary's thoughts on managing a large-scale mobile learning project, as well as a chapter on keeping up with new developments in this field.

This is not an academic book with lots of references and footnotes, or discussions of theory or esoteric concepts. Rather, it is intended as a practical primer of useful thinking and experience with developing mobile learning in the real world. If you read the book using the sequence of sections that we have provided, you will get a sense of the development process for producing a large-scale mobile learning system from beginning to end. However, you may also wish to hone in on a specific topic that interests you today, using the Contents and the Index to find what you are looking for. We hope you enjoy the book and find it useful.

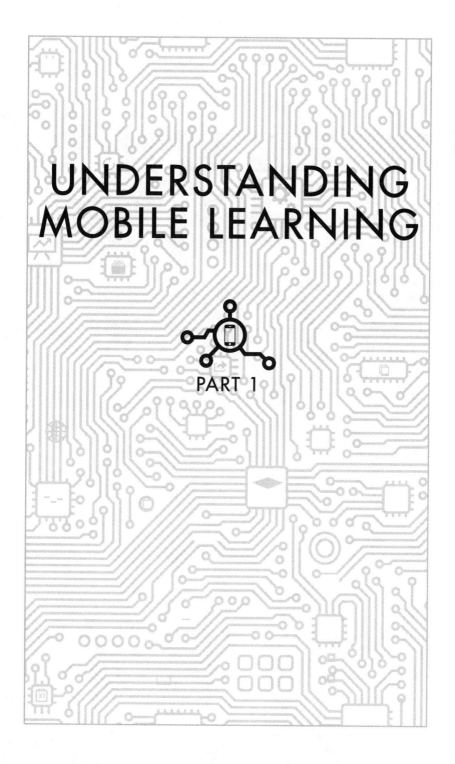

UNDERSTANDING
MOBILE LEARNING

PART 1

CHAPTER 1

Enterprise Mobile Learning
A Primer

Gary Woodill and Chad Udell

Although people have been learning while mobile for millennia, what we mean by "mobile learning" is the ability to move from place to place while using mobile devices to receive from and contribute to a variety of digital information sources. While a large variety of lightweight devices can be used in mobile learning, the important part of this definition is that *the learner is mobile* and not confined to a specific location.

As a society, we've become much more mobile, both as individuals and as groups, than people who lived only a few decades ago. We are nomads, often on the move, but remaining connected to our friends, families, workplaces, and information sources. For many people, such as sales staff, field services workers, consultants, transportation personnel, and high-level executives, being mobile is a major component of their work environments. For many other people as well, commuting to work is part of life and takes up a significant part of the day.

But, as we move about, most of us are equipped, often from our early teens now, with one or more mobile devices connected to a range of information and communication services. The ability to move about while remaining connected is the essence of mobile learning. This change has an impact on both the place and the timing for learning. It empowers learning outside of fixed places specifically designed for learning, such as classrooms and labs, and makes information for learning available any time it is needed. Full-scale adoption of mobile learning will have a profound impact on the structure of enterprise learning and development departments in ways that we are just beginning to understand.

Business Drivers of Mobile Learning

These are early days in the adoption of mobile learning within large enterprises. Some of the business drivers that are moving mobile learning forward in such organizations include:

- *The need for speedier training is evident.* Because we live in a time of rapid technological change, there is often a need for more frequent training as new procedures, strategies, and technologies are adopted by companies.
- *Time available for training has been reduced.* At the same time, hyper-competition and the demand for multitasking by workers has meant that there is less time available for training. Training often has to be done "on-the-fly" or outside work environments. Mobile learning offers one solution to this problem.
- *Mobile learning reinforces a major goal of enterprise learning and development departments.* Enterprise learning is a bit of a misnomer. In reality, most enterprise training is actually meant to increase performance and has very little to do with what is traditionally thought of as acquiring new knowledge. Gaining knowledge and long-term retention of information is often a side-effect of corporate training; but make no mistake, if companies could forego training employees and still maintain or increase performance, they would. Mobile allows resources in the learning and development departments to be spent on efforts to increase performance by having information available when needed, rather retaining knowledge for a long time.
- *The infrastructure for mobile learning is already in place.* The widespread deployment of mobile computing means that the infrastructure for mobile learning is usually in place, and

most workers already carry a mobile device with them most of the time. While some companies want to issue standard, "company liable" smart phones or tablets to their employees, many organizations are taking advantage of the existing situation by using a "bring your own device" (BYOD) strategy.

- *Many workers are already mobile.* For many jobs, the workforce is already "on the road," meaning that it is often expensive to bring them into a central location for training. Still other workers don't go into the workplace every day, but work from home or from other locations. Some are commuters who may be able to work while using public transportation to reach their physical workplaces. Finally, within a large building or campus, employees may move around a specific area as part of their jobs. All this means that, for many workers, mobile learning already fits with their lifestyle and work habits.

- *With globalization, mobile devices may be the best way to reach all employees.* Global sourcing and global labor mean that employees or customers who need training may be anywhere in the world. For some, a mobile smart phone or tablet may be the only computing device available.

In addition to presenting training materials, mobile learning can be used for performance support, research, and learning management. Mobile learning, when properly designed, can be described as "just in time, just enough, and just for me." The capabilities of mobile learning extend well beyond the methodologies of traditional training and allow greater efficiency and effectiveness of the training and development function within an organization.

The Mobile Learning Ecosystem

Many components go into a successful mobile learning experience. Together, they can be seen as a "mobile learning ecosystem." Components include a large variety of mobile devices with many features and capabilities, several types of content, a handful of different operating systems or platforms, a network of mobile communications providers with different standards, offerings, and price structures, a developing suite of tools for content creation, and a set of new concepts and uses for mobile learning that we are just beginning to understand.

Mobile devices come in many shapes and sizes and have many ways of connecting to and distributing information. Input devices include microphones, cameras, keypads, small keyboards, clickable scroll wheels, mini joysticks, touch pads, touch screens, voice, Wi-Fi, Bluetooth, RFID, Near Field Communications, infrared, accelerometers, sensors, magnetic field detectors, and styluses. Output methods include text, sound, video, images, digital signals, LED lights, and various forms of 2D and 3D projection onto surfaces or directly into the eyeball. Work is underway on devices that stimulate the senses of smell and taste using a mobile device.

Mobile Learning Applications

Learning designers and developers have many choices for how to facilitate learning using mobile technologies. The specific techniques that you choose to implement in your mobile learning design will depend on your learning theories, your experience at training or teaching, and the characteristics and needs of the learners you are trying to train. Mobile learning applications can be broken into five broad categories.

Content Transmission and Retrieval

Learning materials relevant to an employee can either be created by the training and development department and "pushed" to the learner, or can be retrieved by a user at "the point of need." Because of the nature of mobile learning, it is best if learning materials are in the form of small "nuggets" of information, rather than large-scale productions or courses. For most workers, mobile learning is something that is usually done in small amounts, but several times during the day. Notifications can be used to alert employees to a required or important piece of information they need to consult.

Capturing Data

In contrast to e-learning, mobile phones and tablets are bidirectional, allowing users to employ them as data-gathering and storage devices as they move about. An inquiry-based pedagogy makes sense for mobile learning and turns a mobile device into a research tool (see Chapter 24). First-person documentation activities can include maintenance of a learning portfolio, monitoring and trend tracking of local phenomena, and the creation of user-generated content.

Communicating and Interacting with Others

Because mobile devices can be networked, they are great for communicating, coordinating actions, and collaborating with others. Networking allows for texting, social media, voice communications, group games, simulations, experiences in virtual worlds, and real-time mentoring, as well.

Computing Algorithms

Mobile devices such as smart phones and tablets can also be thought of as computers in their own right. Many of these are more powerful than many desktop computers just five or ten years ago and, because of that, they can be programmed to do almost anything. This has spawned a mobile app industry that has exploded, with over two million separate pieces of software available in various app stores on the Internet. Thousands of apps now available can be used for mobile learning.

Contextual Inquiry

Not only can mobile devices retrieve information from databases, but they can also be used to interact with "smart" objects and/ or other mobile technology–connecting people in a person's immediate environment. Additionally, the ability of many devices to detect a user's location and orientation allows for new kinds of informational experiences, such as augmented reality and geofencing.

In addition to these five categories of mobile learning experiences, mobile applications can also be used to manage learning activities in the classroom or in the field. Live information on emergencies and instructions on what to do in those situations can be conveyed to a group of dispersed users very quickly. And mobile extensions of more traditional learning management systems allow the tracking of mobile learning by existing learning and development software.

Designing and Creating Mobile Learning Content

At the present time, no rapid authoring tools will easily allow a non-technical person to produce all of the above types of applications. At this early stage of the development of the field of mobile computing, it is usually necessary to use a combination of a designer and a software developer to produce a desired application or to use applications that have been built by others. Once you move beyond creating simple read-only content, you are entering a realm more akin to traditional software design and development than to e-learning or other instructional design and development paths.

There is a recommended process (see below) by which mobile learning content can be built. We start with understanding the

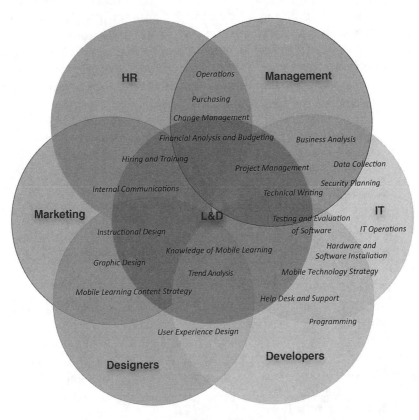

Sample Process

business needs behind the desire to have mobile applications and content produced. Mobile learning creation involves several different design and development skill sets—producing a strategic business analysis of the need for mobile learning, understanding mobile content strategy, managing a sound mobile learning design and development process, leading a solid technology and programming team, and project managing both the development and implementation of an outstanding mobile learning system. Unless you have such a team with these skills sets in-house, you will most likely need to outsource the development of mobile learning to a competent vendor with these skills.

CHAPTER 2

The Seven Shifts
in Enterprise Learning

Gary Woodill

Mobile learning has been involved in at least seven different shifts in enterprise learning in the past decade. While mobile computing is not the only factor causing these shifts, it is implicated in each one. Other factors include improvements and lower costs of computer technologies, the spread of computer networking, the rise of social media, the globalization of innovation, and the information explosion.

1. A Shift in the Location of Learning

Although the 1980s saw a marked increase in the use of classrooms in training and development, especially through the establishment of "corporate universities," this trend has now reversed with the advent of mobile learning. While lots of classroom training still takes place, increasingly the use of smart phones and tablets to look up information "at the point of need" is taking over from classroom instruction. This is particularly true for employees who are already "on the road," such as traveling sales staff, field services workers, and those in various transportation industries.

2. A Shift in Time

The development over the past fifty years of information and communications technologies (ICT) has moved the production and consumption of learning materials from books and binders to a variety of online screens available from anywhere, at any time. Smart phones and tablets have accelerated this trend, as more and more materials are available in electronic formats on a user's mobile device, greatly increasing the speed of access. Instead of waiting for knowledge to be published in print form, which can take up to several months to go through the processes of writing, editing, refereeing, and printing, learning materials can now be written and produced rapidly and sent out to the world within hours. In addition, the adoption of newer, more powerful and faster mobile devices has also accelerated. With the collection of "big data" and continuous monitoring by sensors and user input, new knowledge now can be produced in "real time," while events are happening. As analytics and reporting matures in this space, we can expect that predictive analytics will allow us to respond immediately to learner needs for specific feedback and suggestions for what to do next.

3. A Shift in Context

When learning in a classroom or from e-learning programs on a desktop, users are generally not "in context." That is, they are not immersed in the environment or circumstances about which they are learning. With mobile learning, learners can be in the same context/environment about which they are learning or have questions. Because of this, mobile learning tends to be more relevant and motivating than those forms of training and development that take you out of context. Mobile learning particularly lends itself to inquiry-based learning, because it is able to answer users' questions immediately while they are exploring a particular context. Context, time, location, and learner needs play a much bigger role for mobile learning than they did for previous e-learning applications.

4. A Shift in the Amount of Information

There has been a huge explosion of data created, captured, and stored in the world in the past ten years. "Between the dawn of civilization through 2003, there was just five exabytes (or 500 million gigabytes) of information created," Google CEO Eric Schmidt told an audience in 2010. "That much information is now created in two days, and the pace is increasing. People aren't ready for the technology revolution that is going to happen to them," he added (quoted in Kirkpatrick, 2010). While some critics have disputed the exact amounts of information created up to 2003 and since, there is no doubt that we are in the midst of a massive explosion of data, driven by the ease at which we can collect, replicate, and store it. Continuing on, Schmidt described the search engine's role as becoming more of a "Serendipity Engine," providing information to a user before it is even queried. Google Now is a first salvo in this sort of scenario. Personal agents like Siri on iOS devices are another approach to the problem of having too much information available for any one person to know.

This vast collection of data is now available to specially designed software that allows for "machine learning," whereby computers turn large data sets into useful information and predictions, available at a moment's notice. Increasingly, mobile devices such as smart phones and tablets, are the windows into this new world and are being used in educational settings for "adaptive instruction." The "semantic web" and the inclusion of contextual data for understanding information on a variety of networks is a rich area of research and development. The increasing ability for computers to parse and assign meaning to our written language will open many doors in this challenging area.

5. A Shift in the Location of Information

The digital revolution has shifted the location of information from printed materials and analog recordings to a variety of digital formats. Early computers (including the first personal computers in the 1970s) stored information on tape, then on local hard drives and servers. With the development of global networking, storage of information has now been transformed into "the cloud," a metaphor for the vast "server farms" owned by large companies like Google, Microsoft, Rackspace, Apple, and Amazon, among others. This has the benefit of reducing costs for information storage to nearly zero, and for making information available anywhere, any time. Information that used to be stored locally on a company server is now administered and mined by large corporations and the government. This has implications for privacy, security, and surveillance that we only now are beginning to understand.

6. A Shift in Learning Experiences

As discussed in Chapter 15, the many unique "affordances" (Gibson, 1977) of mobile devices has resulted in the possibility of new kinds of learning experiences. Geolocation capabilities, internal sensors, text messaging, social networking, and miniaturization of mobile computing have all resulted in new possibilities for mobile instructional design and performance support. Learning games using geospatial data, gesture recognition in simulations, supportive messages to people needing help, and collaborative learning opportunities are all real examples of how new affordances are already being used in mobile learning activities. As new affordances of mobile computing are identified and/or combined, other creative experiences will be developed for mobile learning.

7. A Shift in Control

The digital revolution, including developments in mobile computing, has resulted in a new set of powerful tools that can be used in new ways for enterprise learning. One issue that has not been settled is who is going to control the development and use of these new technologies. Is it going to be individuals, who then take control of their own learning? Is it going to be community control, whereby networks of collaborators are able to work together to accomplish their goals? Is it going to be educational institutions, which still retain the power to issue credentials for most professions? Or is it going to be corporations and/or governments, who are now collecting vast amounts of data on each of us, who will be able to analyze this data and turn it into information to influence their employees, other individuals, and communities? The answer to this question has not been determined yet, and the result may, in fact, be a balancing act of shared control among all four groups.

Although they may have had different starting points, the seven shifts in learning discussed above have all converged and are now evolving together. This has resulted in a complex situation for those in the learning and development industry, who must learn new skills and how to overcome new challenges brought on by these shifts.

References

Gibson, J.J. (1977). The theory of affordances. In R. Shaw & J. Bransford (Eds.), *Perceiving, acting, and knowing: Toward an ecological psychology*. Mahwah, NJ: Lawrence Erlbaum Associates.

Kirkpatrick, M. (2010, August 4). Google CEO Schmidt: "People aren't ready for the technology revolution." *ReadWrite*, http://readwrite .com/2010/08/04/google_ceo_schmidt_people_arent_ready_ for_the_tech

CHAPTER 3

The Disruptive Nature
of Mobile Learning

John Feser

When we think of something or someone as being "disruptive," our first reaction may be to paint a negative picture. It could be a child acting inappropriately in a public space or a winter storm that ices roads and forces an evening of cancellations. It could even be something as simple as a telephone ringing that interrupts our train of thought. Regardless of the image that comes to mind, disruptions tend to be things we want to minimize in our lives.

In technology circles, the term "disruptive" often has the opposite connotation when put into practice. Think about some disruptive technologies that have come about in the last several decades: the microprocessor, the microwave oven, cable television, the Internet. The introduction of these technologies all spawned entire industries around them and upset the traditional industries they displaced.

Disruptive is a term commonly used to describe mobile learning. Why is mobile learning considered disruptive? Is this type of disruption a good thing? Answering these questions requires, first, understanding what the term disruptive means in the context of mobile learning. Next is to determine how mobile learning fits into this definition, and, finally, we must investigate the implications for businesses and others looking to implement mobile learning. Once these three areas have been reviewed sufficiently, it is then possible to decide whether, and then how, mobile learning fits into an organization.

What Is Meant by Disruptive?

The World English Dictionary defines the word "disrupt" as "(v) to throw into turmoil or disorder." While there could be some of this with mobile learning, this definition does not truly capture why mobile learning is called disruptive.

In 1997, Clayton Christensen published a well-known and popular book, *The Innovator's Dilemma: When New Technologies Cause Great Firms to Fail*. In his book, Christensen coined the term disruptive technology, which he describes as:

> First, disruptive products are simpler and cheaper; they generally promise lower margins, not greater profits. Second, disruptive technologies typically are first commercialized in emerging or insignificant markets. And third, leading firms' most profitable customers generally don't want, and indeed initially can't use, products based on disruptive technologies.

Here again is a definition that doesn't really seem to fit. Mobile learning may be less expensive in many instances, but the underlying technology certainly is not simple nor is it simpler than current learning technologies. Furthermore, mobile learning has significant implications for large and mature markets, just as it does for emerging and insignificant markets.

James Burke, who wrote and hosted the PBS series *Connections*, explains disruptions occurring from coincidental inventions, changes in regulations and society, exploding demand for new products, as well as growth in complementary technologies created through strange connections. Burke's description seems to fit mobile learning better, but it is a combination of these three that may be the most appropriate way to explain disruption in the context of mobile learning. A more accurate description would be that:

> A disruption is an interruption to the normal flow of an activity, thought, or ideal so significant that it requires a deliberate response to the interruption.

Of course, one response to a disruption is to ignore it altogether, such a cell phone going off in a meeting, but that decision is always conscious and deliberate. This definition is very broad, very deep, and very pervasive, but it easily fits a number of technologies and events that have been commonly referred to as disruptive.

The rapid adoption of DVD technology in the early 2000s forced consumers to decide not only which device they would need to purchase for watching movies at home, but also which format they would invest in for the media itself. Then along comes streaming video like Netflix, and the disruption and upheaval in the market begins again.

With all of this in mind, mobile learning is disruptive in the sense that it significantly interrupts our approaches, ideas, and thoughts on how best to develop and deliver learning content.

How Is Mobile Learning Disruptive?

Mobile learning interrupts the normal flow of our activities, thoughts, and ideas in a number of ways, and each of these contributes to mobile learning being disruptive.

Mobile devices are ubiquitous. The evidence is clear: mobile technology is becoming more and more pervasive in people's daily lives. For many individuals, their cell phone is the first thing they look at in the morning and the last thing they check before going to bed. How often do we sit in a meeting and see people checking their email, sending a text message, or looking up additional information related to the presentation or discussion at hand? The fact is, every day humans are becoming more and more dependent on mobile devices, to the point that they don't even realize just how much they use them to learn. Take, for instance, turn-by-turn navigation, whether it is using a dedicated device such as a Garmin or TomTom GPS receiver, or if it is the navigation system built directly into an Android device. When a destination is programmed in, there is an expectation that the device will show how to get to the location directly, quickly, and accurately. Whether it is a friend's new home or somewhere we never plan to go again, there is still learning occurring in the sense of learning how to reach the destination, including any alternate routes that may be available. The point is, regardless of how much people realize it or how deliberate they are in their use, mobile devices are playing a big role in helping individuals learn and discover new things every day.

Mobile learning is challenging traditional views of teaching. For hundreds of years, teaching has focused on the concept of "learn now, use later" or "learn now, just in case you might need it later." These ideas, which have driven the design of many learning theories, have a strong emphasis on memorization and retention. For instance, many would agree on the importance of learning CPR, but unless you work in the medical field, this knowledge is something we likely will never have to use.

Mobile devices, however, support the notion of "need now, learn now." Many of today's automatic external defibrillators (AEDs), which are becoming more prevalent, especially in places like public buildings and larger companies, have voice synthesis built in that will actually walk you through the process of using the device and giving CPR. This is not to suggest that CPR training is no longer necessary, but now the in-class instruction can focus more on proper technique and less on memorizing the exact cadence and timing of the breaths and compressions. In this way mobile computing is helping to shift teaching from face-to-face instruction to "performance support."

Mobile devices are enabling more self-directed learning. Most learning theory is based on the concept of an instructor teaching a student. The instructor determines the learning objectives, the curriculum, and the pedagogy to be used. The student is then the recipient of this information in the form of instruction. The instruction can happen in a classroom or on a computer in the form of e-learning. It doesn't matter; someone other than the learner predetermines the learning content.

With mobile learning, instruction can be very personal and individual. Imagine two people in downtown Chicago standing in front of the Willis Tower (formerly the Sears Tower). One may be very interested in the history and physical aspects of the skyscraper, when it was built, how tall it is, why the name was changed, and so forth. The other person may be interested in knowing how the building has been used, what corporations have had offices there, the cost to lease space, and the historical occupancy rate. By looking for the information they want on a mobile device, both individuals are learning what matters and is most relevant to them. Their learning is not being dictated by what someone else thinks is important.

Mobile devices are changing how and when information is accessed. Let's say a parent is waiting to pick up her child from school. She hears a song on the radio and is really interested in the performing artist. Fifteen years ago, aside from hoping the DJ says the name of the song and the artist or waiting until she is home to call the radio station, this person may be out of luck. Today, with the Shazam app loaded on a smart phone, not only are the name and artist of the song available, but it is possible to instantly purchase the song or album, find tour information for the artist, read reviews, and find a whole host of additional information right from the app.

Carry this technology a little further and imagine someone heading to a business meeting two hours away. He suddenly hears a noise coming from the engine compartment of the car and is not sure whether it is serious enough to warrant stopping and having it looked at or whether to keep going in order to make it to the meeting on time. As of early 2013, people can keep tabs on their cars with a remote monitoring device from Verizon. It's only a matter of time or innovation before the Shazam for engine noises exists.

There is no question that mobile technology is taking the world by storm. For the past few years, mobile phones have held the distinction of being the most prolific electronic technology humans have ever adopted. With more than six billion mobile subscribers worldwide, smart phones continue to sell at an ever-increasing rate, resulting in a global society that is becoming more and more connected in many different ways. One of the most significant implications of this surge in connectedness is in how people access information and how they learn.

The Impact on Organizations

How should organizations and their HR and training departments react to the disruption caused by mobile learning? The high-level answer to this question is straightforward: keep an open mind and get smart. Mobile learning represents significant differences from the approaches used in traditional learning. These traditional approaches have been in place for many years and are an ingrained part of how training developers think and work. Helping organizations see the potential in mobile requires a change in how people view learning and a fundamental shift from the idea that the instructor is in control to one where the learner is in control. Unless training managers and developers understand this critical point and are willing to give up control, the power of mobile learning will never be fully realized.

Where should those interested in embracing mlearning spend their energies and resources? The answer lies in moving beyond your comfort zone and thinking differently. The pace of change today is not just filling people's pockets, offices, and living rooms with new gadgets, tools, and toys, but changing how people think, learn, and interact. Understanding and embracing these sociological and behavioral changes is every bit as important as the rapid improvements in technology. As companies look at how to incorporate mobile learning into their learning and development needs, the following ideas should be in the forefront of their thinking.

Significant Opportunities for Mobile Exist, But They Are Not Always Immediately Obvious

Organizations considering mobile learning must come to grips with the idea that mobile learning represents opportunities for learning and performance enhancement that previously did not exist. However, identifying these opportunities is not as straightforward as one might think. While there are always a number of situations for which benefits can be easily found, these are often too generic to be practical or too specific to apply to another organization's needs. The reality is that successfully taking advantage of a disruptive technology like mobile learning is an iterative process requiring both an understanding of the technology and, at the same time, being in tune with the business needs of the organization. By focusing solely on the technology, companies risk a situation in which they have a "solution looking for a problem." On the other hand, ignoring the technology until "someone else figures it out" is not the best option either. The most effective answer is recognizing that the best opportunities will not present themselves all at once, but will materialize over time as an organization's experience with mlearning grows.

As an example, digital video recorders (DVRs) represented a disruptive technology to the hugely popular videocassette recorder (VCR). When DVRs first appeared on the market, a number of features and benefits gave them an advantage over VCRs, but they were largely seen as an upgraded technology to what already existed. Then along came TiVo, a company that was creative and identified numerous opportunities for providing benefits to its customers. Features such as the ability to recommend shows similar to those a user normally records, the ability to request a program be recorded remotely from the Internet, the ability to transfer recorded shows to a mobile device, and the ability to automatically extend the recording time of live television shows are all examples of ideas resulting from this disruptive technology, but they did not all come at the same time.

HR and Training Departments Must Change How They View and Create Learning

Mobile devices are changing traditional views of learning from a directed experience defined by the person creating the training, to a self-directed experience where the learner is in control. This idea will have a profound impact on the role of HR and training departments in most organizations. In the past, these departments have had to focus on the content that had to be learned: curricula, courses, job aids, and so forth. With mobile learning, the focus is not just simply on what has to be learned. Now, consideration must be given to factors such as when the information will be most useful, how to provide easy access to information, and presenting content in a way that matches the context of the situation in which learning is needed. Essentially, trainers must move from the idea of telling people what they need to know to helping them learn what they want to know.

A related impact is the working relationship between learning developers and those departments that will benefit from the learning. Much of mobile learning is about delivering information at the moment of need, in the context of the situation, and in bite-size chunks. As a result, training developers will be forced to work more closely and collaboratively with those groups who are requesting that learning materials be developed. In many ways, traditional forms of training, where information is pushed to the learner, are much simpler to develop because there are only two key variables: the audience and the content. With mobile learning, these two variables still exist, but now there is a third variable: context. Adding this third variable requires a much more thorough understanding of the situation in order for effective learning to take place. As a result, a much tighter working relationship between learning development and other parts of the organization must be developed.

Organizations Must Recognize the New Efficiencies and Limitations Associated with Accessing and Sharing Information

Vast improvements and changes in how people communicate with each other are having a profound impact on how learning happens. Those responsible for delivering training must find ways to leverage these improvements. Traditionally, learning content has been static; once delivered it would not change. Content developers could fix on a format, a delivery method, and, to a certain extent, on the environment and be assured that anyone accessing that content would receive it in the way in which it was designed. With mobile technology and many more ways to access information, learning content providers must plan for myriad ways that information can be accessed and passed along.

An obvious example is the various screen sizes and technologies associated with mobile devices. For instance, most PDF documents look great on an iPad, are very difficult to read on a mobile phone, and only show up in monochrome on a Kindle. The de facto standard for publishing documents on a computer is not nearly as useful on many mobile devices in their various default presentation formats. On the flip side, better connectivity between people can enhance learning in ways that were never before possible. Think about a doctor looking at an MRI trying to diagnose a patient's condition. Instead of trying to research the situation in books or online, the image can be sent to a colleague across the globe who can provide advice and suggestions simply by looking at an image on her phone or tablet.

Conclusion

Mobile devices are having an enormous impact, interrupting long-held approaches to how people learn, what they learn, and when they learn. This disruption is causing many different reactions.

The disruptive nature of mobile learning provides tremendous opportunities for organizations willing to embrace this new method of providing information and performance support.

But make no mistake: mobile learning is disruptive, and to take advantage of this disruption, a proactive response is required. By stepping outside the box of traditional instructor-led training and e-learning, HR and training departments can provide tremendous resources to employees. But doing so will require a commitment to thinking differently and trying new ideas.

Reference

Christensen, C. (1997). *The innovator's dilemma: When new technologies cause great firms to fail.* Boston, MA: Harvard Business School Press.

CHAPTER 4

Why Executives Should Care About Mobile Learning

John Feser

The world is a busy place, and people's time continues to become more and more a scarce resource. This is especially true for corporate executives, who are often presented with numerous opportunities that require assessment and problems that require fixes. In many cases, they spend a significant amount of time in meetings being inundated with mounds of information and data that they must sift through in order to make sound decisions. With all that is on their plates and all the issues they have to deal with, why would or should corporate leaders care about mobile learning? Here are ten reasons:

1. *With mobile devices, your employees always have their learning tools/devices with them.* Mobile phones are ubiquitous and pervasive in today's society. Why not take advantage of devices employees have with them and use all the time? In many cases, they have paid for the devices themselves, and all you might have to do is help to subsidize a better data plan. Concerned that everyone has a different device and is on a different platform? Fair enough, but there are many ways to overcome this limitation, most not as complicated as you might think.

31

2. *Mobile is global.* With over six billion subscribers, no other technology is more accessible around the globe than mobile devices. For a company that has a distributed or multinational workforce, learning materials and activities can easily be distributed using mobile technology. Even in third-world countries, where running water and electricity might be scarce, mobile infrastructures are growing at an amazing rate.

3. *Performance and productivity improvements are a fact of life.* As trite as it might sound, a key component of ongoing business success is finding ways to do more with less. Putting the right information in people's hands by making that information available when they need it is an important component of mobile learning. Identify where the information gaps are for your employees, especially when they are on the go, and then find ways to fill those gaps through mobile content delivery. Make a list of the main inefficiencies you are dealing with in your organization today, and you will most likely discover that the lack of easy access to information is a leading contributor to many of those inefficiencies.

4. *The volume of information your employees need to know is increasing at an incredible rate.* Take a step back for a moment and think what most people had to know fifty years ago in order to be effective versus what they need to know today. Whether it is knowing about more tools (Excel, PowerPoint, Word, Access, etc.), expanding product lines with additional features, or understanding 401(k) investment options compared with company pension plans from the 1960s and 1970s, it is undeniable that most people must remember, understand, and utilize much more information today than ever before. Any time you can reduce the amount of information or cognitive load people have to remember by making it readily available elsewhere, you are going to realize benefits through increased accuracy and efficiency.

5. *Mobile learning is contextual.* Much of the time spent in instructor-led training (ILT) or in front of computers doing e-learning can be replaced by "learning while working." Classrooms and e-learning must create an imagined context for the information being taught, whereas, with mobile devices, learning occurs when a real context presents itself.

Think about the difference between trying to create a "what if" scenario for your children as opposed to taking advantage of a "teachable moment." For a concrete example, consider showing your child a video on how to ride a bike versus actually being by their sides. I think that, as parents, we would agree that the teachable moments are much more effective. Workplace learning is no different.

6. *Mobile learning is cost-effective.* Considering the time employees spend participating in instructor-led training or e-learning, it is apparent that development costs are only one of the expenses that result from these forms of learning. That doesn't make these forms of instruction bad, but when the costs of delivering training are factored in, mobile learning can have a real advantage. In addition, the costs to develop mobile learning rarely exceed more traditional forms of training, and in some cases can be much less.

7. *Mobile learning is reusable.* Think about how much material from a classroom training session is never used again by the people attending the training. Sure, there are often handouts or a binder full of information. But are those handouts and binders really designed for ongoing use and reference? In some cases, the answer is yes, especially if the instructional designer has paid close attention to creating solid reference materials. But the accessibility of information in mobile learning makes creating training that has a life beyond initial use both practical and beneficial.

8. *Mobile learning has adaptability and speed.* With properly designed mobile learning, new or updated information can reach your audience almost instantly. Imagine an SMS text message that alerts your sales force that new product information has been released. The next time they log onto the mobile web or native app that contains product information, the new information is downloaded and is available to the user. When appropriate, content can be updated behind the scenes with no action required by the learner.

9. *Mobile devices allow improved data capture.* We tend to think about training and learning in terms of a traditional teacher-student model where instructional material is prepared ahead of time and then shared with or communicated

to learners. But mobile devices can be an excellent way to generate content and share information gathered or learned. There are many examples of this. For instance, a camera phone can easily be used at a job site to send information about a problem to a colleague. Or, using applications like Twitter, information can quickly be shared with a group. In one example, an insurance company was looking to improve their agent recruiting efforts through the use of mobile devices. By providing recruiters an easy way to capture information about prospects and recruiting efforts, management hoped to gain valuable information about which techniques and locations were most successful and which needed to be refined.

10. *Mobile learning is convenient.* Unlike PCs that have to be turned on and booted up, or classroom training that must be scheduled, mobile learning takes advantage of devices that are usually on, within reach, and in most cases connected to the mobile network. The convenience factor allows for creating learning content that is more likely to be used when needed.

This is not an exhaustive list, of course, but it should serve to illustrate that mobile learning is not a passing fad or trend that can be easily dismissed or ignored. For executives who are serious about leveraging opportunities as they present themselves, mlearning certainly deserves a closer look.

CHAPTER 5

mLearning Is *Not* e-Learning on a Mobile Device

John Feser

With the proliferation of mobile devices and the increasing capabilities of today's smart phones, mobile learning (or mlearning), has been getting a lot of press. Given the similarity between the terms e-learning and mlearning, one might be tempted to assume that mlearning is little more than e-learning on a mobile device. This assumption could not be further from the truth.

Clearly, we don't use our cell phones, e-readers, and tablet computers in the same way we use our desktop or laptop computers, or even their technological predecessors, books, CDs, or tape players. So it follows that the type of learning that is appropriate on a mobile device is very different from what we do at our desks. In fact, the differences between mlearning and e-learning are at least as great as those between e-learning and instructor-led training. The differences between those two deployment paths are so significant that it requires a completely different approach to instructional design, graphic and user experience design, and information presentation. So what makes mlearning so different from e-learning, and why is mlearning such an important development?

Understanding the differences between e-learning and mlearning begins with first defining mlearning. While there are many opinions and ideas surrounding this topic, when our company first started in 2010, we defined mobile learning as:

> ". . . the use of mobile technology to aid in the learning, reference, or exploration of information useful to an individual at that moment or in a specific use context."

At that time, we talked about cell phones being ubiquitous and pervasive in society, but April 2010 was the same month that the Apple iPad first went on sale. The explosion of tablet devices and the miniaturization of laptop computers over the past three years have greatly blurred what we typically think of as "mobile technology." With wearable technology such as fitness bands and Google Glass, this blurring has only increased. We are now every bit as mobile in our homes and offices (check out the number of mobile devices in any conference room meeting) as we are outside of them.

How does this affect our definition of mobile learning? The biggest change is that it is not the technology or device that puts the "mobile" in mobile learning, but the combination of learners themselves and the approach to learning. As a result, the pedagogy is completely different.

What makes mobile learning different from other delivery channels for learning content is that it can happen at any time, anywhere, and in ways that are vastly different from what can be achieved in a classroom or traditional e-learning, in which a single learner sits and interacts with a teacher or computer.

Mobile learning is able to combine the best aspects of self-teaching with group learning (as in a classroom setting), with the technological aspects and advantages of e-learning, and more. The combination of these areas makes mlearning both unique and distinct.

Initially, we saw that the primary differences between mlearning and e-learning fell into four main categories: timing, information access, context, and assessment. With hindsight and experience, we have added three more categories to the differences between mobile learning and e-learning. The new categories are performance support, user-generated content, and design for the unique affordances of mobile technologies. Let's briefly look at each of these seven categories in turn.

Timing

The first major difference between e-learning and mlearning is the time when learning is expected to take place and the anticipated duration of the learning session. Most e-learning is designed for the learner to sit at a computer and progress through a specified amount of material for a period of time. The length of time required to complete a particular e-learning module varies, but generally the duration ranges anywhere from fifteen or twenty minutes to two hours. Because the instruction is designed to run on a desktop or laptop computer, a specific time is usually chosen to complete the module. Usually, this seems to be as close to the deadline for compliance as possible.

But mlearning, by its very nature, is untethered and can be done any time and anywhere, at the time of need. In addition, the small screen sizes of today's mobile devices mean individual interaction sessions and, by extension, learning sessions, are much shorter in duration. Individuals don't want to spend an hour staring at their phones just to complete preselected learning objectives. Instead, mobile learning is ideal for conveying smaller chunks of information that can be absorbed while waiting for the bus, standing in line at the grocery store, or located on or around a job site. These chunks are chosen by the learners when they need them.

An example of this type of training is a quick reference guide. Imagine a new salesperson who has just completed her company's online sales training course. The course was comprehensive and covered a lot of material, including the company's custom sales process. Now she is on her first sales call. Arriving fifteen minutes early, she pulls out her smart phone and reviews a checklist of the five key elements of a successful sales call. Seeing that the number one element is to know the name and title of the person she is calling on, she quickly checks her notes and reviews the information about her sales contact. This sort of just-in-time experience exhibits the value in making your learning content mobile.

Information Access

When taking an e-learning course on a topic, such as a sales training or a new product introduction, two key learning objectives are comprehension and retention. Because the information being learned will be applied at a later time, it is critical that the material be understood and remembered until it is needed—what we might call "just-in-case learning." Mobile learning, on the other hand, is more about accessing information at the moment it is needed. This implies that successful mlearning is more about easy and convenient access to information and less about committing information to memory.

Take healthy eating as an example. A lesson on the benefits of healthy eating would make an excellent e-learning topic due to the amount of information and the level of compression necessary to convey the key points. This type of learning would most likely not be appropriate for a mobile device. On the other hand, learning whether the Caesar salad or a bowl of black bean soup has more calories at a local fast-food restaurant via a simplified interface tailored for the device is an ideal application for mobile learning.

Context

There is no doubt that mobile devices are being used for tasks that extend far beyond talking on the phone and sending text messages. The capabilities of these devices extend across a wide spectrum from geolocation to photography to Internet access. As a result, our context drives how we use our mobile devices. If it is lunchtime and we are in an unfamiliar city, we may use a mobile application or the Internet to find a suitable place to eat or relax at a park.

Context is one of the key areas in which mlearning is distinguished from e-learning. With e-learning, as with instructor-led sessions, it is critically important to establish the context so that the learner understands the importance of the subject matter. For instance, take an e-learning module about the importance of performing a safety check before using a piece of equipment. You would most likely start the instruction with a discussion of why safety checks are important and, specifically, how they relate to the particular piece of equipment being discussed. Once the context has been established, information on the actual safety check process can be presented.

With mlearning, however, the context has already been established. For example, the defense company Lockheed Martin has recently developed an iPhone app that includes a full pre-flight checklist for the C-130 Hercules Transport plane. The app contains a rotatable, zoomable image of the plane, as well as a visual step-by-step guide to each task required prior to flight. The idea is that a visual checklist is easier to use and interpret than a written document. When you add in the ability to clearly see close-ups or levels of detail that simply wouldn't be possible in a traditional checklist, the value in leveraging the context of being next to the item you are inspecting or using becomes obvious.

Assessment

With e-learning, the gap between when learning occurs and when it is applied in practice can be significant, especially when compared to mobile learning. As a result, the methods of assessment are very different for the two learning methods. While Donald Kirkpatrick's four levels of learning evaluation are applicable to both e-learning and mlearning, the approach to evaluation is different.

When assessing an e-learning module, it is relatively easy, through a series of questions, to determine success at the first two stages in Kirkpatrick's levels of training evaluation (Kirkpatrick & Kirkpatrick, 2006): Level 1–Learner Reaction (what the learner felt about the training) and Level 2–Learning (the resulting increase in knowledge or capacity). However, with Level 3–Behavior and Level 4–Results, it becomes much harder to assess the impact of e-learning. This is not to say that behavior and results are, in and of themselves, hard to measure. But so many other factors can influence a person's behavior or an organization's results that it is difficult to tie these changes specifically to e-learning.

The time span between when mobile learning actually occurs and the application of that learning is usually very short; often it is immediate. As a result, it is much easier to assess mlearning's impact on both an individual's behavior and the ensuing business results. In addition, because mlearning is less about comprehension and retention and more about easy access to the right information, Level 1 and Level 2 assessments are less important if the behaviors and results are appropriately changing.

Performance Support

The accessibility of mobile devices has not only decreased the need for rote memorization, but has increased our ability to capture and share information. This is huge when it comes to on-the-job performance support.

Whether it is having access to the latest information, such as a UPS or FedEx driver knowing the latest traffic information on his route, a doctor being able to quickly access a formulary to determine drug contraindications, or a company's sales force making real-time updates into a CRM system aided by inline help and performance support aids, people are now able to be more productive at work. This is a result of their ability to find and communicate information that helps them do their jobs. Because communicating valuable and useful information is the basis of all learning, performance support clearly falls into the space of mobile learning.

User-Generated Content

Traditional e-learning is primarily unidirectional: a person sits at a computer and receives the information that was placed in the course module. In most e-learning, there is little or no feedback from one learner that can be shared with others, except for the occasional "smiley" that accompanies the course. This is weak feedback, given that it is basically communication to the course authors and doesn't really contribute to the learning process. However, the social and collaborative nature of mobile devices changes all of this with mobile learning.

Consider the State Farm Driver Feedback app as an example of the ability for people to share their personal experiences with others. It provides a means for people in a common situation to connect and learn from each other. Imagine an entire high school driver's education class using the app to improve their driving and then sharing their experiences. This is learning occurring, being shared, and affecting behavior—jumping from Kirkpatrick's Level 1 or perhaps 2 to Level 3 in a very real and measurable way. The assessment occurs, but in a very different way than the one to which you may be accustomed.

The Unique Affordances of Mobile

Many of the mobile learning enhancements over previous learning tools have been made possible by technologies that simply haven't been available or practical in classroom and e-learning.

Features such as geolocation, cameras, accelerometers, and other sensors turn our mobile devices into multi-purpose tools (can the Star Trek Tricorder be far off?). But more than that, these devices are also computers that can be programmed and, in turn, help program us for better performance.

Consider the State Farm's Driver Feedback app. This tool uses the sensors in an iPhone to assess how a person is driving. It records how fast the car accelerates, corners, and brakes—all useful information for helping someone become a better driver. While an e-learning module can certainly teach someone about the importance of not accelerating or taking a corner too quickly, mlearning can actually help someone recognize he or she is doing it!

Different Doesn't Necessarily Mean Better

The differences between mlearning and e-learning may suggest that one learning approach is better than the other. Each can be appropriate in different situations. For instance, no one would want a cardiologist to need a refresher on the different valves of the heart prior to doing surgery. But you might feel a little bit more comfortable if your doctor pulled out her iPhone to confirm all the side-effects of a new blood thinning medication that had just been developed while she was about to prescribe a new course of treatments for you.

Similarly, an e-learning module on the history of Chicago may be both interesting and educational. The depth of content that could be revealed might require multiple viewings, with each one bringing forth myriad fascinating details. But a walking tour of Chicago that uses the GPS feature of your phone to point out and explain important landmarks based on your current location is much more engaging than learning about them at home sitting at your desk.

The point is that the capabilities and features of today's mobile devices are now allowing us to create entirely new ways of learning than were previously possible. When you start thinking about your phone or other mobile device from this perspective, you'll be amazed at the creative ideas that will start to flow and the many ways to enhance the learning process. The key in transitioning the learning objectives and content lies in your ability to assess the learners' goals and understand their context and the delivery methods you have available to you as the learning creator.

Conclusion

Mobile learning certainly is not a replacement for instructor-led learning or e-learning. Both still have their place. Furthermore, there may be many legitimate reasons for making most, if not all, of your e-learning content accessible on mobile devices.

But it has become clearer as time has progressed that the mere act of publishing e-learning on a mobile device is not mobile learning. Genuine, newly conceived mobile learning has its own unique qualities, characteristics, and pedagogy.

It's not a case of trying to teach an old dog a new trick, but an entirely different animal—one that can often teach tricks to itself with just a little push.

Reference

Kirkpatrick, D., & Kirkpatrick, J. (2006). *Evaluating training programs: The four levels.* San Francisco, CA: Berrett-Koehler.

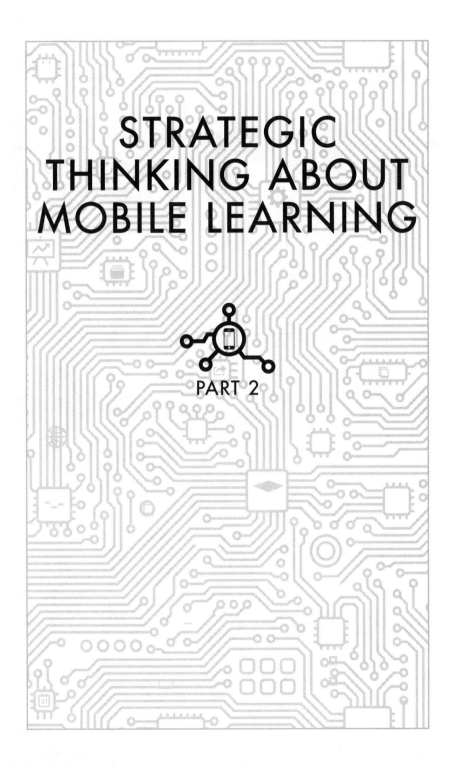

STRATEGIC THINKING ABOUT MOBILE LEARNING

PART 2

CHAPTER 6

The Six Ps of Mobile Learning Strategy

Chad Udell

Most of the questions about mobile learning I have answered over the past few years fall under one of the categories in a group I like to call the "Six Ps": Platforms, Policies, Procurement, Provisioning, Publishing, and Procedures. In this chapter, I present these six categories and some thoughts about how they fit into an effective mobile technology strategy.

Choose the Most Appropriate Mobile Platform

The first category, platforms, sounds like a simple one. Android, iOS, BlackBerry, Windows 8—pick a platform and go with it. But it isn't that simple. Perhaps the CEO has an iPad that she loves and now wants the entire company to use them. Maybe there is an existing installation of BlackBerry Enterprise Server that the IT department has already paid for and insists on sticking with. Or maybe the organization has a huge investment in Samsung products and can buy new phones and tablets at a huge discount. Everybody has an opinion, and sometimes the strongest voices come without the proper research. Be careful not to rush into a specific platform without careful consideration and strong evidence for what is most appropriate for your enterprise.

Another concern in choosing a mobile platform is deciding whether to embrace or reject the backdoor introduction of mobile devices by users adding their personal smart phones or tablets to the network. This trend, known as Bring Your Own Device or BYOD for short, is changing the way business technology services and solutions are conceived, designed, developed, and delivered. If you ignore this, you run the risk of creating a de facto policy of allowing any device onto the network, which creates a possible security risk and support headaches for your IT staff. Establishing an official mobile platform reduces that risk. It will also help determine your policies on accepting outside devices into your organization.

The biggest question that must be answered is whether it is even possible to settle on a single platform or whether you will be supporting more than one. That will change how you answer the questions that come when discussing the rest of the "Ps." For a small company, it might be easier to say that you only have the resources to support Android devices or Apple's iOS, but not both. Perhaps a large company has the resources to purchase and deploy iPads to every mobile user in the organization. Then it is possible to plan a single platform strategy. On the other hand, you may need to support contract employees who use different platforms, or you may want to be able to handle any mobile platform on the market. In that case, your future plans for provisioning devices, developing apps, and supporting the devices are entirely different from a single platform strategy. But be mindful of the consequences of supporting multiple platforms—it complicates things.

With the increasing number of tablets on the market, you also have to decide how that decision affects your planning. Is it possible to create a single mobile strategy for smart phones and tablets, or does it require separate rules for each type of device? Just as developers have found that many apps don't scale up from a phone to a tablet, your mobile strategy might not either.

It also is important to take the future of any chosen platform into consideration. Worldwide, the Android operating system is far ahead in terms of sales. The market for all mobile devices is quite dynamic and can change radically in just a couple of years. Choosing an appropriate platform means one that is more likely to be around in the future. There will also be far more apps and accessories developed for a platform with a large market share. The larger a mobile ecosystem is, the more useful it can be for your organization.

So what is the best strategy in terms of choosing a mobile platform? There isn't a single correct answer to that question. The best response is to gather information throughout the organization. What is the reason for using mobile devices and deploying mobile learning? What devices fit into the enterprise infrastructure? What will the total cost of ownership (TCO) be for the mobile platforms? Who are the developers? Who and where are the end-users? How will you manage the devices and apps? Answering these questions requires talking to your IT staff, developers, and users to obtain an accurate idea of what will work best. Doing the proper research and planning up-front is essential to choosing the platform that will work best for your organization.

Implement Proper Procurement

The next important "P" is procurement. In some ways, this is a simple topic, but it is worthy of thoughtful consideration because it can be puzzling at times as well. Each of these steps is an interlocking part of the mobile strategy and influences the choices you have to make in the other areas.

When you hear procurement, you probably are thinking that it just means an end-user makes choices and then goes out and acts on those choices, right? Sure, those are the basics, but different factors can always affect those choices. If, back in the platform stage, your organization decided to adopt a single, standard mobile platform, this can be an easy step. This follows the traditional, familiar model of standardizing on a single software package or hardware vendor, which is why it is often recommended in mobile strategy plans. Several variables are similar when purchasing mobile devices. For instance, what type of organization are you buying for? Most educational institutions have separate channels to go through. Apple has many schools and colleges listed in their online store. Many large vendors have a GSA-approved channel for government organizations, too. Keep in mind that there are also volume enterprise programs to consider, if you are making a substantial purchase. There may be a process to request a quote and a possibility to negotiate on the price. It could be time-consuming, but it really is no different from the process of purchasing any other technology hardware for the organization.

You need to consider whether you have to purchase smart phones and service. If so, you will need to work with one of the wireless carriers. This adds the issue of negotiating for the service rates, and possibly a service level agreement (SLA) or guarantee policy. If the device or platform selected for your organization is exclusive to one carrier, you may have less negotiating power. Initially, if you wanted iOS, AT&T was the only carrier in the United States with the iPhone. There was no leverage for the consumer in comparing multiple vendors (and when it comes to Apple devices, there still really isn't: one manufacturer, one price). Or perhaps your organization is locked into a contract with a carrier already. In that case, you may be limited to the smart phones available on that provider's network. If your organization has chosen a platform that is not available with that carrier, it would be necessary to negotiate an early termination fee (ETF) to break that contract. Depending on how many devices are under the contract, it could add a large expense for your organization to change carriers.

If your organization has chosen to support multiple mobile platforms, the issues around vendors and carriers are multiplied. Also, with exclusive devices being tied to specific carriers due to hardware availability, international trade laws, or contractual restrictions, the actual devices to choose from may be restricted.

Much more common today is for a company to have a bring your own device (BYOD) policy. Rather than the company supplying a smart phone or tablet for everyone in the organization, employees have the choice to use their personal devices within the organization. More companies are choosing to support multiple platforms, and a BYOD policy allows an organization to implement this at a lower cost. Some policy issues, such as creating a list of supported devices that will be allowed on the company network, determining who is responsible for the cost of data plans, and approval for applications, must be determined before implementing a BYOD policy. Once you have chosen your platform and devices, you will have to consider the management policies for your mobile devices. Using one of the several mobile device management (MDM) products and/or mobile applications management (MAM) products that supports multiple platforms can be a good way to handle your mobile management strategy. Once again, this shows that these are all pieces of the same puzzle. Your policies will determine what you want to use for device management, based on the features offered in the MDM and MAM products on the market. Your organization will have to determine the delivery method that works best: software as a service (SaaS), software and data installed on local servers, or appliance installations (installed in your mobile devices). While procurement can seemingly be a simple part of your mobile learning plan, it illustrates how each part is woven into the others. Each subsequent decision in the development of a mobile technology strategy builds on the last. Without vision, perseverance, and documentation it will be difficult to achieve success, no matter how simple the procurement step seems.

Adopt Sound Policies

Policies are the third P to consider in your strategy. Remember that these pieces all work together to help build your strategy, and the choices made in one area influence the others.

Some parts of a mobile strategy are similar to traditional technology policies in your organization. For example, the University Information Technologies department at Villanova University has a mobile device/PDA policy that covers the purchase, deployment, and support guidelines for mobile devices. The initial section of this policy states that users are expected to follow the existing Acceptable Use and Network Security policies. Because mobile devices are accessing your organization's network the same as any other computing device, it is important that you make your users aware that the same policies apply for those devices as well.

In some ways, certain parts of a mobile policy are actually determined before you reach this point in your planning. By your choosing a mobile platform (or multiple platforms), a policy for what devices can be used on your network was established. The procurement method that was selected helps determine the policy on how those devices can be provided. One additional piece that may need to be added to your organization's policy is whether you have elected to allow a bring your own device (BYOD) plan. In this situation, there will likely be policy differences between company-supplied devices and user-owned devices. Some recommendations for creating user-owned device policies include limiting what devices will be allowed, requiring management rules to be applied to user-owned devices, and limiting support offerings to those devices.

At the root of your organization's mobile policy is a decision on what information can and will be on mobile devices used for company business and how securely that information needs to be protected. Because mobile devices, by their very nature, can leave the physical location and network connections that you have secured, they pose a significant risk of your information being lost or stolen. In your organization's policies, you will have to decide what information is allowed on mobile devices, and furthermore, how that data should be protected. Do you require devices with encrypted file systems to protect the data at all times? What about during transfer of the data? In order to protect the data, you may define a policy that requires users to use an encrypted data network at all times. This can range from requiring WPA-secured wireless connections to using secured virtual private network (VPN) connections any time a device is used while not connected to the company network. Beyond these more apparent security policies, additional technologies, such as configuration profiles, SAML authentication, or various other domain authentication practices should be considered as part of the overall mobile technology policy you are crafting.

Some policies also must be considered for legal reasons. One issue that has occurred involves hourly or non-exempt employees using personal mobile devices to access their email. In a well-known case, one employee claimed and was paid for eight hundred hours of overtime in four months for viewing and replying to emails outside of business hours. Another issue with mobile devices involves distracted driving laws. Setting aside the obvious safety risks involved, there have been cases when the company that provided the phones was found liable in accidents involving their employees. Some state laws banning the use of cell phones while driving explicitly state that an employer can still be held responsible for an employee who is negligent. As a side note, my company does work with a couple of organizations that have actually made mobile device usage while driving a terminable offense. Because of these types of issues, it is crucial that your organization set policies for issues with potential legal implications.

Another part of your planning should involve your organization's mobile support policy. It is not enough to simply provide a list of approved devices; you will also need to determine what apps are supported, who will service issues with supported devices, and replacement procedures when devices are lost or stolen. When phones are involved, there are also issues to consider in dealing with service providers. If a phone needs to be replaced, a new device may have to be assigned and the phone number will have to be transferred to maintain usage. There should be a policy for replacement and upgrading of devices as well. New devices come out faster than ever, and your organization must have a plan for moving to newer devices, including how to transfer applications and data to these new devices.

If you allow users to bring in their own devices with a BYOD policy, your organization will have to determine how much support to provide for user-owned devices. It may be as simple as stating that support personnel will provide a best-effort attempt, but that results are not guaranteed. A time limit on support for user-owned devices could be listed, or the policy might be to only support software on the device that is required by your organization. Placing limits on supporting user-owned devices can help limit the liability for supporting those devices.

A very important part of your support policy covers your organization's response to lost devices. Due to the potential for your data being lost or exposed, a "remote wipe" process should be considered. You must have a procedure for reporting lost or stolen devices and a policy on when and how devices are wiped. These should be included in any BYOD policy and applied when employees leave your organization. For example, your policy might be to issue a remote wipe command to all mobile devices owned by an employee when that employee leaves, to prevent unauthorized data removal. If you choose to implement this policy, your users could complain due to its restrictiveness, but it may be important for the protection of your organization.

It is easy to see that defining policies for your mobile technology strategy is a must; however, those policies don't help your organization if they cannot be monitored or enforced. There are ways to monitor and require compliance with almost any policy, including some that may seem unenforceable, such as distracted driving policies. It is important to find a way to implement those configurable policies. The best way to do this is to use a mobile device management (MDM) solution. An MDM system that supports multiple mobile platforms will allow your organization to create profiles that configure and enforce your device policies.

It is also possible to create multiple profiles to allow for some variances in your policies. Some users can have fewer restrictions than others due to job requirements. Using an MDM can allow you to quickly assign a device to a category so that each employee receives the appropriate profile and policy settings. If you use an MDM solution, it is important to inform your users that your company's BYOD policy requires them to have their devices added to the MDM system. It may be intrusive to your users, but it is a must to be able to enforce your policies and protect your organization's network and data.

Creating mobile device policies for your organization can be a long, and sometimes tedious, process. As you can see, though, it is a must to properly secure your data and protect your organization and your employees. The policies that you create are another block in building your mobile technology strategy.

Properly Provision Your Devices

Provisioning mobile devices consists of everything from getting ready for deployment, creating and managing device profiles, configuring and enforcing device settings, to, finally, establishing a method to monitor and report on your organization's devices. It is the last step in your organization's strategy before you put the devices in users' hands. All of this can sound like a daunting task. Provisioning is a mix of items that involve some strategic planning when you first decide to bring mobile to your organization, and grunt work such as taking devices out of the box, creating an inventory, and activating all the devices. However, you can simplify a lot of your provisioning tasks with the previously mentioned MDM system. Such a system is useful for maintenance, inventorying, and decommissioning mobile devices. If your organization has a large number of mobile devices to support, a proper MDM system is a necessity to configure and support them.

Depending on the needs of your organization, an MDM can be used to help with almost all of your provisioning requirements except for taking the devices out of the box and activating them. For that, you will still have to be hands-on. Most mobile devices require activation as well, although the activation method varies depending on the device platform. Android, BlackBerry, and Windows 8 devices can be activated directly on the device. Older iOS devices required a connection to a computer running iTunes to be activated, so, depending on your IT infrastructure, you may still need to connect your mobile devices physically. One step that can speed up this process is setting up an activation station with iTunes configured in an activation-only mode. That sets iTunes to activate the device without syncing it with the computer, which greatly speeds up the process.

Once your devices are activated and ready to configure, then it is time to configure them to comply with your organization's policies and standards. Network settings, email accounts, security restrictions, and other settings could make this a time-consuming process, especially for a large organization. This is where an MDM system makes your job easier. Create your provisioning profile once in the MDM, and then add each device to the MDM list of supported devices. The joining process varies from one system to the next, but it is still much less time than configuring each device by hand. A good MDM solution also makes it easier for your organization to be flexible in configuring mobile devices. The needs of a sales representative are not the same as those of your trainers, IT staff, or executives. You can create a separate configuration profile for each role and then assign the devices to those in the proper roles. This type of configuration gives your organization greater control over who has access to specific information and applications.

While each mobile platform has its own methods to build and deploy configuration profiles, third-party platforms typically offer more flexibility, as they often support multiple mobile platforms. One platform offering that most people are familiar with may be changing that strategy. With their purchase of Ubitexx, Research in Motion (now BlackBerry) announced that it would add support for iOS and Android devices to their BlackBerry Enterprise Server (BES) platform. For organizations that have a long-term investment in BES, this may provide a chance to broaden their support for other devices. The only sure thing about this space is that change is going to continue.

Another issue comes up if your organization has decided to support a BYOD policy. Users with personal devices that have already been activated and set up may not conform to your organization's policies. In a recent survey, only 35 percent of companies are maintaining a strict limit on mobile devices accessing their networks, but nearly half either do not have, or do not enforce, a security policy on user-supplied devices. Creating an official BYOD policy for your organization that requires all devices to be registered with your MDM system will help keep your network more secure. You will be able to implement and enforce your policies on those devices, as well as protect your information when they leave the organization. For users who are worried about losing personal data because of your MDM's remote wipe capability, many systems now offer the ability to "sandbox" personal information from your business organization and wipe only the private data from your organization.

Is it possible to do all of this without an MDM system? Of course, but it becomes much more time-consuming and difficult to enforce. For a small organization, it may be possible to get away with developing configuration profiles manually and applying them before deploying a device, but that will not prevent a user from modifying the settings. It also becomes nearly impossible to enforce your security policies when you have a BYOD policy without a management system. It doesn't hurt to plan for growth. If you implement MDM when your organization or mobile deployment is small, you are establishing a good foundation for the future.

Publish Content for Your Users

At this point in your mobile strategy, you have chosen a platform for your organization, procured the devices, developed your mobile policies, and provisioned the devices for deployment. Now that mobile devices are in your users' hands, you have to get your apps and media to them. Publishing your information is the next step in your mobile planning.

Publishing your mobile apps and media inside your organization can require a significant amount of planning. There are a number of steps to consider, from the deployment process to updating and securing apps. In your mobile strategy, you must find a distribution method that allows you to manage all of these steps.

Putting apps and media onto mobile devices has typically been done using one of three methods: (1) the online marketplace method, such as Apple's App Store or Google Play, which are effective for distributing apps to a large and spread-out user base, but really only suitable for consumer media and applications; a large number of app marketplaces from both mobile platform developers and third-party sources, in which case your organization needs either to choose a marketplace that best serves your requirements or use several online locations that will each have to be monitored and maintained, as enterprise apps, with sensitive or confidential information or a limited number of users, don't fit well in a publicly available distribution location; (2) the ad hoc installation method, also known as sideloading or manual installation on some platforms, requires downloading the application installer or media file and then manually installing it on the mobile device (note that some platforms are easier to manage manually than others, but users could find the process confusing or too time-consuming to keep things up-to-date); and (3) the third method is to build a private app catalog to install apps wirelessly. A private app catalog lets you distribute your apps and media to mobile devices in a more user-friendly manner. The problem with this method, at first, was that it was just an automated way to perform ad hoc distribution. Users would receive an email or SMS that contained a link to your organization's private app server. They had to hit that link and download the installer and put the applications on their devices manually. It helped to get the apps out to users faster and to a geographically diverse user base without putting them in a public marketplace, but there was still no way to tell whether people downloaded and installed the apps or files. In the Enterprise IT world, organizations need to know what is installed where, and ensure that proper updates occur for security and licensing requirements. How can you make that happen in mobile?

A rapidly growing answer to that question is to use mobile application management (MAM). These systems allow organizations to create a private application catalog that works similarly to the public marketplaces. Media files and documents that are useful to your mobile users can often be included in a MAM system as well. Apps can be categorized and only visible to specific users, as they would in a traditional enterprise application deployment system. Apps can be updated, either by notifying mobile users or even by push updates without user intervention, if the platform supports it. Apps can also be removed or disabled from mobile devices if a user leaves the organization or has accessed the application improperly, without requiring a full device wipe. This can give you more flexibility in making sure mobile devices comply with your policies.

Mobile application development can also benefit from having an application management system in place. When it comes time to test on the actual devices, being able to publish updates for each build is easier than connecting each device and loading the app manually. This can dramatically speed up the development process in your organization.

MAM systems also can be helpful in monitoring and ensuring compliance with application licensing. Your mobile systems administrator can use a MAM's reporting features to see which users have installed apps or downloaded available media and keep track of or limit how many users install a specific app to comply with licensing issues. In conjunction with an MDM system, you can have a variety of tools to keep your organization in compliance with your mobile strategy. MDM is not the same as MAM, however. Several mobile device management platforms offer some application management features, but a dedicated mobile application management system usually has more features and will serve your organization better.

Mobile application management is a tool that can help with your organization's mobile applications lifecycle, from development and testing to deployment and updating. With a bit of planning, MAM can make it a lot easier to publish the apps and media in your organization.

Standardize Your Procedures

Procedures are the end result of standardizing the first five Ps so that everyone in your organization is on the same page. Without choosing a platform, carefully documenting policies, setting up steps to purchase and provision the devices, and publishing content, there is no hope to achieve standard operating procedures. Every time you execute the steps, there will be variations in the end results that will lower quality, increase costs, or in some other way limit the true return on investment. So it is in creating standardized procedures that "the rubber meets the road." With proper procedures, you will have the following:

- A planned platform or platforms to support, with no surprises as new mobile handsets and tablets are released;

- A procurement process that takes into account equipment lifecycles and replacement planning, as well as buying discounts and service level agreements (SLA);

- Policies that can be enforced and are legally defensible. This should protect your company's intellectual property and your employees' rights. The procedures should cover the "What If's" when policies aren't followed and spell out the enforcement steps that will be taken;

- You will have a technology solution and business process in place to provision the devices as they are brought into the workplace. This should cover and enforce your policies, making BYOD devices and company devices equal when it comes to accessing information needed for performance support. This solution should not be dependent on any one individual for its implementation, but must be institutionalized;

- Putting your apps out to your audience shouldn't be a problem either, because the publishing procedures spell out whether and when you are targeting the mobile web, private app catalogs or MDM/MAM solutions, or putting your apps into public marketplaces like the Apple App Store or Google Play.

As you can see, this is the culmination and standardization of all of your hard work. Standardization improves efficiency, because everyone knows what to do, without having to work through all these decisions each time there is a change or addition to your mobile system. You've come this far, and you owe it to yourself and your company to finish the job.

Here are some key points to keep in mind when developing a procedures document. Your procedures document must have the following characteristics to succeed:

- *It must be accessible.* Put it in a centralized repository or on the organization's intranet so that all parties who need to read it have access.

- *It must be collaborative.* One person is simply not knowledgeable about all aspects of a company's mobile strategy to manage everything. Establish a workflow for editing the document or use a team environment like a wiki to store this vital resource.

- *It must be updated as time passes.* Mobile moves fast. No document is going to be etched in stone, because the mobile industry just changes too quickly to assign arbitrary update cycles to this.

- *It must be workable.* If your procedures document is so loaded with jargon and legalese that it makes it tough to implement, you'll never see the benefits of its creation and rollout. Keep it simple!

- *It must be transferable.* This is, after all, your company's policy, right? This is not a single person's domain, even if you only have one person manning the servers at your company. Because very sensitive data may be being sent on these devices outside of the company's firewall, it's important that more than one person know how the process works.

The six Ps represent the main components of a mobile learning strategy. Of course, there are a lot more issues to consider when it comes time to create and implement a specific strategy for your organization.

CHAPTER 7

The Business Case for Mobile Learning

John Feser

We have just come out of one of the most severe economic recessions since the Great Depression, with unemployment higher than has been seen in decades and companies looking to cut costs in every way possible. In these circumstances, how can an investment in mobile learning make sense? In difficult economic times, training budgets are one of the first areas to be reduced or eliminated. Employees tend to be more focused on being heads-down and productive and doing their jobs than on taking training. Given this situation, how does a learning professional present a compelling case to management to spend money and invest in new skills and new technologies? In today's environment, many people would expect to hear a stern reminder of budgetary restraints at such a request.

However, with a modest time investment on your part and a critical look at your organization's operations, you might find that now is the perfect time to make an investment in mobile learning. Business fundamentals tell us that companies improve their bottom lines in one of two ways: increase revenue or decrease costs; if you can do both, all the better. This chapter on the business case for mobile learning takes an in-depth look at how mobile learning can benefit both sides of the business equation.

First, a quick disclaimer: there is no silver bullet here. Every organization is different, from the products it sells to its organizational structure to its unique operations. I cannot possibly provide all the answers, as the best and appropriate ways to increase revenues and decrease costs are specific to each business. However, I can provide a few key tips and logical techniques for uncovering the opportunities for growing revenue and reducing costs in your company using mobile learning.

Mobile learning is about accessing useful information any time, anywhere. So the key to building a strong business case for mobile learning is to identify ways to provide better and timely access to the right information, which can help your company increase revenue or decrease costs.

Mobile Learning and Increasing Revenue

Companies generally have three basic ways to generate more revenue.

1. They can sell more of an existing product or service,
2. They can offer additional products or services, or
3. They can increase the prices of their products or services.

But none of these methods work magically; there has to be an underlying, fundamental change in the demand for your products or services for any of these options to work. Selling more or being able to charge more for the same product requires raising the demand for your product or service through better sales and marketing efforts or a perceived differentiation in the marketplace. Mobile devices can help increase the demand for your products and services by providing both your customers and your sales force with better access to information about what you sell.

In this chapter, you will notice that the lines between what is considered mobile learning and what is known as mobile marketing are blurred. This is to be expected. It is difficult to talk about growing sales or increasing the demand for products and services without talking about marketing in some form or another. For instance, does the idea of making your company's website accessible on a mobile device strike you as being a marketing activity or a mobile learning task? Most people would contend that a company's website falls within the marketing department's domain.

However, if you subscribe to the idea that mobile learning is about "making useful information available any time, anywhere," then it becomes less clear whether a mobile version of your company's website is learning or marketing. The good news is that it really doesn't matter. The same concepts of context and access to information apply whether we are talking about mobile learning or mobile marketing.

Therefore, if businesses are going to find ways that mobile learning (or marketing) can help increase revenue, there has to be a plan for increasing demand through the immediate access to information that mobile devices offer. This is true both in terms of how you sell to your customers and what you sell to your customers.

How You Sell

In order to find ways that mobile learning can help you sell more, you must first think about and understand what makes your product or service relevant and unique. Three key steps or questions come to mind:

1. Why would someone want to spend money on what you have to offer?
2. What information does a client or a customer need to make a well-informed decision? How can they find this information?
3. When do they need to access this information?

By understanding what your customers base their purchasing decisions on, you can be in a better position to provide that information via a mobile device. Amazon.com and Target are both excellent examples of this. Both have superb websites that are optimized for mobile devices. Both provide access to product information, price, and availability. Amazon.com's mobile customers even have access to the same user reviews that you can find through the full browser version.

Imagine yourself in a store like Best Buy considering the purchase of a new inkjet printer. You might have thought about doing some research before you left your house, but you didn't and now you are standing in front of a row of ten printers trying to decide which one to buy. You might ask a salesperson for some suggestions and he or she might be able to give you a good answer, but chances are the salesperson hasn't used all ten products, so knowing which one is the best for you might be a guess. But having access to reviews and information about the various printers you are considering through your mobile phone allows you to make a much more informed decision.

Supporting Your Sales Force

Another key mechanism by which a business can improve its revenue is through supporting its sales force. If a business goes to market with a trained sales force, then those people have a focused job description—to generate demand and bring in sales. What information needs do they have? How can they best be supported in the field? Do you have a diverse product line that changes regularly? Do you have frequent turnover in your sales force, requiring a heavy investment in regular training? Can some of this training be done on the road, as a podcast or a series of tip sheets accessible from a mobile phone? By thinking of mobile devices as small computers with instant access to information, the possibilities are numerous. Like your customers, the key is to think about what information your salespeople need to access and how you can improve their ability to find information quickly, when they need it.

What You Sell

We've talked about ways to increase demand through how you sell. But what about adding value to what you sell? Just as there are many ways to inform and influence the buying decision before a purchase, there are equally many ways to use mobile devices to enhance the buyer's perception of your product or service before, during, and after the sale has been made. Doing these activities well can lead to repeat business and referrals to other potential customers.

Mobile learning offers opportunities to provide a richer, more valuable experience with your product or service. To identify these opportunities, think about what information you can provide your customers that will improve how they use your product or service. Also think about the context for how they might access that information. For instance, do you want your customers to know how to contact the customer service department if they have a problem, or do you want them to be able to solve most issues on their own? Do you provide troubleshooting tips? Are there user forums on which people can share ideas and tips about best practices for using your product?

Maybe you already provide this information on your company's website. It may be tempting to think that, just because information is available via the web on a desktop or laptop computer, it doesn't need to be accessible on a mobile device. However, considering the rate at which mobile devices are increasingly being used to access the web, this may not be a good idea. According to a recent Morgan Stanley report, analysts expect that the "mobile web" will overtake desktop Internet access by 2015. As more and more people access the web from their mobile devices, you have to ask yourself: How well can they get to the important information about my products and services?

Cutting Costs

The other way of improving profits for a company is to cut costs. To quote Benjamin Franklin, "A penny saved is a penny earned." While there are many ways for organizations to manage their costs, learning and development efforts usually involve helping people do their jobs faster, better, or cheaper.

How does faster, better, cheaper translate into cost savings? Working faster means more is done in a shorter period of time. This results in fewer people being needed for a particular task, more time for other tasks to be completed, and, just as importantly, the ability to handle more (more warranty work, more service calls, etc.) with the same number of people. Working better translates into higher quality output, which results in fewer service calls, warranty claims, and rework, not to mention happier customers. Working cheaper means using fewer resources to complete a task. This could mean anything from using fewer raw materials to using less expensive computers or software. For any of these improvements to actually reduce costs, a reduction of costs in one of these areas cannot be offset by an increase of costs in other areas. For example, it doesn't help to simply work faster if there is a corresponding drop in the quality of the final product. So what are some of the ways that mobile learning can help people work faster, better, and cheaper?

Reference Materials and Job Aids

One form of mobile learning consists of reference material and job aids. Mobile devices, with their instant-on, always connected qualities, can offer a rich library of information for service technicians and others who travel for their jobs. Imagine a new washer and dryer repair person who has been trained on the latest models produced by his company, but has not been in the business long enough to see the differences from washers and dryers that were made five or ten years ago. By putting repair manuals online and making them easily accessible through a mobile device like a smart phone or a tablet, the need to carry and keep track of potentially hundreds of paper repair manuals is eliminated. In addition, if designed properly, these reference materials can provide significantly faster access to information and offer much more detail than what traditionally has been produced with paper manuals.

This same basic principle can be used in other industries as well. Arborists, who have to identify and diagnose many different forms of tree diseases, can benefit from having diagnostic pictures available on their mobile devices, along with prescriptions for treatment. In addition, the geolocation feature on many smart phones can help by automatically sorting and filtering the information based on the arborist's location and the types of trees that are most common to that geographic area.

These forms of reference materials can reduce costs in a number of ways. First, the cost to update electronically available materials is significantly less than the cost for updating and reprinting paper versions of manuals and reference guides. Second, when designed properly, access can be much faster and easier than for traditional paper-based materials. The geolocation feature is one example; a well-indexed and fully searchable reference guide is another example of how companies can save costs by providing faster access to information. Finally, the opportunities for collaboration and communication with a mobile/electronic version of various reference guides and job aids should not be overlooked. Imagine if the washer/dryer repairperson found an error in the manual or a more efficient way to make a repair. By his having the ability to comment on or rate that section of the job aid, others could easily benefit from the experience. In essence, the experts are continually updating the repair manual of the future. It's the Wikipedia for washer/dryer repair manuals; it's the Bing for HVAC technicians.

Performance Support Tools

Another related, but distinct area of mobile learning that can help organizations reduce costs are performance support tools. Performance support tools, like reference guides and job aids, help people do their jobs better and more efficiently. For example, in the construction industry, equipment safety checks are a critical part of preventing accidents and keeping workers free from injury. Organizations such as OSHA in the United States require these safety checks to be documented as part of standard start-up procedures for various types of equipment. Often, the documentation is misplaced or forgotten. Lack of compliance can lead to fines and increased insurance costs or worse—accidents that have severe ramifications. One need only look a little closer at the recent oilrig disaster in the Gulf of Mexico to hear how shortcuts were encouraged and safety practices were not followed in order to bring the oil platform online faster. An electronic checklist created for use on a mobile device can have several advantages to ensuring compliance. First, there is an electronic record that the inspection has been completed that can be sent to a centralized database. If an inspection has not been completed by a specified time, a reminder notice can be sent to the machine operator or the safety manager. If a safety issue is detected, it can be recorded using the camera.

A company called Earthrise Technology has developed an innovative mobile performance support tool. Earthrise is a subsidiary of Digisec Group (www.digisecgroup.com), a leading supplier of after-market automotive security products in China that also develops and distributes state-of-the-art telematics products for the transportation industry. Earthrise recently released a product called Eco-Way that combines a personal navigation system with an on-board diagnostic system that monitors a number of factors related to how efficiently a vehicle is operating and how economically the driver is operating the vehicle. This tool provides real-time data to those driving the vehicle as well as a web portal for others to review, making it ideal for transportation companies wanting to better manage their fuel consumption costs. For companies that have large fleets of vehicles and spend significant amounts on fuel, this tool can serve as an excellent training device to help drivers maximize their fuel efficiency and help vehicle maintenance workers keep vehicles properly tuned. Earthrise estimates that, through the use of Eco-Way, drivers can improve their gas mileage and reduce their carbon emissions by up to 45 percent.

Applications for Your Company

If your company doesn't repair washers and dryers or have arborists who examine trees for disease and infection, what applicability does this have to you and your organization? What if you are not part of a construction company or one that has a large fleet of vehicles? How do you apply the principles of mobile learning to manage costs in your company? With any organization, the process of managing costs begins by first looking for opportunities. Set aside for a moment the idea of mobile learning and examine how employees are spending their time and the quality of the work they produce. What information do they require on a regular basis to do their jobs and do those jobs expertly? Focus on the time they are away from their desks and don't have access to a traditional desktop or laptop computer. What must they do while they are at their desks that they cannot currently do elsewhere?

Remember, today's mobile devices have as much computing power as the desktops from just ten years ago and, in many cases, they have a much faster connection to the Internet. Can you provide them with better access to information? Are there ways to combine learning with their daily activities (like Eco-Way does for drivers)? Taking a step-by-step approach best solves cost reductions, like many other business challenges. Start by breaking the problem into parts; then look for opportunities for improvement. When all the features of today's mobile devices are combined with the information needs required by many of today's jobs, practical opportunities present themselves. With patience and a questioning attitude, there is no doubt that cost reduction opportunities exist with the use of effective mobile learning.

Conclusion

When it comes to growing the top line of your business, mobile learning and mobile marketing have a lot in common. Whatever you call it, the key is to make sure your potential customers and those who have purchased your products or services have access to the information they need. By putting yourself in the shoes of your customers or your sales force, you can identify ways that providing "useful information any time, anywhere" can enhance people's experience and perception of what you sell. With some focused time investment and a critical look at the company's sales activities and practices, a business can most likely improve its top line through the use of mobile learning. At the same time, there are many ways for mobile learning to support cutting costs, contributing directly to a company's bottom line. Doing both is optimal and possible with the implementation of mobile learning.

CHAPTER 8

The New "Nomadism" as a Driver of Mobile Learning

Gary Woodill

The idea of mobile learning has been talked about seriously for only about twenty years, but the dream of using mobile electronic devices to communicate is at least one hundred years old. In the past two or three years, there has been a rapid increase in both the visibility and publicity surrounding mobile learning. What is driving this recent surge in interest?

One obvious answer is the explosive growth of mobile phones, particularly smart phones, in recent years. The number of mobile phone subscribers has far outstripped the number of Internet users since the mid-1990s. There are now more than six billion mobile phone subscribers worldwide. Eighty-five percent of that growth has come from emerging markets, such as Latin America, Eastern Europe, the Middle East, India, and China. In these countries, many people cannot afford a computer, but often they can afford a mobile phone. In North America, the dramatic growth of the use of smart phones and tablets has allowed mobile learning to become widespread.

Another driver for mobile learning is the fact that people are more and more on the move. In 2008, *The Economist* magazine published a special report on "The New Nomadism." Because of our increased mobility, people are less likely to want to stay in one place in order to attend school or train in a specific location. With the new possibilities of connectivity to information from wherever we are, there is no need to hang around home base.

This new ability to move using improved transportation systems has led to the creation of entire categories of mobile workers, especially those in field services and in sales. As well, our ability to move has led to people living at an increased distance from their workplaces, making telecommuting very attractive. The shedding of permanent full-time jobs and their replacement by temporary and part-time service jobs that can be done at home or by virtual teams has also increased the attractiveness of learning from any location at any time.

Of course, much has been made of the new generation that is entering the workforce in terms of their intimate knowledge of computers and mobile devices. But I think this has been overblown as a driver, in that the use of mobile learning needs to make business sense, rather than simply catering to the desires of a new set of workers. Yet, there's no denying that many of us, of all ages, become very attached to our mobile phones and tablets. There's even a psychiatric condition called "nomophobia" to describe those who become anxious when not in the presence of their mobile phone, or when their batteries run out. The British Post Office has actually done a research study on this condition.

Finally, and perhaps most importantly for the corporate training audience, there are solid business reasons for the adoption of mobile learning. First, the widespread deployment of mobile phones means that an infrastructure for mobile learning is already in place. This means that there are already communication devices in the pockets of most workers, with access to email, texting, and the Internet.

Mobile learning, when properly designed, can be described as "just in time, just enough, and just for me." Researchers have found that it improves retention in learning, because what is learned is relevant to the situation at hand. Mobile learning has the potential to leverage the "idle time" of workers on the move, who would likely otherwise be unproductive. On the other hand, people need time off, and the use of mobile learning can be seen in some situations as a way of unfairly increasing workloads without compensation.

Mobile learning has potential to change the way people work together. It can result in increased collaboration and a sense of community, and it can give employees up-to-date information that they need in their jobs. At the same time, such information can be personalized and contextualized according to each person's work situation. In short, mobile learning has "come of age."

Reference

Nomads at last. (2008, April 10). *The Economist.* www.economist.com/node/10950394.

CHAPTER 9

Creating a Mobile Learning Content Strategy

Chad Udell

What is content strategy? In its simplest terms, content strategy for formal learning is a holistic plan for content, the knowledge that you want the learner to receive and retain. The strategy should include the planning, creation, governance, publication, and long-term maintenance of the desired content. In bigger terms, content strategy is looking at the material you produce for your audience from the perspective of an "information steward" and making informed decisions that improve the transfer of the knowledge shared and the sustainability of the information source that provided it.

This emerging and critical aspect of instructional design is part of the new normal of being learning professionals in the connected age of ubiquitous access and user-generated content. It is simply not enough to create once, publish, and then move on. We must think through the lifecycle of the content and plan for its optimal delivery through the mechanisms we have available to us, regardless of technology or platform.

Content strategy may seem unrelated to learning professionals. However, this topic has been long studied and employed in the marketing and web worlds to great success and deserves a place in our essential skill sets. Numerous blog articles have been written on it, the most notable being "The Discipline of Content Strategy" by Kristina Halvorson at *A List Apart*. A number of books have been written on content strategy, as well. I recommend Karen McGrane's (2012) *Content Strategy for Mobile* as an excellent, easy-to-read introduction to the subject that offers a clear plan to action.

Karen McGrane's steps for a content strategy include:

1. Perform audience research.
2. Perform competitive research.
3. Perform content inventory and analysis.
4. Choose delivery platforms appropriately.
5. Don't fork your content, yet edit to meet delivery needs.

An important takeaway is that our roles as learning professionals responsible for the delivery of content are changing (and, incidentally, will continue to change). We must continue to evolve and work to create a content framework that is scalable and strong, flexible yet authoritative. Candidly, it's not easy, but the very challenge is what makes the role so interesting and important. This is definitely different from the "set it and forget it" approach to creating curriculum and courseware we have used in the past.

This new approach to content creation and lifecycle is needed if we are to keep up with ever-tightening product cycles. It is a must if we hope to deliver content on the devices and platforms of today and tomorrow. With appropriate planning, it is possible. A bit of time in research and planning pays big dividends here.

We have to create a systemic (meaning deeply ingrained in the system) and systematic (carried out using step-by-step processes and procedures) approach to delivering content to our learners. This is the How and When of What we are going to share with our audiences.

Consider the various ways you interact with websites or platforms, such as Facebook, Twitter, Flickr, CNN.com, Netflix, or Amazon. Every one of those companies has a different experience for the users, depending on the device each user employs to access the content. An app is different from a set top box, which is also different from a web browser, which is different from the mobile web. Pumping their respective sites through some kind of magic transformer didn't create these experiences. Some features are omitted or tucked away, as they may be unneeded in a particular case, but the key functions the user requires in that particular case—desktop, web, mobile, or other—are accounted for and designed.

So, too, will your carefully crafted mobile learning experiences need to account for these platforms. Running your Flash course through some sort of HTML5 mill is not the answer. You must redesign and adapt your applications to fit within your content strategy for mobile. Beyond basic considerations, such as user interface, element size, and scale, there are more dramatic shifts you will have to make in your thinking.

Some of the content from your original software may stay largely intact. A thoroughly indexed and well-manicured company wiki may require only a new mobile theme, and perhaps the addition of some basic contextual awareness (geolocation could be really useful, for example) to make it a valuable mobile learning tool. Other items—immersive software simulations, for example—may require more thought prior to porting the content to mobile handsets (or perhaps skipping this approach for more effective uses of resources). Mobile devices do have constraints in terms of screen size, bandwidth, and processing power, and in order to match the experience to the target platform, you may have to take these factors into account in your design process.

On the topic of straight content conversion from e-learning to mlearning, I have mixed reactions. While, yes, it's great to be free to leverage your content and repackage it for a new class of users in need of it, none of the simple paths to mobile learning I have seen truly put mobile considerations into the design up-front. They may apply a new mobile-friendly skin to the content, sure, but that's the easy way out. Seldom do I hear of learners impressed by mobile content delivery. On the other hand, I do hear people impressed by Urbanspoon's scope feature, Path's streamlined feel on smart phones, or Twitter's ease of uploading images or adding location data to posts. This sort of smart user experience design, coupled with content strategy, takes work. If page-turning e-learning were a sure-fire way to create snoozeware on the desktop, then it is death on the mobile side.

If we want to escape that perilous trap, we must plan our path to the mobile learning landscape of tomorrow.

References

Halvorson, K. (2008, December 16). The discipline of content strategy. *A List Apart*, (274). http://alistapart.com/article/thedisciplineofcontentstrategy.

McGrane, K. (2012). *Content strategy for mobile*. New York: A Book Apart.

CHAPTER 10

Seven Easy and Inexpensive Ways to Launch Mobile Learning

John Feser

Your initial foray into mobile learning doesn't need to be complicated, require a five-figure budget to implement, or dramatically alter how your company conducts training. The great thing about mlearning is that it encompasses so many forms of knowledge transfer and sharing that there are many creative implementations, all of which fit neatly into the category of mobile learning. Here are seven easy and relatively low-cost (in some cases free) ways to implement mobile learning. My hope is that these will not only be useful, but will also help to trigger other ideas that can be implemented and shared.

1. Micro-Blogging

Micro-blogging is a web-based service that involves sending or broadcasting short messages to a specific group of individuals who are signed up or have "subscribed" to be a part of that group. Twitter and Yammer are examples of two popular micro-blogging services, the former being free yet public and the latter offering paid subscriptions to set up a private group. Both services are easily accessed on mobile devices, making them accessible wherever a cellular or Wi-Fi connection is available. Micro-blogging works great as a simple messaging and collaboration tool. For instance, a salesperson could send a message to his or her colleagues such as, "Getting a lot of pushback on our recent price increases. Anyone have a suggested response?" Others who see the message can easily weigh in on the conversation. Because these services work with SMS, virtually any mobile phone user can have access to this information and participate in the conversation.

2. Create a WordPress Website or Blog

WordPress is an open source publishing platform for the web. It was started in 2003 as a blogging tool, but has since matured into a very robust content management system. Because it is open source, it is free to download and use. From a technical standpoint, all that is needed is a web server running PHP and MySQL. What makes WordPress so useful for mlearning is the wide variety of mobile-friendly themes and plugins. Using a responsive design based theme, for example, a list of a company's safety rules and regulations could easily be documented using WordPress. When workers on a jobsite need access to those rules and regulations, they can easily pull up the site and search for the information they need.

3. Start a YouTube Channel

While someone will often read a recipe in a cookbook or magazine, think how much more powerful it is to watch a chef demonstrate how to make a particular dish on TV. In many situations, video can be used as an excellent learning tool. When being able to visualize a task or view a series of steps is easier and more efficient than a text description or static photos, videos can work extremely well. Creating a YouTube channel provides a way to organize videos that are created for a specific purpose or company. YouTube videos play on many of today's mobile devices, making this a great site on which to put mobile content.

4. SMS (Text) Message Alerts

Today, virtually 100 percent of all mobile phones have the ability to send and receive text messages. This capability, along with a relatively low overhead cost, makes text messaging an ideal way to distribute bite-sized learning nuggets. There are numerous examples of how text messaging can assist in the mobile learning arena. One example is reminders for a group or team. Imagine a safety manager on a construction site. At 5 a.m. he notices the weather forecast for the day is hot and humid. So using a service to send SMS messages to a group of people, he sends a reminder to all the members of his crew, "Forecast for today is hot and humid. Don't forget to bring adequate sun protection (hat, sun block, etc.) and extra water." In sending a message that costs his company around 5 cents or less, he may prevent a worker from having heat exhaustion, heat stroke, or something worse.

Another example of SMS usage in a corporate setting is in the on-boarding of personnel. In this situation, text messages can be scheduled to be sent over the first week or month of a person's employment. The messages can be anything from a reminder to complete specific paperwork to providing additional information about the company that may not have been presented during the initial orientation. This type of on-boarding can create a connection that eventually leads to a more engaged (read productive) employee. There are a number of text messaging services that offer a variety of ways to send text messages.

5. Create a Mobile Version of Your PowerPoint Slides

It is generally not recommended to simply convert a PowerPoint presentation to something that can be viewed on a mobile phone and call it mlearning. There are many instances where this would be wholly ineffective. Who wants to look at a two-hour, 150 slide presentation on a company's strategic initiatives on an iPhone? However, there are other instances when a PowerPoint presentation specifically designed for a mobile device can make sense. Reference documents are a great example. Think of information like product data, tip sheets, or quick reference guides as information that could be made available on a mobile device through the conversion of a PowerPoint document. There are a number of ways to make a PowerPoint mobile ready. The methods that are most appropriate depend on whether the document must be resident on the phone so that it can be accessed when the phone is not connected, and on the types of phones used by the target audience. One option is to use SlideShare. SlideShare has a mobile version that works on iPhone and Android operating systems. Another option is to create a video of the PowerPoint presentation. This method has the added benefit of being able to easily handle audio narration. The video can then be published to YouTube or downloaded directly to a mobile device. One option for this is to use a tool like authorSTREAM to create a video version of your PowerPoint. Creating videos with an authorSTREAM watermark is free. If you want videos without the watermark, there is a fee.

6. Audio Podcasting

Podcasts can be a great form of mobile learning because of their flexibility. Whether mowing the grass, driving to work, or waiting at the airport, audio podcasts are a great way to communicate information or share knowledge because they only require one sense: hearing. Depending on the content and the type of information being shared, this allows the learner to be engaged in other activities while learning. Obviously, audio podcasting is not an effective approach to mobile learning in all cases. Certainly, situations that involve visualization or learner interactivity are not appropriate. But audio podcasts work very well when presenting information to an interested audience and when engaging storytelling can be incorporated into the content. A number of free tools are available for creating audio podcasts, and some excellent step-by-step tutorials are available as well. The basic steps involve creating the audio file, converting to the correct format, and publishing the podcast.

7. Poll Everywhere

Poll Everywhere is a web-based audience response service that allows a presenter or trainer to ask a question and receive audience feedback via SMS text messages or Twitter or the web. Responses can then be displayed in real time in PowerPoint, Keynote, or on a web page. The advantages of Poll Everywhere are (1) it is easy and (2) it is relatively inexpensive (or even free!), depending on the size of the audience you wish to poll. Polling during a presentation is an excellent way to engage your audience, gather feedback, and allow them to participate in the discussion. Give it a try!

A word of caution: just because something is easy and inexpensive does not necessarily make it the right tool for the job. One can easily go to a local discount store and purchase a child's wagon for a relatively low cost. But if you try to use it to haul five tons of rock from the landscaping company across town, you will find your wagon is not very effective. However, borrowing your neighbor's pickup truck may be equally easy and cost you nothing more than a friendly beer shared on the back porch or a gift card to a local restaurant. The point is, no matter how easy and inexpensive something is, you still have to select the right tool for the job or, in the case of mobile learning, the right design to meet the learning objectives.

The seven ideas presented here can all be effective in certain situations and not at all effective in others. When implementing mlearning, be sure to think of the contextual goals of the learners to make sure they are using the right tool for the job.

CHAPTER 11

Building Brand Advocacy Through Mobile Learning

Scott McCormick and Chad Udell

Educational marketing is a concept that has been around for a long time. The basic concept can be explained simply as "An educated customer is an engaged customer." An informed customer is more likely to understand and appreciate the value of your product or service offerings and, therefore, more likely to buy or recommend your product to others. This is known in marketing circles as "brand advocacy." Writers and bloggers like Word of Moss, Seth Godin, and many others have been writing about this concept for some time.

Most of the time, brand advocacy takes place in one of two ways. It can be an organic process, with customers becoming advocates by virtue of the product being great. This usually results in them telling others about the product or service. Brand advocacy can also be seeded, with companies sending freebies, samples, and other offers to influential bloggers and Twitter users. These influencers then share their feelings on the product (positive, one hopes). Either way, there is no debate that brand advocacy is an effective way to turn more people on to your product and that it does matter in a modern marketing effort. These types of advocacy are considered authentic and real and therefore carry much more gravitas and weight than traditional commercials or ads. They have longer term and more lasting effects than viral campaigns and cost virtually nothing in comparison to other more conventional marketing, such as radio, print, and television. This type of marketing takes advantage of the social media concept, "wisdom of friends," putting stock in the fact that people take their social network's recommendations very seriously and that it definitely influences and impacts their buying habits.

What does this all have to do with mobile learning, you might ask? Well, what if you could harness the power of mobile learning to help create brand advocates among your existing customers? What if you could produce great content that empowered your customers? Content that informed them and helped them see the value of your products, even more than they already do? This content should instruct users on how to make the most out of your products, whether home improvement tools, a vacation package, or electronics. By giving users useful and fresh educational content, your mobile application ("there's an app for that") is more likely to be reused. In Josh Clark's excellent book *Tapworthy* (2010), it was revealed that users download ten apps per month on average, and most are not launched more than twenty times. After two months, only one-third of apps are used at all. Gimmick apps are used only a handful of times. Consider this example: a virtual circular saw is cute, but will only be used three to five times; however, an app with videos on how to actually use a circular saw may be used two or three times more than a non-video-based app. Couple that content with social media sharing features and you can help to create your own little army of brand advocates.

In an article published in *Learning Solutions* magazine, Float's John Feser (2010) asked, "Who Owns Mobile in Your Organization?" Based on our observations of the marketplace and paying attention to what our contacts are telling us, more often than not, sales and marketing departments are very influential in getting mobile initiatives rolling in the enterprise. You can see this in a quick search of various mobile app stores; it is clear that product catalogs and simple gimmick apps abound. Who funded development of these apps? Well, it certainly wasn't IT, or learning and development. Very likely, the marketing budget paid for these experiments in mobile learning. This really needs to change going forward, especially if you want to build brand advocates and empower your customers to help you sell to their social networks. Why? Well, who knows more about how to use your products than the learning department? Who knows how to pull together the subject-matter experts (SMEs), content, resources, and talent to produce great content that is useful to people? You should be pointing at yourself right about now.

So what should you do? One easy thing would be to take a look at your industry and see how online educational content is being packaged to consumers. Hardware companies frequently have "Projects and Advice" sections on their websites, and electronics resellers have question-and-answer sections on how to connect the devices they sell. Use this research to frame up some easy ways to bring useful information to your customers. Then, after you have some ideas, talk to marketing. Perhaps there is a way to partner and share your budgets and resources to produce something truly great and a game changer to boot. Executives should see an application that truly sets your organization and its products or services apart as distinct and valuable. Often, the content that the learning department is creating for owner manuals and sales training is not really that different than the brochures shipped to the customers or the videos on the site showing the features and benefits of the product.

Some basic things to consider in the content you provide are listed below. This is, after all, training, not a hard sell, so please remember that in order to build advocacy your content needs to:

- Provide real, timely, and actionable help information,
- Use the product as a user would, that is, don't feature it as a "star,"
- Use the product safely, and just as you would want a consumer to use it, and
- Subtly reinforce your product's value proposition.

We strongly recommend using high production values in the content. Such a mobile app is more likely to have a much larger audience than you may be used to targeting. A typical internal sales module may only have an audience of hundreds of employees who are accustomed to internal jargon, photography, and video styles. Externally facing content needs to be more polished. You may want to consider hiring professional talent and scouting for a shooting location, rather than the typical talking heads in non-professionally produced content.

In preparing to deliver this content, please remember to set yourself up for success. Plan for measurement and metrics. In-app analytics are a must; creating a landing page at your site for the app store traffic is a basic requirement; using simple ecommerce conversion tools like promo codes is a viable option; and using a social media measurement platform like Owl.ly would be a smart thing to do. This will enable you to know who is sharing content from your app and, more importantly, who is buying based on their experience with the app. Remember, satisfied customers tell three others about how they feel about your product, angry ones tell three thousand.

Your next step should be to consider how brand advocacy could work for your brand. Are companies in your vertical space using it or experiencing the benefits of putting educational content onto their customers' smart phones? You should talk to marketing. Are they using brand advocacy in their efforts? How are they building it? Could they benefit from your content and expertise on creating learning? You have the great opportunity of bringing a very powerful audience to your company via a partnership between the marketing and learning departments and their respective audiences.

A Case Study of Brand Advocacy: State Farm Insurance

Let's take a close look at an application that is a great example of brand advocacy. Did you know that State Farm Insurance is in the moving business? Of course not. They aren't and have no plans to be. So why do they have a full-featured mobile application called MoveTools in the Apple App Store? MoveTools is an interactive planner that helps the user through all of the details of a house move. It comes with sections like "To-Do List," "Pack Up," and "Moving Tips," and it has a planner to remind you of the different steps you should be taking in the weeks leading up to the move. It not only provides helpful content, but it allows you to input your own information about your move. In the "Pack Up" section, the user can create a packing process parallel to their actual box packing, which results in a digital list of all the boxes and what is contained in each. The user can print out labels with bar codes that can be read by a smart phone that contains a list of the contents for each box! It is a complete app to make any move significantly smoother.

All analysis of the content, functionality, and construction of the app aside, why is State Farm, a leading insurance company, making this app available to the public? Your first answer might be so that they can sell more insurance. Certainly, that is an ultimate goal but any type of "sales" content within the app is contained within a very small popup menu that is revealed when the user touches the State Farm logo in the bottom menu bar. It's inconspicuous and, in fact, almost hidden. The obvious motivation for the application is for State Farm to strengthen their brand to a target audience. The application itself is conveying a message that has a positive effect on users such that they will associate the good experience with State Farm. Because of this, the MoveTools app is an excellent example of brand advocacy. Let's take a look at how that works.

First of all, the MoveTools application solves a problem; it relieves pain or stress. Have you ever met anyone who likes to move? In fact, usually when people move, at some time during the move they proclaim, "We are never moving again!" The entire moving process is a stressful experience. State Farm tries to alleviate some of that anxiety by providing an app that helps the user be organized and more efficient in the multitude of steps it takes to execute a move. The availability of the app creates all sorts of positive touch points between the target audience and State Farm. When the user opens the app, the State Farm logo is apparent, but not obtrusive, so it serves as a constant reminder of who is providing relief at a difficult time. The app is designed in the State Farm branding guidelines so it has the "look and feel" of State Farm. If used correctly, the app is needed throughout the whole moving process so dozens, if not hundreds, of impressions take place over the move. After successful use of the app, the user tells a friend about it and two more friends, and before long they have become brand advocates as well. They might not even be State Farm customers! When a mom learns that her neighbor is moving and she recommends the MoveTools app, then brand advocacy is in action.

A mobile application can also reinforce a brand's core qualities. As mentioned, State Farm is not in the moving business. But, as any insurance company would like to be known, they are in the "help you with big life decisions" business. They want their customers to think of them first if they have a critical or difficult experience or change in life. Whether it's an auto accident, a tornado disaster, or knowing loved ones are taken care of if the head of the household dies, there are answers and security in the brand. That's why MoveTools is such an appropriate brand advocate. It reinforces the fact that State Farm is a brand of strength and expertise—a leader in their industry.

A mobile application can also be a significant differentiator for you in your market or industry. If you have a message to put out, you need to find ways to stand out, especially if you are broadcasting your message in a cacophony of other messages. Because mobile content delivery is still a nascent technology, there is a good chance you are delivering your message on this platform before your competitors or from whomever you need to distance yourself. Mobile also says you are progressive and forward-thinking. Let your audience know that you care enough about them to deliver information to their mobile devices so you can get the message right into their hands any time, anywhere. Like any longstanding company, State Farm fights an image that they are conservative. The MoveTools application sends the message that, as a company, they are adapting to new technology to meet the needs of their target audience. This result shows that the mobile application not only reinforces the core qualities of the brand, but it can also start and fortify new qualities, too.

One final clue that the goal of this application is to strengthen the State Farm brand: it is available for free. State Farm wants it in the hands of anyone who wants to use it or even thinks he or she might use it. The messaging about the brand is meant for public consumption—for customers and non-customers alike. So what is the ROI for this app? After countless successful user experiences, State Farm has "hired" an untold amount of brand advocates, working for free in their neighborhoods and towns. Not a bad ROI!

References

Clark, J. (2010). *Tapworthy: Designing great iPhone apps*. Sebastopol, CA: O'Reilly.

Feser, J. (2010, October 28). Who owns mobile learning in your organization? *Learning Solutions*. www.learningsolutionsmag.com/ articles/550/who-owns-mobile-learning-in-your-organization.

CHAPTER 12

Developing a Mobile Management Strategy

Gary Woodill and Scott McCormick

We all know the scene. Row after row of cubicles as far as the eye can see with each one looking almost exactly the same. That may describe a corporation you have visited, or perhaps you can look down the aisle from where you sit and see that very landscape.

You'll also notice that each cubicle contains a computer. From desktop to desktop, the PC is the same make, same model, and if you were to boot it up, the same applications are locked and loaded. Why is everything the same? Why can't employees have a little hardware and software freedom of expression in their jobs?

You don't need to go much further than to ask the first company IT technician who walks past your cubicle. It is his or her job to keep your computer and all the hardware and software in the company running smoothly and to keep it stable and manageable. Yes, that charge does keep you restricted to a specific PC and on a predetermined operating system (OS) that may all seem hopelessly out of date, but it also keeps you and everyone else in the company, well, up and running (for the most part).

But what if all the rules changed? What if everyone had different computers, different models, different brand names, different operating systems, a different assortment of applications, different email clients, different . . . everything?

That dilemma is what IT departments are facing in the mobile age. A plethora of devices, operating systems, and applications are all coming to play in the corporate workspace. And their job is to manage and maintain all of these devices, as well as keep them working for you properly so you can do your job. Mobile content delivery in the workplace has caused IT departments to expand their knowledge base exponentially to accommodate the new technologies, or to put a stranglehold on multiple platforms in order to keep things under control.

Traditionally, the IT department is accustomed to exerting control over computers within an organization. IT controls the software installations, licensing, backups, patches, versioning, upgrades, and security. IT also acts as a guarantor for information systems. They ensure maximum availability and information integrity, act as a policing system for violations of policy or threats to security, offer technical expertise for swift problem resolution, and maintain technical relationships with partners. These tasks and services have become dependent on their ability to maintain centralization. The sudden influx of privately owned mobile devices into the workplace has become a threat to the established order.

Bring Your Own Device (BYOD)

The advent of smart phones and tablets at affordable prices means that high-capacity computing outside the control of IT is entering the workplace. This new upstart technology has less overall capability than the old PC-based systems, but greater flexibility afforded through peripherals, specialized apps, texting, imaging, and voice. The portability and sheer convenience mean that these devices are being used in employee functions.

For example, outside salespeople have become dependent on these devices to keep them connected, at any time, to their clients and sales support teams. They use them to touch base with the customers, run conference calls, maintain their contact lists, organize their leads and sales funnels, text their technical staff, keep up with industry announcements, follow professional publications . . . the list goes on.

A side-effect of mobile is that these devices are effectively substituting for traditional computers and their software systems in many day-to-day tasks. Laptops, in particular—which are less convenient to the mobile worker than the average mobile device (they must be removed from a case, powered up, and physically supported)—are being replaced for some activities, often by the employee's own decision. This is not simply an issue of redundancy of equipment. This movement can have serious consequences for IT because established systems begin to unravel when replaced by external, independent alternatives. This risk is pronounced when IT is slow in accommodating innovation.

In the case of salespeople, who are totally focused on making sales and generating revenue, there may be a risk of them adopting their own personal sales support systems on their mobile devices and not using the corporate-sponsored software packages. This is clearly an issue and, should this person be a high-performance employee bringing much value to the bottom line, a difficult one to solve.

First, mobile technologies may enable a salesperson's success; therefore, interference may be detrimental to the organization's income. Second, it's difficult to discipline a renegade for being successful and "A" players may choose to move on rather than conform. Mobile device users need to be accommodated, and this must be in a manner that also addresses the concerns of the organization.

Accommodation of mobile technologies can be accomplished through issuing standardized, corporate devices (also called corporate liable devices), or through the concept of "bring your own device" (BYOD), where the organization embraces the idea of a mobilized workforce, but the workers supply their own hardware, such as an iPhone or Android device. Many organizations are finding that their employees are pushing for this (Messmer, 2012). Ricoh America, in response to the mobile tsunami, recently opened the door for BYOD for its sales, field engineers, and administrative staff. Ricoh CEO Tracey Rothenberger states:

> Technology is moving very fast with the introduction of new devices every month, and we didn't want to sit down and maintain a refresh strategy on something that was a personal decision for each employee. . . . We do not care what employees bring to work as long as they follow our corporate policies for usage of the device and protection of proprietary information. (Miller, 2012)

Mobile technology, especially BYOD, raises new problems that need to be resolved. These include security, software interoperability and data sharing, ownership and control, and who pays for what.

Security and Bring Your Own Technology (BYOT)

A related trend, bring your own technology (BYOT), is an extreme form of BYOD. It allows a user to bring his or her own device, software, and usage patterns to the workplace. For example, BYOD allows employees to make their own selection of smart phones and/or tablets, but IT and other stakeholders establish software and usage patterns. BYOT extends the BYOD concept by allowing employees to select their own software combinations in ways they feel enable them to perform their duties.

BYOT, like BYOD, is becoming more prevalent in organizations. This adds yet another element of complexity to IT because of the sheer distance from corporate-sponsored software. Each organization needs to decide whether they wish to take active measures to stop it, control it, or facilitate it.

Lost/Stolen Devices and Ex-Employees

An organization's private data is its property, and is the "soul" of the business. Mobile devices may contain customer contact lists, technical data, and even sensitive material about the state of the business. Because of this, these devices pose a substantial threat in the wrong hands. A lost or stolen device could be used in fraud or corporate espionage. A personal device, owned by a former worker, could be the source of abuse should that worker try to leverage corporate information for his or her own benefit (e.g., a former employee using a client contact list to steal business for a competing company), or in retaliation for a perceived wrong (e.g., a disgruntled former employee publicly leaks sensitive information to damage the organization).

Banks and financial institutions, faced with the risk of unmanaged devices and their possible loss, are very concerned about finding a solution (Violino, 2012). They seem to be aware that this solution will have to evolve alongside the rapidly changing technology it addresses.

Software and Information Homogeneity and Control

Organization efficiency requires that information technology staff standardize its software. This allows for effective training, usage guidelines, and cost control, compliance with licensing agreements, support for contracts, maintaining interoperability, and data sharing. Mobile devices, living outside these standards, create a risk of destabilization of this regime.

First, mobile adds an additional layer of technology that IT must address. Second, it introduces hardware and software variability into the existing workspace, already pressed for people and expertise. Third, without controls, IT can no longer guarantee the completeness of company data. How do they know what is going on in those devices?

Consider the issue of malware prevention software. Not yet a major problem with mobile devices, it is only a matter of time before a major incident occurs that compromises a large multinational or public institution. IT departments are responsible to maintain information security; therefore, they will be on the hook for system disruptions or security breaches.

A great deal of investment has been made in selecting, implementing, and optimizing corporate information systems. This investment has not only consisted of time and money, but in developing a vision that is closely tied to organizational goals. These goals originated from the top decision-makers. The idea that this order, which was hard to achieve, will suddenly fall because of the potential chaos of mobile technologies is about as welcome as a dam bursting in a rainstorm. With the arrival of mobile, both IT and executives will want to keep as much of their control structure as is possible.

Private Property, Corporate Property

In BYOD environments, mobile devices are often the property of workers, and this leads to conflicts when corporations wish to exercise control, at any level, over these devices. Another concern is that not all workers own mobile devices. Mandating ownership at the worker's personal cost may be resented, and this would be a prickly issue in a unionized workplace. This is likely to be seen as an attempt at cost reduction by offloading business expenses to the employees. Attempting to enforce brand choices and/or control the device would inflame the situation.

Organizations can provide standardized devices to their workers, and this is an excellent solution for some businesses. Institutions and corporations requiring specialized security (government, research) or rugged devices (warehousing, manufacturing) would likely follow this approach.

This is not so simple in other cases because it presents two problems. One, the organization may now incur the cost of a personal computer *and* a mobile device for each employee—an expensive proposition. Two, people don't want to carry two mobile devices (one for business and one for personal use); the extra bulk is contrary to the idea of mobile.

Once again, a company's outside sales force provides a good example. They are highly mobile people who want to minimize the weight they carry, especially through airports, while maximizing their connectedness. Allowing limited personal use on a business-issued device is an option, but it's not an ideal situation for either party.

The issue becomes even more complicated when information services are provided to partners, affiliates, and customers. An acceptable compromise between private ownership and corporate ownership must be found.

Circling the Wagons: Mobile Management Strategy

Because of the sudden increase in mobile technologies, there has been a sharp rise in the need for enterprise mobile device management (MDM) and mobile application management (MAM) as companies strive to maintain order in employee use of mobile technologies.

There is some confusion about the difference between the two types of technology management, but there doesn't need to be. Just as it sounds, MDM is the setup, allocation, and support of the mobile devices used by the employees for company purposes, and MAM is the deployment, management, and support of the applications on the devices used by those same employees. That may sound overly simplistic, but misunderstandings are becoming more prevalent as the two fields become bunged together. This problem is mostly the result of solution vendors who are selling products and services that offer a "one size fits all" combination of MDM and MAM. The issue is only going to become more complicated when companies start selling mobile data management platforms.

Mobile device management provides a series of challenges. First, which mobile devices are employees going to use for their company activities? This doesn't just pertain to mobile learning, but also to their email, alerts, calendaring, company intranet usage, and so on. Because MDM governs the device itself, it is concerned with the activities of the entire device; it makes the device secure and controlled, but can be seen as intrusive. For example, MDM can prevent users from performing activities that are viewed as counterproductive, such as playing games or using Facebook. Device content can also be controlled. This is not an ethical solution when BYOD is mandated. Simply put, it's bad form to try to manage devices when you don't own them. MDM may also present significant stumbling blocks when partners, affiliates, and customers are involved; they may be opposed to an IT department viewing or having access to their data.

If employees use devices that they personally own, the enterprise will need to determine the right balance for the employee between company and personal usage. If a company does follow the BYOD model, the devices can be smartly provisioned to make it easier for the user to separate business and pleasure. BYOD does make life easier for end-users because they are comfortable on their own devices, but it creates challenges for IT because it is harder to support the variety of devices that result. BYOD can also have a bearing on your application development as apps will have to be designed for many different devices and operating systems, which can mean a substantial amount of development time.

The other alternative is for the enterprise to purchase and equip all the employees who will participate in mobile learning with identical mobile devices, an approach sometimes called "corporate liable." Obviously, there is an expense involved for this approach, but it also allows for much greater control, as all users will have the same device with the same OS and have access to the same applications. IT will also be able to build layers of security that function the same across the entire audience and that make the devices safer and more secure. All of the devices, no matter what the make, will have a specific ID number. For instance, Apple devices have a UDID number that allows for management and security to be device-specific. All devices have unique identifiers of some sort, whether a serial number, IMEI, or some other manufacturer-specific number.

Mobile Device Management Strategy

Mobile device management is primarily intended to fulfill a security role (Murray, 2012). In the event of a lost/stolen device, or should an employee leave the company, the mobile device can be blocked, locked, or erased to protect organizational information. It also allows IT staff to administer mobile devices in a manner similar to PCs in order to maximize standardization, minimize downtime due to problems, and enforce usage policy. Functions include application installations, firmware and software upgrades, scheduled backups, remote diagnostics, device history logging, and policy enforcement.

BlackBerry Enterprise Server is an example of an MDM solution designed to provision, audit, and protect smart phones and tablets through a centralized administrative interface. Their newer product, BlackBerry Fusion, is intended to work in a BYOD environment and supports BlackBerry, iOS and Android devices. With Fusion, there is limited allowance through a component called BlackBerry Balance to separate personal and business information. This is biased toward the protection of corporate data, is only available on Playbook 2.0 and enabled BlackBerry smart phones, including the Blackberry 10, and is optional. There are many other MDM providers, particularly for iOS devices. Examples include AirWatch, BoxTone, MobileIron, and Good Technology, to name just a few.

Mobile Application Management Strategy

We are used to going to an app store and downloading an app for free or for a small fee. But do you want your employees to be going to the Apple App Store or Google Play for their company mlearning? Probably not. Some vendor solutions are available that allow you to set up your own app store that has your own branding. This is a big plus for those enterprises that have spent a lot of time and money building a company "university" identity. Your development team and IT work together to set up the store, and your learners simply tap the store icon to retrieve their apps. The whole process works the same as the retail app stores, but this store is the company's and gives the needed security and management options. The ease of downloading gives your learners a positive user experience, which is important, especially on your first rollout of mlearning.

Good mobile application management demands other requirements so your learners have access to the best and current versions of apps. You will want to push notifications to let them know when a new iteration of an app is available with new content or bug and security fixes. They'll also need to know when a totally new app is available.

Your application management will help in other areas, such as security and metrics. There is greater control over the apps, as it becomes possible to disable and even wipe an app remotely if something appears wrong in the authentication of the user or the device. Mobile apps can actually be more secure than e-learning, and that will be good news for executive management and the IT department.

It's also important knowing who specifically is using your app. Mobile application management will give you helpful metrics, such as who is downloading the app, whether the app has launched, how many times it is used, and other critical measures of effectiveness. If you have goals related to your mobile learning, such as ROI, these metrics can be extremely beneficial to building an mlearning success story.

Mobile application management (MAM) is a strategy based on governing specific mobile applications deployed on a device, not the device itself. The functions are similar to MDM, but less intrusive on the user's private space. Because MAM is not concerned with what is globally occurring within the mobile device, it is well adapted for a BYOD environment when property and privacy rights are to be respected.

MAM does not have all of the capabilities of MDM, because it functions at the application level. This may be an issue if a company wants to enforce usage policies and device wide audits. MDM and MAM are not necessarily exclusive and may complement one another in some workplaces, but they are quite redundant (Faas, 2012).

MAM typically controls distribution and upgrading through a distribution API or an enterprise app store. Security can be applied to individual apps through MAM, whether an MDM solution is employed or not, and can protect against breaches or violations of policy. There are three basic approaches:

1. *Using a MAM SDK:* This requires recoding apps to communicate with an administrative server, a process that requires additional resources and therefore restricts apps to corporate selections (Gruman, 2011). App updates may present additional problems, as IT will need to rebuild new versions for each distribution. This is a very customizable solution and may be well suited to organizations that build their own custom apps. An example of an SDK solution provider is AirWatch.

2. *Containers:* This approach requires IT to fit the app into a security "container" within the device, where all of the contents are subject to a predetermined security paradigm, including access and encryption (Faas, 2012). Container contents can be selectively wiped by IT, when necessary. This is not very customizable, but can be simpler and easier to maintain. As an example, Accelian uses a container in its mobile management solution.

3. *Cloud and Middleware Solutions:* Some solutions are able to work with existing apps, without changing their source code or using a container, by relying on the cloud and middleware. When data and sensitive services reside in the cloud, middleware can be employed to create device transparency for IT and solutions developers, as well as handle many security issues. This higher degree of flexibility may prove very useful when BYOT is permitted. The additional layers may prove problematic, particularly in isolating support issues. An example of a product using this approach is Apperian's EASE product. (Disclosure: Float Mobile Learning, where the authors work, is a partner with Apperian.)

Making a Decision

In response to BYOD and BYOT conflicts, perhaps an organization would be in the position of greatest advantage to offer a stipend for mobile users to accommodate some of the mobile device costs. This is not a perfect solution and not everyone will be happy with it; however, it would allow the organization and worker to treat the mobile device as a "shared space."

MDM is a good choice for devices that demand high-security features or complete uniformity. It is also a good choice for issued devices when it need not concern itself with a user's personal data. Quite simply, personal usage is not the organization's responsibility; personal usage may even be against policy, and MDM can help enforce this.

MAM may be a better choice in many cases. In a BYOD setting, the corporate information is still protected without compromising privacy and property rights. It is also worth considering that mobile devices free the users and allow them to perform their jobs in creative and effective ways. There are many innovation opportunities for mobile devices, and the number of apps available for mobile users is steadily increasing; excessive control can defeat this advantage (Murray, 2012). For an organization wanting to leverage this advantage, an approach using containers or the cloud-and-middleware combination may be the better option.

In spite of all that we have said about mobile device management and mobile application management, the first step is to build an overall mobile learning strategy for your specific needs. You won't be able to make an informed decision about MDM or MAM until you know what requirements you have that are unique to your enterprise. A vendor solution might be just right, or a custom solution might be in order. Be careful of being shoehorned into a solution that makes you compromise on your priorities.

References

Faas, R. (2012, April 17). Why apps (not MDM) are the future of iPhone management. Cult of Mac. www.cultofmac.com/183151/why-apps-not-mdm-are-the-future-of-iphone-management-feature.

Gruman, G. (2011, April 26). Mobile application management without the heavy hand. *InfoWorld*. www.infoworld.com/d/mobile-technology /mobile-application-management-without-the-heavy-hand-770.

Miller, R. (2012, November 5). Ricoh CIO explains why he let 9,000 employees go BYOD. *CITEworld*. www.citeworld.com /mobile/21026/why-richoh-lets-9000-employees-go-byod.

Messmer, E. (2012, September 5). How BYOD has changed the IT landscape. *Network World*. www.networkworld.com /news/2012/090512-byod-262146.html.

Murray, A. (2012, June 5). Mobile application management (MAM) has put MDM in its place. *Network World*. www.networkworld.com /news/tech/2012/060512-mam-mdm-259877.html.

Violino, B. (2012, September 24). Forecast 2013: Setting a mobile risk management strategy. *Computerworld*. www.computerworld .com/s/article/9231488/Forecast_2013_Setting_a_mobile _risk_management_strategy.

CHAPTER 13

Change Management Strategies for Mobile Learning

Scott McCormick

It's not easy instituting change in any organization. There are a lot of expectations placed upon you, and some of them can be unrealistic if people are uninformed. Although you'll be a hero if the change brings success, you are also out front to take any of the arrows. If you have stepped up or been given the charge to evaluate or implement mlearning in your company, you are going to bring about change. But that doesn't mean it has to be a stressful or daunting experience. There are some steps you can take to be well equipped and smartly positioned to assure that you are headed down the right path and prepared for the challenges that come with any new endeavor.

By educating yourself on the characteristics, benefits, and challenges of mlearning, you will be able to determine how your company or organization can best use this form of learning. In addition, you will be positioning yourself to develop a business case for mlearning and be prepared to answer the inevitable questions that will arise as you work to institute a change in how people think and work. Here are the key steps you should be taking.

Immerse Yourself in the Field

You will need to take off your water wings and jump into the deep end. If you are going to be the point person for mlearning, you'd better understand it to a depth that you can have informed conversations and answer most of the questions that will be thrown at you. Start frequenting mlearning blogs and participate in the conversations. Use the comments section to ask questions, give your opinions, and let others know you are out there and want to collaborate. Follow mlearning colleagues on Twitter by using the hash tag #mlearning. Many tweets and retweets will catch your eye with links to interesting articles, blog posts, and statistical information. You can attend mlearning conferences and gatherings of associations in your area. Begin to connect with other people in the mobile learning field on sites such as LinkedIn and build your network. All of these activities should have a ripple effect on your knowledge capital and visibility in the field.

But you need to be active. You can't just add your name in a couple of places and sit back and wait. Go to the world; don't expect the world to come to you. If you become active, you will have more information and connections than you know what to do with. It can be helpful to persuade a colleague in your organization to get involved, too.

Start Using Your Own Mobile Device—A Lot

That may sound like funny advice, but how much of your device do you actually use? If someone asked you to input a custom URL into your mobile browser, could you do it? Could you change your Wi-Fi settings or pair your device to a new Bluetooth speaker? Could you scan a QR code if you were asked to? Today's handheld units have so many features that you'll be amazed at the power you have been carrying around with you. Download applications that are applicable to your daily needs, and even some that are not. How about a kid's game or a game you play against someone else at a distance? What about an app that uses features like push technology, GPS (Google Maps), augmented reality software such as Layar or Aurasma, or alerts? How about fitness tracking apps or photo sharing communities? When you take your next business trip, do as much as you can on your mobile device: book a cab or rent a car, schedule meetings, find a restaurant and make a reservation (try going to OpenTable. com or Yelp.com on your smart phone and see what happens), or check your flight status. Listen to an Internet radio station (Pandora, iTunes Radio) while you are waiting for your plane. The best part about this advice is that it won't bust your budget. Most apps are cheap or even free (just watch your data consumption if you are not on an unlimited plan). Also, don't just limit yourself to smart phone apps, try some SMS (text messaging) applications, such as getting Redbox updates, local restaurant deals, or weather.com.

Another interesting element of the app stores is that every app has its own usability group in the reviews section. Go ahead and try this: search for an app that you want to download and then read the reviews. What do people like and dislike? What works and what bombs?

The more you become familiar with the capabilities of your own device and the devices your colleagues are carrying, the more ideas you will have about how mobile learning can best be used by your organization. It is hard to find uses for a tool if you don't know all it can do.

Do Some Informal Polling

Let's face it: you are going to become the company evangelist for mlearning. You are going to have to walk the walk, and talk the talk, among your colleagues. You need to learn what kind of reception your new initiative will receive. As you interact with your co-workers in the hallway, at lunch, before and after meetings, get a feel for their attitudes and perspectives about mobile content delivery. Here are some questions you can try: "What kind of phone do you have?" "What OS version is it running?" "What do you like or not like about it?" "What are your favorite apps?" "Do you text message a lot?" "Hey, you know those compliance courses we all have to take? What would you think if you could take parts of those on your smart phone?"

Every once in a while, we have a "Lunch and Learn" where one of our employees gives a presentation about a topical subject or new piece of cool technology and everyone brings lunch into the conference room (sometimes we buy to help entice participants). Try one of those with your group and give a fun and informative talk about mlearning.

There's obviously a lot to do if you are going to be the front-runner of change in your company or organization regarding mlearning. But you can be much better prepared to lead that change if you take these steps at the beginning of your journey.

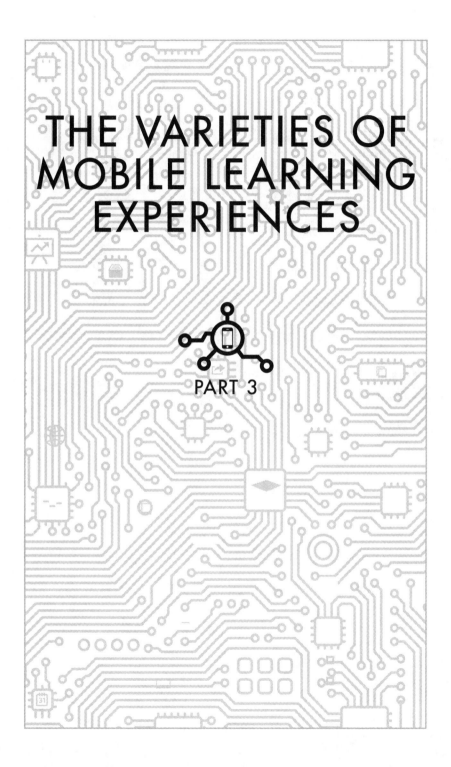

THE VARIETIES OF
MOBILE LEARNING
EXPERIENCES

PART 3

CHAPTER 14

Categories of Mobile Learning Content

Gary Woodill and Chad Udell

While it is a good idea to ensure that your employees carry mobile devices at work, what about the "mobile content" that goes on them? The current concept of content comes to us from the "instructionist model" of mobile learning, that is, the approach based on classroom metaphors or presentations of "learning materials" and testing.

But content for learning can be almost anything, including web pages that were not specifically designed for education and training, access to databases of information of interest to the person who is asking for it, or any online mobile experiences that we can learn from. Content can also be "real-life experiences," where mobile devices are used to augment the information in the physical environment, or where mobile devices are used to store and transmit information that the user wants to save or send to others.

Keeping these distinctions in mind, what most people mean by mobile content is what appears on the screens of users when they connect to specific learning materials that are designed for their use. As we shall see, it goes way beyond that.

There are many ways to slice and dice the types of mobile learning content. One way is by starting with the simplest kind of messaging and moving to the most complex:

- *One-way text-based messages:* examples include SMS text messages and email. Almost from the beginning, mobile phones have been able to send simple text messages of up to 160 characters through a function called "short message service" (SMS). This is the facility that is being used when people "text" each other. Texting can still be used to send short messages of educational value to learners on demand. Also, text-based learning games have been developed or text messages can be used as additional information (such as providing clues) for real-life games. For longer messages, email to mobile devices also can work well, although it doesn't seem to have the immediacy of texting.

- *Bi-directional text and data messages:* examples include text chat, surveys, tests, and mobile data collection. The next level of complexity for messages is two-way communications. In addition to receiving information, mobile devices are capable of sending back information to a database, to an instructor, or to a learner's peers. There are educational uses of live chat and mobile methods of gathering information for research purposes, such as surveys, polls, and other forms of mobile data collection.

- *Voice-based content and/or responses:* examples include synchronous calls and broadcast messages. Of course, we should never forget that mobile phones are first and foremost voice-based communications devices. That means we can use them to speak with people or to send spoken messages. Mobile devices can also be used to record podcasts for learners that can be listened to at will.

- *Presentation materials:* examples include instructor-designed learning materials that are often in the form of slides, graphics, or animations. This type of mobile learning content is probably closest to the model of e-learning that has developed over the past ten years. Here, successive screens of information are presented to learners in the form of courses or learning modules. Often, a test follows these presentations to show that the information has been retained at least until the test is finished.

- *Just-in-time information to be searched and retrieved:* examples include database content and web pages. Vast stores of information can be accessed via a mobile device. The real problem is finding the right information when the mobile learner wants it. This problem is being solved through sophisticated algorithms and tagging procedures that are starting to build semantic intelligence in mobile networks so that information can be more easily found. The concept of just-in-time information has its primary application in supporting the performances of individuals and groups.

- *Rich media:* examples include asynchronous, animated audio and video productions that can be downloaded or streamed to a mobile device. With the development of large storage banks for video and audio on the Internet, we've seen a huge increase in the availability of educational animation, audio, and video. In addition to rich media that are specifically produced for educational purposes, we now have vast amounts of lecture material and conference presentations available to mobile users. With the increasing capabilities of mobile devices to record and edit rich media productions, we're also seeing a huge increase in the amount of user-generated content available in this form.

- *Interactive and immersive media:* examples include games, VR, AR, and interactive apps. An additional level of complexity is to add interactivity and immersion, along with rich media, to produce educational games, virtual reality, augmented reality, and other forms of interactive applications. Many productions at this level are in the form of downloadable apps, proprietary programs that run with specific mobile operating systems, or cross-platform applications that are available on any mobile device (such as those authored in HTML5).

- *Collective/collaborative experiences:* examples include "flash mob" instructions, collaborative learning projects, and social movements supported by social media. Mobile content is aimed at groups rather than individuals. Examples include instructions for group actions such as meetings of flash mobs, mobile collaborative learning projects, and large-scale social movements that have developed as a result of users meeting in coordinating their actions using mobile devices.

Each of the above types of content requires different methods of authoring and production. Some forms of mobile production can be created by tools that come with mobile devices, while others require additional sophisticated hardware and software. For you as an instructional designer working with mobile learning, all of the above types of content should be considered in your strategic planning for the implementation of mobile learning in your organization.

CHAPTER 15

Unique Affordances of Mobile Learning

Gary Woodill

The concept of an affordance was first coined by psychologist James J. Gibson in his 1977 article, "The Theory of Affordances," and in his 1979 book, *The Ecological Approach to Visual Perception*. Essentially, an affordance is a quality or feature of an object, or of an environment, that allows an individual to perform an action. For example, the handles on a teacup allow it to be lifted without burning one's hand. This is a key affordance of a teacup. The speakers on a home theatre system allow us to hear high-fidelity sound. This is a key affordance of those speakers.

All learning technologies have a set of affordances that makes some actions possible while limiting others. If we look at three different learning technologies—a physical classroom, self-paced e-learning, and mobile learning—we can immediately see that the actions of both teachers and learners are enabled, shaped, and also limited, by the features of each of these technologies. Table 15.1 shows some of the differences (and similarities) among these three learning technologies.

Several writers have pointed out that when a new technology is introduced, the first impulse that many of us have is to apply the same methods and content we have been using to the new technology. As Marshall McLuhan noted, "We look at the present

Table 15.1. Comparison of Three Learning Technologies

Physical/Virtual Class	Self-Paced e-Learning	Mobile Learning
Teacher control	Software control	Learner control
Learner is immobile	Learner is immobile	Learner is mobile
Learner is NOT in context	Learner is NOT in context	Learner is usually in context
Information is presented, learning is facilitated	Information is interactive, can be repeated	Information is pulled as needed, or pushed as required
Books and papers are the main external source of information	Television, computers, monitors are the main external sources of information	Social networking and databases in the cloud are the main external sources of information
Assessment uses exams, homework, observation	Assessment uses short quizzes, games, tracking of interactions with learning materials	Assessment uses quizzes, games, behavior tracking, search queries, gestures, geolocation, sensors, portfolios

through a rear-view mirror. We march backwards into the future" (McLuhan & Fiore, 1967).

In the case of mobile learning, this tendency is reflected in the early applications for mobile learning, which included traditional instructional uses such as the delivery of courses, lectures, video, and notes; use of devices as personal organizers by both students and instructors; provision of assessments on mobile devices, especially multiple-choice questions; and attempts to make mobile devices terminals for collecting data for learning management systems. All of these uses of mobile technology are based on a 250-year-old classroom instruction methodology.

In order to do things differently, we need to understand the *unique* affordances of mobile devices. In 2013, the U.S. Department of Defence's ADL group issued a report on their MoTIF Project that included an inventory of "capabilities of mobile devices," a similar concept to affordances. If we broaden the concept of capabilities to include features of mobile environments and look for additional features of mobile devices, we can see that there are at least twenty-five possible affordances of mobile devices, as shown in the list below:

- Camera(s)
- Clock
- Cloud storage
- Computing functions/apps
- Document production and viewing
- Embodiment
- External sensors
- Geolocation
- Individual addressability
- Input/output peripherals
- Internal sensors
- Internet connectivity
- Media viewer/playback
- Memory
- Messaging
- Microphone and audio recording
- Microprojection
- Networking
- Notifications and alerts
- Portability/mobility
- Short-range communication
- Touchscreens
- Ubiquity
- Voice/phone communications
- Wearability

Detailed suggestions on how to use a number of these affordances for mobile learning are outlined in the next few chapters by Chad Udell. I'm sure there are other affordances of mobile devices and environments that can be identified and discussed in terms of their usefulness in learning and development. The future will also bring new functionality that we haven't even thought about to the mobile world. As technology evolves and costs to bring advanced features and sensors to devices decrease, hardware will gain functionality currently impossible. Let's briefly look at each of the above affordances to see how each might be used in learning and development.

Camera(s)

One of the big shifts with mobile learning is the fact that people both enjoy and learn from making their own personal audiovisual productions. Many people then post these images and videos to sites like Instagram, Vine, YouTube, and Flickr. Some people, known as LifeLoggers or LifeBloggers, even wear cameras twenty-four hours a day seven days a week, capturing every aspect of their lives. Others are now using mobile equipment, such as Google Glass, to provide a first-person point of view on the world in which they are moving. This facility can be used in training for recording actions and words for later critique by supervisors or trainers, or could even be broadcast live over the Internet, with instant feedback coming from the person who is observing at a distance. First-person point of view (POV) telepresence is now possible with wearable computers containing the right optical and networking capabilities.

Cameras are also at the core of "augmented reality," a technology that adds text and/or virtual objects to the scene or object that the camera is focused on. Augmented reality is in its infancy, but has huge potential for training and development by providing supplemental information for any scene.

Cameras and mobile devices are also used to capture and interpret Quick Response (QR) codes, which can then provide additional information about a particular object or environment, including instructions on how to operate or understand a piece of equipment.

Clocks

Virtually all mobile devices have a built-in clock that can be used for telling the time (converted to any time zone), as well as used as a timing device for events or recordings. Clocks are integral to the provision of alerts, alarms, and triggers, which can all be used in the development of educational activities. Content and activities can be altered, allowed, or disallowed based on this vital aspect of use context. And, of course, the clock in mobile devices can be used for teaching time.

Cloud Storage

The provision of huge banks of servers by large providers like Amazon, Google, and Microsoft has led to the concept of "cloud" storage and programming. The cloud metaphor simply means that this vast resource is available from anywhere, one of the technologies that make modern mobile learning possible. Information can be stored anywhere. You rarely know the actual physical location or the source of the information that you are receiving. Because of the cloud, the cost of digital storage is virtually nothing, which is why many services give up to a terabyte in the cloud for free. Cloud storage is one of the unique affordances that makes mobile learning possible, available anywhere, any time.

Computing Functions/Apps

Mobile devices such as smart phones and tablets are full-scale computers in their own right. In fact, a typical smart phone is ten to fifteen times faster than the Cray 1 supercomputer of 1979 (Croucher, 2010). The iPad 2 is about as powerful as the Cray 2 supercomputer, the world's fastest computer in 1985 (Markoff, 2011). Because of this power, and the mature and robust software development kits (SDKs) available for these platforms, mobile devices can be programmed to do almost anything within imagination. The number of programs for mobile devices, known as apps, has exploded, with over two million apps available in the Apple iPhone App Store and Google Play. While many of these apps are not applicable to enterprise learning and development, a large number are useful for mobile learning of any kind, ranging from support for school curricula to enterprise training and professional continuing education.

Of course, mobile devices such as smart phones and tablets already have built-in computer functions, such as calculators, databases, memory, and the ability to be programmed locally. At this stage of the development of mobile learning, you really need to be a programmer to produce anything significant, but drag-and-drop programming for non-technical people is already in the prototype stage and will be available shortly for production-ready deployment.

With the advent of "big data," there is talk of "machine learning" in addition to using mobile devices for training and development.

Machine learning refers to the ability of mobile devices to process large amounts of data in order to discover relationships that previously were unknown. As mobile devices become faster and more powerful, knowledge will be developed in real time, and decisions will be made or relevant information provided as events happen. This cloud-based computing largely takes place outside of mobile devices themselves, but contextual data from mobile devices and/or user input can be used in such calculations and push new or different output to users in the field as circumstances change.

Most importantly, mobile devices as computers are being used to augment human memory and thinking abilities. As Clive Thompson (2013) has argued in his recent book, *Smarter Than You Think*, "hybrid thinking" using the unique abilities of humans combined with the unique abilities of computers will become more powerful in the near future than the use of human experts or computers by themselves. Basically, we are all "smarter" with mobile devices at hand, giving us immense computing power, and the entire Internet in our pockets.

Document Production and Viewing

Most mobile devices such as smart phones and tablets are equipped with keyboards and have some word processing software available for them so that they can be used in both document production and document viewing. Text still remains a primary way of communication and delivery of knowledge, and most mobile devices support this method of communication. Text-based materials come in many forms, such as e-books, PDF files, chat rooms, SMS messaging, other messaging systems like Snapchat and WhatsApp, and mobile websites. Mobile makes these texts available from anyplace, anywhere, at the "point of need." While the nature of reading has changed, the amount of reading in the world has not declined.

Embodiment

Embodiment of mobile devices, whether swallowed, attached to parts of the nervous system, sensed through brain waves, or placed on or under the skin, are all in the testing phase of development. Right now, Motorola's research division has announced a prototype indigestible pill that transforms your body into an authentication passcode transmitter by broadcasting information from your stomach. Perhaps less radical than that idea is the use of a temporary password tattoo. Also, stretchable circuits can be used for skullcaps to detect concussions in sports, or baby thermometers can be attached to the skin in order to track an infant's vital signs. Other embodiment technologies that can be built into mobile devices include eye tracking, voice recognition, and fingerprint identification. While many of these technologies are not ready to ship soon, these developments indicate the direction of embodied mobile technologies.

External Sensors

While internal sensors in mobile devices detect movement and location of the device itself, there's no reason why external sensors cannot be hooked up to a smart phone or tablet. If this happens, we all can become nomadic monitors, gathering data as we move through the world. This possibility was discussed about five years ago in the *Economist* magazine, in a report called "A World of Witnesses." At that time, there were already prototypes of the concept working in the world and, since then, more examples have been developed.

One area for future growth is to equip mobile devices with "sniffing" capabilities, which can be activated automatically and without user command. The *Economist* wrote in 2008 that:

> . . . researchers at America's Purdue University reported that they are building a system for the state of Indiana designed to use a network of mobile phones to detect and track radiation. In the event of a nuclear leak or a "dirty bomb," the sensors of large numbers of phones, all identifying their location through the global-positioning system (GPS), would point authorities to the source of the radiation.

Such tracking systems rely on the collective information from large numbers of phones, whose owners may not even be aware of the part they are playing in this. If, say, a car is carrying a dirty bomb and driving down a street, it passes other cars. The mobile phones inside those passing cars would send information to a database. The signal would grow weaker as the distance from the source increased, whereas the signal from phones in approaching cars would grow stronger. The software would then use the sum of this information to pinpoint the bomb.

In the same article, *The Economist* suggested that mobile devices could be attached to taxicabs that move around a city, automatically sniffing out problems and reporting on environmental data. Carbon monoxide levels, amounts of ozone, pollen count, intensity of ultraviolet rays, ambient noise, and temperature or barometric readings are relatively easy to detect by sensors in mobile phones in such a way that users would not even notice, or they could be used for alerts to hidden dangers. External sensors can build a profile of our immediate environment and show it to us in a visualization that helps us to understand the world we are living in.

Geospatial Data

One of the major differences between mobile learning and e-learning is the use of geospatial data, including the user's location, orientation, and movements in the space and relevant physical information about the features of the environment in which the user is located.

Specifically, geospatial data from mobile phones and tablets are emerging as a special kind of data that link many other kinds of information together, integrating them into a holistic view of what a person is doing or has done. This built-in feature of many mobile devices—the generation of geospatial data—is transforming learning in ways we are just starting to imagine. In 2012, Jeff Jonas, distinguished engineer and chief scientist for IBM's Entity Analytics group, described geospatial data as "analytic superfood." "Geospatial data," he said, "is going to rip the lid off what's computable" (Jonas, 2012). It is the basis of what is served up in augmented reality and provides much of the context that can be used to determine what information is relevant to the user.

Already, educational uses of geospatial data include mapping and navigation, games like geocaching, and apps that use geofencing to restrict access to files unless a person is at a specific geographical location.

Individual Addressability

Each mobile device has a unique phone number or other address-able messaging identifier and, usually, is owned by a single individual. As well, most individuals have their own email addresses. Both mean that, while on the move, a specific individual can be located and communicated with as needed. Each individual can call (or be called), regardless of his or her actual location. In a traditional landline system, we "come to the phone." With mobile, the excuse of not being near a phone is not available as a reason for not answering a call. As Ling and Donner (2009) explain:

> Having a mobile phone—along with caller ID and voicemail and texting functionality—means that we can call or text directly to the individual. If we are "indisposed" at the moment, we can still see who is calling and make a snap decision as to whether we should enter indisposition in order to take the call or simply send it to our voicemail account. The problem is even easier with texting, which is by its nature asynchronous. . . . The mobile phone puts each of us into play. We are remotely accessible to others . . . whenever and wherever [we] happen to be.

There are several implications of the availability of individual addressability. There is an interlacing of mediated and co-present activities, for example, we can be reading text messages while we are listening to someone speak to us in the same room. Throughout the day, we can maintain a unique "connected presence" with family and friends, communicating at a moment's notice.

From an educational point of view, individual addressability makes the personalization of content possible, both by being made available to a learner and by being tracked to evaluate learner engagement and responses to specific learning materials.

Input/Output Peripherals

If we think of smart phones and tablets as small computers, then it makes sense that a number of mobile peripherals can be added to them for increased functionality. Small peripherals that can be added include card readers, tiny printers, miniature speakers, micro projectors, and small scanners—both 2D and 3D. While learning uses for these peripherals have yet to be developed, it is important to think about them when planning new and innovative uses for mobile learning. How could you connect existing sensors, tools, and other work aids to your mobile devices to better inform your workers?

Internal Sensors

Most smart phones and tablets have internal sensors that calculate the position, orientation, and movement of the device itself. The sensors include an accelerometer, a compass, gyroscope, and connections to a global positioning system (GPS). Because of the sensors, the software in the device can detect the location of the device and what the cameras of the device are pointing at. This capability has all sorts of uses in learning, including augmented reality, simulations, gesture recognition, and navigational guidance.

Internet Connectivity/Search

Almost all mobile phones and tablets being sold today have a mobile browser that connects to the Internet and World Wide Web. From any location, provided the user is connected to a mobile network, searches can be undertaken on any topic. For those users who subscribe to social media, social search can be used to ask other users for information. From a pedagogical point of view, mobile devices lend themselves to quick reference material, inquiry-based learning approaches, and learning at the "point of need" when an immediate answer is required.

Media Viewer/Playback Function

Nearly all mobile communications devices today include media viewers and playback functionality, in order to see and hear images, animations, video, and audio. Early forms of mobile learning included the creation of "podcasts," although this terminology is now fading as the ability to create and provide video and audio experiences is taken for granted. The field of mobile learning is moving into "multi-screen experiences," whereby the user moves freely among a variety of screens (such as phones, tablets, monitors, and televisions) and audio playback devices while software keeps track of where the user is in order to maintain continuity. Also, the quality of video and audio is improving with new generations of devices, enhancing the user experience and making it more realistic.

Memory

Mobile smart phones and tablets are devices for augmenting human memory, allowing data capture and storage. The amount of memory available in a mobile device is steadily increasing so that now it is not uncommon to have several gigabytes available in your mobile device. Vastly increased memory (or connections to miniature hard drives) is necessary if mobile devices are being used in a continuous 24/7 fashion to record all aspects of a user's life. The memory functions of mobile devices can be used for surveillance whereby authorities or organizations collect and analyze information about citizens, but they can also be used for "sousveillance" whereby citizens capture and store activities of agents of the state or corporations.

Having large memory capacity and increasingly faster chips allows for "brute force computing" and "machine learning," wherein large sums of data are analyzed on the fly for near real-time decision making. More likely, mobile devices with greatly increased capacities will be paired with human decision making, creating a form of "hybrid thinking" that utilizes the strengths of humans combined with machines (Thompson, 2013).

Messaging

Text and multimedia messaging have been built into mobile phones almost from the beginning. Short message service (SMS)—also known as "texting"—is very close to a universal medium for receiving questions from users and sending immediate responses. This is being used in a number of ways for teaching, including homework support from schools and universities, after-hospitalization care for patients who have been discharged, alerts to students on campus, and informational support for pregnant women and new mothers. Messaging in the form of chat applications and social media is also increasingly playing a role in learning and development.

Microphone and Audio Recording

Most mobile phones and tablets have a microphone and include built-in applications for sound recording. Sound input can be used in a number of ways in learning apps. It can be used to identify a specific soundscape, a particular piece of music, or a voice. These capabilities can then be used as input for additional programs, such as the ability to play musical instruments on a mobile device. Text to speech and speech to text are powerful technologies to both leverage existing content in new ways and to generate new learning content.

Microprojection

Microprojection is an emerging capability of mobile devices and is related to the concept of "surface computing." Micro projectors can be built into a smart phone or tablet, or can be small external peripherals. They can project images onto any surface for instant presentations. Prototypes of micro projectors used to add video to print newspapers have already been developed. As recent research at MIT has shown (Mistry, 2009), when images are projected onto a user's hands, the results can be used in gesture detection. All these possibilities are in development at the present time and will be available within the next five years.

Networking

While networking is not unique to mobile computing, the fact that users can remain connected to the network while moving around is a unique affordance. This means that social media can be used to connect two or more users and for the development, coordination, and collaboration of mobile communities. Because of the individual addressability of each mobile device, specific people can be contacted at will through the mobile network, at any time and wherever they may be located.

Many users value their mobile devices because of their ability to keep users connected with each other. Texting and chat are widely used to keep in touch, and the loss of the ability to connect to others can lead to emotional upset.

Notifications and Alerts

Most smart phones and tablets have built-in clocks that allow alerts and notifications when appropriate. These alerts may be in the form of sound signals, flashing LED lights, or vibration. Prototypes have also been developed to have mobile phones change their shapes or shift their weight to one side or another as signals. These capabilities can be used in educational games or in teaching users navigation and way-finding skills. Notifications can also be used in "proximity detection" to indicate when a user is near a specified object or person.

Portability/Mobility

The portability of mobile devices makes mobile learning possible. While the term "portable" has a long history in computing, calling something mobile simply means that a person can carry it continuously, ready for use when needed. The portability of mobile devices has been made possible by the miniaturization of electronic components and new manufacturing techniques that have allowed this shrinkage of devices while increasing their functionality and power. The concept of portable is changing to a concept of "unconsciously mobile"—meaning that the user doesn't even consider whether to take the device along. He or she simply does. The fact that most mobile devices today are attached to a person's belt or can be carried in a pocket or purse means that mobile learning is truly ubiquitous. Future developments include even smaller devices, the modularization of distinct components of mobile computing, wearable and embodied electronic devices, and developments in nanotechnology.

Short-Range Communications

Short-range communication abilities of mobile devices are used to connect with nearby peripherals, such as printers, keyboards, mice, scanners, and headsets. A variety of methods are available for short-range communication with mobile devices, including Bluetooth, radio frequency identification tags (RFID), near field communications (NFC), infrared beams, and Wi-Fi connections.

This also allows for unique shared group experiences simply impossible before; one can now share audio, video, photos, and documents seamlessly via mobile applications and communications like iOS's built-in AirPlay and AirDrop functionality.

Touchscreens

Almost every smart phone or tablet purchased today is equipped with a multi-touch screen that is used to control and interact with the device. Because they are multi-touch, more than one finger can be used to control and interact with what is on the screen. This enables new applications based on gestures or stylus use. Some multi-touch screens even measure pressure on the screen that can be used in haptics-based learning applications.

Ubiquity

Mark Weiser (1991) articulated a vision for ubiquitous computing in the early 1990s. Ubiquitous computing is already here, seen by the fact that a majority of people in developed countries have mobile devices available to them at all times. As electronics become wearable and are embedded in human bodies and into appliances, tools, and other objects (the "Internet of Things"), mobile learning will become even more ubiquitous. The vision, which has almost been achieved, is to have the ability to pull information from any location at any time, as well as to be able to send information back into a network. Ubiquity also denotes the fact that mobile technologies become "invisible" as they meld into the everyday world.

Voice/Phone Communications

Because of the variety of things that can be done using a smart phone or tablet, there's a tendency to forget that mobile phones were originally designed for voice phone calls. In fact, the acronym for ordinary landline use of telephones is "plain old telephone service" or POTS. Of course, voice communication using mobile devices now uses a variety of technologies, including voice over IP (VoIP) and various forms of online calling or conferencing, such as the services offered by Skype, Adobe Connect, Google+, WebEx, and many others.

Wearability

Mobile learning through wearable technologies is just taking off, in spite of the fact that it has been around since the 1980s. As mentioned earlier, mobile learning has become ubiquitous because of the fact that mobile phones are generally worn or carried on one's person at all times. In addition to "belt wear," we are increasingly seeing mobile devices being attached to people's wrists, integrated with their glasses, pinned to their clothing, worn as hats, built into their underwear, or used as jewelry. Multiple wearable devices can be connected to a "body area network" (BAN). A BAN can store data and be coordinated through a mobile phone or other miniature computing device and can co-mingle data collected by other users throughout an enterprise.

New Possibilities by Combining Affordances

If we combine two or more of these affordances, new possibilities will emerge. As instructional designers, it is important that we understand these various possibilities, and all their combinations, before embarking on the design and development of mobile learning experiences. Learning is complex, and the design of effective learning materials requires an understanding of objectives, the capabilities of the technologies and environments we are in, and the kinds of learning activities that both motivate and teach in a way that is engaging and memorable.

References

A world of witnesses. (2008, April 10). *The Economist.* www.economist.com/node/10950499.

Advanced Distributed Learning (ADL) Initiative. (2013). *Mobile learning survey report.* U.S. Department of Defence. www.adlnet.gov/wp-content/uploads/2013/09/MOTIF-SURVEY-REPORT-3.pdf.

Croucher, M. (2010, June 2). Supercomputers vs. mobile phones. *Walking Randomly* (Blog). www.walkingrandomly.com/?p=2684.

Gibson, J.J. (1977). The theory of affordances. In R. Shaw & J. Bransford (Eds.), *Perceiving, acting, and knowing: Toward an ecological psychology.* Mahwah, NJ: Lawrence Erlbaum Associates.

Gibson, J.J. (1979). *The ecological approach to visual perception.* Boston, MA: Houghton Mifflin.

Jonas, J. (2012). How big data is changing the world. Online video. www.youtube.com/watch?v=aopf7kZ9rcc.

Ling, R., & Donner, J. (2009). *Mobile communication.* Cambridge, UK: Polity Press.

Markoff, J. (2011, May 9). The iPad in your hand: As fast as a supercomputer of yore. *Bits (New York Times Blog).* http://bits.blogs.nytimes.com/2011/05/09/the-ipad-in-your-hand-as-fast-as-a-supercomputer-of-yore.

McLuhan, M., & Fiore, Q. (1967). *The medium is the message: An inventory of effects.* New York: Bantam Books.

Mistry, P. (2009). The thrilling potential of SixthSense technology. Online presentation. www.ted.com/talks/pranav_mistry_the_thrilling_potential_of_sixthsense_technology.html.

Thompson, C. (2013). *Smarter than you think: How technology is changing our minds for the better.* New York: Penguin.

Weiser, M. (1991, September). The computer for the 21st century. *Scientific American: Special Issue on Communications, Computers, and Networks,* 265(3). http://wiki.daimi.au.dk/pca/_files/weiser-orig.pdf

CHAPTER 16

Leveraging Geolocation to Make Your Content More Relevant

Chad Udell

I hope, by now, it's clear that mlearning is *not* e-learning on a mobile device. Instead of teaching students "just-in-case" they need specific knowledge at a later date, mobile learning is focused on "just enough, just in time, and just for me." This shift reflects that mobile learning is more often about performance support and adaptive personalized learning than the study of materials for later use. It is also being driven by the move to use some of the unique affordances of mobile devices in ways that have never been possible before.

One example of a unique affordance of mobile devices is the fact that most of them have built-in GPS, giving them geolocational capabilities. Almost all mobile devices—phones and tablets alike—have some sort of global positioning system (GPS) feature available to use in order to help users ascertain where they are and what is around them. This feature can be used to tailor a learner's user experience in a very direct and effective manner.

Give Your Learners "Just Enough"

Mobile learning is best suited for smaller bits of information. More accurately, good mlearning is more granular than most material used for e-learning. The chunks of information are usually digestible and complete by themselves.

How do you know that small bits of information are accurately chosen and displayed to be useful in a specific geographical context? A couple quick tips on how to use GPS data in mobile learning might help.

Keep content short and focused, based on where you are. Different use cases can have distinct content needs based on where the user is at the time. For this exercise, let's explore jobsite safety. In the jobsite equipment safety training world, a piece of general courseware may have to provide an exhaustive list of things that the learner needs to know across all conditions and worksites. In practice and onsite, only the pieces of equipment available at a site really have to have their safety information available as a quick reference. Does your jobsite have a concrete saw or a backhoe present? No? Then don't provide safety information to the mobile device user about those pieces of equipment.

Combine your location-based curation with the current time to produce a winning combination. The learner's intention when accessing information at home after work hours is likely different than when accessing the same site or app during work hours at the office. Think about your habits. When you use the AA.com or Delta.com sites for your travel needs from home, you probably are looking for different information than when you are en route to the airport in a taxi or when you are strolling through the terminal. Infer intent via triangulation of location and the setting or time of the access, and you can tailor much of the content to match the user's needs.

Make Sure Your Information Is "Just in Time"

Only in sci-fi productions like *Dr. Who* or *Looper* do time and space typically cross over, but there can be direct linkages to geolocation and time-of-information access in mobile learning. If this concept sounds like it came from the future, just follow me for a moment.

With some planning and design, you can create mobile learning that not only puts information at the person's fingertips when it's needed, but also can let the person know when and where she might need to know something she hasn't specifically requested. For example, here is a serious and very effective use of such a notification: If you have an Android smart phone or iPhone with iOS 6 or newer, and your carrier supports it, you may have at one time received an AMBER Alert for a missing child. This is important just-in-time information, and it is targeted to specific geographical regions.

Weather alerts can be delivered like this, as well, turning your phone into a weather radio of sorts. This is highly effective for situational awareness enhancement, since the mobile device rarely leaves your side.

You could take a similar approach with work-related information—letting your employees know about emergency situations in an office or even giving your outdoor employees updated weather information so they come to the job ready to work with the adequate clothing or protective gear.

Just-in-time reaches new heights when you explore the world of geofences (a virtual perimeter for a real-world geographic area) for your mobile learning. For example, Apple's Reminders app on iOS is capable of telling you to water the garden when you return home or to reboot the servers when you get to work, because it knows where you live and where you work (provided you've told it that information ahead of time). Entering and exiting geofenced areas could trigger a nearly infinite number of workflows, announcements, and information delivery.

The required APIs for creating geofences are available to be used in most major platforms, with Android's LocationManager and iOS's CoreLocation fitting the bill nicely. Mobile web browsers are also capable of discerning the user's location, so it is not confined to just apps. With the advent of Siri and the coming rise of intelligent personal digital assistants, this type of just-in-time information is only going to increase.

Take Advantage of "Just for Me"

Mobile, in essence, is always a personal thing. These devices are always with us, within reach, and often owned by us. Because of this, we've made them ours by customizing the devices and setting up accounts and preferences. The device can store this information and compare it with GPS data to create a customized mix of learning content never before possible.

Searches for information can be confined to a specific radius around the user, sort the results found by proximity, and even hide or omit irrelevant distant information, which could be construed as noise. You have the power as the designer to tailor information presented to the users based on where they are and provide personalized content that is pertinent and timely.

Taking Geolocation Further

When you get the basics, doors open to you that you likely overlooked in your earlier mobile learning designs. Consider these possibilities:

- Files tied to GPS coordinates
- Location tied to actions, such as sending messages and emails
- Geofenced reminders to check things or perform specific tasks
- Integrating calendars with locations and vice versa

Once you've tapped into device capabilities like GPS in your mobile learning, you are well on your way to maximizing your workers' performance by making their information just in time, just enough, and just for them.

CHAPTER 17

Incorporating Multi-Touch and Gestures into Mobile Learning

Chad Udell

We live in a touchy-feely, device-driven world. Your phone, tablets, and likely your laptop have some ability to interpret and use multi-touch input to assist with using your devices in a wide variety of ways. These types of inputs help us interact with on-screen elements, mimic real-world gestures, and lower the wall between the metaphor of icon-driven graphics and physical objects. You've likely seen videos of new computer users, children, and even animals interacting with smart phones and tablets naturally, easily, and with few troubles at all. These devices are intuitive and natural to use for people (and creatures!) of all ages and skill levels. In fact, toddlers who have experiences on a multi-touch tablet will often see a magazine as a mobile device that doesn't work, or a television as broken, as they push on objects on a page to see what they will do. Reflect on this for a moment in the scope of your experience as a designer for other screen-based experiences.

When the original e-learning experiences, such as CD-ROMs and web applications, were created, these courses often would be accompanied by an introduction that was more like "Using a Computer 101" than it was related to the core learning objectives for the course. Tutorials like "here is how you use a mouse" (and more) all permeated these interactive pieces. This was largely needed, because many users had either little computer experience or they had moved from an experience based on monochrome "green screens" or terminals to a GUI-driven personal computer.

These tutorials were also needed because using pointer devices like a mouse and a cursor is nothing like anything in the real world. There is no physical parallel, and the metaphor of files, folders, and clicking and dragging is an artificial contrivance at its root.

Why tap "Next" when you can swipe right to left? Why click or tap a magnifying glass icon when you can pinch and zoom? The rotate or flip buttons are pointless when you can grab an object and spin it with two fingers. With touch-based interfaces, the possibilities are incredible.

So, with the new vocabulary of input and control at our fingertips, why are so few of us taking advantage of these new features in designing our mlearning experiences? In my view, I think there are three primary drivers holding the industry back from adopting true multi-touch and gestural inputs in our mlearning work:

1. Lack of design thinking and commitment to creating a mobile-first experience,
2. Lack of experience and vision creating or designing for a multi-touch and gestural metaphor, and
3. Lack of support for these input methods in common authoring tools we use to produce typical learning products.

Let's explore these issues and suggest some ways to overcome them.

Creating a Mobile-First Experience

In my book *Learning Everywhere* (2012), one of the four main content types I explore is "Content Converted from Other Sources."

This approach, while valid and appropriate for many pieces of content in your library, is by its nature not a mobile-first experience. This is evident when interactions and elements are brought over from a mouse-and-keyboard-driven environment.

Artifacts like mouse hovers, prompts to "click here," "Next" buttons, and many other elements that are needed or helpful on a computer have no place or are completely inappropriate and unusable on a tablet or smart phone.

Consider the cliché of an exploratory or metaphorical interface that requires you to hover over items to gather more information on them. This simply will not work on a mobile device.

How to get away from these conventions? The answer is stop "converting" and start redesigning. Take into account the target device's capabilities and re-examine all and any user interface or user experience factors that could or should change. On-screen prompts, user interface controls, and deeper interactions in your applications and websites need to be used instead.

Designing for Multi-Touch and Gestural Metaphors

Design disciplines all have their own sets of patterns and conventions, visual languages, and approaches to standardization for how the design should be conveyed to engineers, developers, or manufacturers who need to interpret the plans to create the final product.

Software designers use Garrett IA and UML diagrams. Architects use a standard set of views, elevations, or projections, and specific types or elements for plumbing, doors, and the like. Electrical engineers all use the same sets of figures to relay items like transistors, resistors, and other items needed for the schematics.

A similar sort of vocabulary for gestural and multi-touch, and a set of conventions on when, where, and why the various types of gestures should be used, has emerged. Covered in great length and amazing detail in *Designing Gestural Interfaces* (2008), by Dan Saffer, this set of rules, and the accompanying visual vocabulary that informs developers how to employ them, is something new to most of the training community.

A quick Google image search for "multi-touch gestures" results in a wide array of visual depictions of these gestures.

Sample Gestures

To begin incorporating these gestures intelligently into your work, it would be wise to read up on this topic, but you can also find libraries of ready-made graphics to incorporate into your sketches and wireframes. Stencils for common diagramming software programs like Visio, PowerPoint, Keynote, or OmniGraffle are readily available, so you can start designing with a gestural language immediately. Just having access to the templates certainly doesn't make you an expert, but it does give you a framework you can start to explore and an expanded toolkit to enable you to design mobile-first interfaces.

Supporting Gestural Input in Your Development Workflow

If you have started creating mobile-first experiences and documenting your design process with properly annotated gestural inputs, you may be wondering where to take things next. If you are primarily a rapid e-learning tool user, you have no real options available to you at this time. At the time of this writing, no major software packages out there—regardless of whether they state they support mobile or not—can directly address gestural or multi-touch input out of the box.

This certainly throws a wrench into the works, but it doesn't need to completely stop you from trying out long presses, swipes, and more in your next mobile learning project. For the most part, HTML authoring tools don't support this sort of input directly either. There might be documentation for a specific device, and operating system developer areas on the web to show you how to support these gestures, but you are going to be mostly on your own when it comes time to write the code.

Some tutorials can help you get started with multi-touch and HTML5, and some mobile-friendly JavaScript libraries already have support for these gestures. Recently, some enterprising and bright developers have risen to the challenge to make this easier and have created some third-party libraries that make developing web experiences with multi-touch and gestural input capabilities much easier. For example, the library Hammer.js adds robust support for the most common gestures and touch events. On top of that, it has the rather puny tagline, "You can touch this!" to boot, if you like that sort of thing.

Summary

The world of multi-touch is an expanding and interesting place to explore. The intuitiveness of the use of gestures for interacting with content is real and demonstrable. Your users will value the time you take to craft mobile-first interfaces. With some minor adjustments to your design workflow and attention to the changes needed in your development toolset, you can accommodate and embrace these new ways to empower your users.

References

Saffer, D. (2008). *Designing gestural interfaces.* Sebastopol, CA: O'Reilly.

Udell, C. (2012). *Learning everywhere: How mobile content strategies are transforming training.* Nashville, TN/Alexandria, VA: Rockbench /ASTD.

CHAPTER 18

Storing Preferences and Inferring Intent in Mobile Learning Experiences

Chad Udell

Mobile devices are personal. We bring them to work with us, but in most cases, still own them, unlike laptop computers provided by our companies. We personalize the home screens and wallpapers. We install apps and widgets. We add our own contacts and take photos of people we know and places we visit.

These devices know our most intimate details. You bank with them. You check on your medical data. You text family members updates on your latest news and whereabouts daily without a second thought. You perform video calls and maybe even send Snapchats for someone's private consumption.

Our learning on these devices has mostly been devoid of this level of personalization. In the pursuit of just in time, we have mostly been neglecting the just for me aspects of mobile learning. Learning on these highly personal devices should be individualized, as well. A number of sites and apps understand this.

With Yelp, you log in and receive a list of restaurants around you and have easy access to comments and reviews. The Weather Channel app knows your favorite locations for instant retrieval of weather conditions at your parents' home or your upcoming vacation destination.

Apple's Passbook app is indispensible to me, and it may be the current ultimate example of inferring intent. It knows where

I am going next, what coffee shop I frequent, and when my credit card bill is due. It knows what I want to do on the day I do it, and whether my flight is delayed.

This schism between our real-world activity and learning isn't that surprising. Our previously created learning content rarely took any aspects of personalization into account either. One size fits all was the de rigueur standard.

e-Learning has had some success at personalization, modest as it might be. Most courses can restart where we left off, know when we completed them, and probably even remember what we answered on practice exercises or the final assessments. But does the course really know about us? What we need? What we are trying to accomplish today?

Properly programmed, our mobile devices can know this. From providing us email, tracking calendar events, listing contacts, knowing our location and syncing with our time zone, the mobile device you have with you already knows more about you than your grade school friends ever did.

Mobile learning can leverage this deep knowledge of us for our benefit. Even the simplest HTML5 mobile web experiences have rich, powerful databases available to them to store data, preferences, and history. WebSQL (now deprecated), Indexed DB, and various tutorials for offline programming and databases for iOS and Android are out there offering examples and tips on how to tailor a web experience for the user to help personalize and store information about the user's needs.

Just as many web content management systems and social sites capture our history and reflect it back to us, we need to start tailoring our mobile learning, performance support, and job aid experiences to take into account the users' true needs and preferences. On a large scale, this requires data storage and bandwidth. These are two things we currently have in abundance.

Data storage aside, there is need to use some powerful algorithms if we are truly going to provide information that is "just for me." A growing list of articles, SDKs, engines, and APIs is emerging to help you do just this.

In 2010, Eric Schmidt took the stage and talked about the next logical step for search. "Think of it as a serendipity engine," Schmidt said. "Think of it as a new way of thinking about traditional text search where you don't even have to type" (quoted in Boulton, 2010).

What we are really talking about is inferring intent via context, past expressed intent, our tastes, and our social network behavior. This is a powerful recipe to create a perfect learning experience for anyone, no matter where he or she is located.

It doesn't stop there. Natural language processing and digital agents will definitely revolutionize the way we receive information that is important to us. Why do I need a copy of *USA Today* outside my hotel room door when I have Flipboard and Siri? Almost all of the information in an average newspaper is not relevant to me, but with a user-agent-assisted or personalized account that knows my interests and history, nearly everything is something I want to read, share, or even comment on. Certainly, there is a danger that looking at the world only through a lens created by you could induce a sort of tunnel vision, but with some filters and additions, you can obtain a blend of items that remains relevant with little extra filler. Tell Siri to find articles you might want to read? Maybe not yet, but soon.

A lot of research is going on in this area, of course. Public relations firm Ruder Finn published an exhaustive survey in 2009 that outlines a wide array of use cases segmented by demographics. Their Mobile Intent Index asked respondents how frequently they use their mobile phones to go online, based on 295 possible reasons. The primary reason to go online was "instant gratification." While the study's excerpt states that "mobile phones are not a learning tool," 64 percent of all users say they go online with their mobile device for education or research.

Intent has been an area of research for human-computer interaction (HCI) for some time, starting with a 2004 doctoral dissertation that covered a "method of programming robots to automate motor tasks by inferring the intent of users based on demonstrations of a task" (Dixon, 2004), and a very interesting piece from 2012 on "Language intent models for inferring user browsing behavior" (Tsagkias & Blanco, 2012). New books by Bin Aftab and Karim (2014) and Sukthankar, Goldman, Geib, Pynadath, and Bui (2014) are adding to the growing research in this area. Recall Schmidt's quote on searching without having to type? Google I/O 2013 unveiled just that.

Not to be outdone (at least not too much), Yahoo! Labs also has a great research area on this topic. Tracking trends, providing context for search, and much more are just around the corner, if not already here in one shape or form already.

It's clear there are fantastic developments in this area coming shortly, as well as a number of ways to try out things already, available for you to start on inferring your learners' intent in order to improve mobile interface design. Just don't forget it.

References

Bin Aftab, M., & Karim, W. (2014). *Learning Android intents.* Birmingham, UK: Packt Publishing. www.amazon.com /Learning-Android-Intents-Muhammad-Usama/dp/1783289635

Boulton, C. (2010, September 28). Google CEO Schmidt pitches autonomous search, flirts with AI. *eWeek.* www.eweek.com/c/a /Search-Engines/Google-CEO-Schmidt-Pitches-Autonomous-Search-Flirts-with-AI-259984.

Dixon, K. (2004). Inferring user intent for learning by observation. Doctoral dissertation, Carnegie Mellon University. www.cs.cmu .edu/~krd/papers/postscript/Dixon_Thesis.pdf.

Ruder Finn. (2009, February 10). New study shows "intent" behind mobile internet use. Press release, PR Newswire. www.prnewswire .com/news-releases/new-study-shows-intent-behind-mobile-internet-use-84016487.html.

Sukthankar, G., Goldman, R., Geib, C., Pynadath, D., & Bui, H. (Eds.) (2014). *Plan, activity and intent recognition: Theory and practice.* Waltham, MA: Morgan Kaufmann. www.amazon.com /Plan-Activity-Intent-Recognition-Practice/dp/0123985323

Tsagkias, M., & Blanco, R. (2012). Language intent models for inferring user browsing behavior. *Proceedings of the 35th International ACM SIGIR Conference on Research and Development in Information Retrieval,* Portland, Oregon. http://ilps.science.uva.nl/sites/ilps.science .uva.nl/files/fp372-tsagkias.pdf

CHAPTER 19

Using a Mobile Camera as a Powerful Learning Tool

Chad Udell

The old cliché goes something like this: "the best camera is the one you have on you." As trite as this sounds, I do think this is true.

I've gone from camera to camera, each getting smaller and smaller. Of course, this increases the convenience of carrying them around. It's just easier to bring them with me when they fit into a pocket. Until recently, I carried a stand-alone camera with me almost all of the time.

However, the latest generations of smart phones have dramatically improved their imaging capabilities. Capturing images with 5 to 8 megapixels is considered baseline functionality in 2014. Phones are often better cameras than the point-and-shoots we own because they offer HD video recording, flash, high dynamic range imaging (HDRI), and sometimes even 3D or slow motion video.

Because of these new capabilities, and the fact that I always have my phone with me, I rarely take my point-and-shoot with me, never mind my larger SLR camera. The key for me is that I have my phone with me and don't need to think about bringing the camera. The SLR still is used because it has capabilities beyond my phone camera, but taking it along with me is a very deliberate planned activity. The point-and-shoot collects dust.

Images and video are powerful learning tools—viewing and creating them can be a great way to learn. When you couple the image-gathering capabilities of an up-to-date smart phone with the network connectivity and other features on board, you have a very capable platform for creating and consuming visual content.

New affordances like heads-up display (HUD) and augmented reality (AR) are additional dimensions to your image-based learning content that only mobile devices can provide. This is a brand-new world of performance support and just-in-time information, as well as social and informal learning. Visual assessment via computer vision and object detection are also new avenues we have open to us in the learning world.

Exploring in More Detail

The device's camera is only a camera in the loosest of terms. Sure, it can capture images as both stills and video, but really, it's also a digital visual input device that allows the output to be processed and presented in a multitude of ways.

We see this already in everyday uses like scanning QR codes, cameras autofocusing on faces in frame to enhance your photos, adding filters to Instagram images, and on and on. Some other examples that are out there that are exciting from a learning point of view are apps like Leafsnap and Word Lens.

Leafsnap, a project from Columbia University, the University of Maryland, and the Smithsonian Institution, is a mobile field guide that helps you identify trees of the northeastern United States based on the shape of their leaves. This is accomplished via a technique known as computer vision and, even more specifically, a trained object-recognition process. In another example, Word Lens, launched in 2010, allows you to point your camera at signage and have the message on the sign translated into your desired language.

Now the wheels are spinning, I hope. So much more than a simple camera, the visual output from the sensor can also be coupled with on-screen elements to show way-finding clues, visual overlays for geolocation, temperature, or any number of things and can even be processed to alter the image for easier understanding of what you may be looking at.

For some examples outside of the mobile device realm, consider some heads-up display and image-processing examples:

- These types of wearable displays have been augmenting vision and providing real-time information to pilots and military applications for years.

- With a smart phone, you can enhance images and add useful overlays to assist your learners in finding where they need to go, or even where to grab dessert, by combining the image with geolocation data.

- With Google Glass on the horizon and with other wearable technology coming soon, I expect this sort of view to become even more common.

- Augmented displays offer many things that make them a really useful performance tool: repair instructions, facial recognition, real-time video chat, and even visual checklists could all become common working and learning tools.

- Consider the possibilities of applications that both inform you how to set up a workstation or retail shelf, and then verify that you have set it up correctly through pattern recognition using computer vision. I fully expect the use of augmented vision and glasses to be a must-have job accessory for technicians and people who work with their hands by 2020.

I realize this may all seem like science fiction now. You can begin today, though. Think about creating an internal image database where co-workers share best practices. Or maybe you could create a video-sharing portal where people narrate their work and share how they do things. These ideas, and much more, are all relatively easy to set up with common content management systems and some modest application development effort.

Some of these use cases may require building an app, because they will not work as mobile web experiences due to browser security issues or capabilities. As always, determine whether your technology strategy and your audience goals align.

The really cool thing about all of this is that it clearly shows that mobile learning is a two-way street. Both consuming and creating images can be enlightening and add to performance outcomes for your organization.

CHAPTER 20

Employing Mobile Device Sensors for Enhanced Learning Experiences

Chad Udell

Many new features make mobile devices unique and particularly well-suited to provide just-in-time information to a mobile learner. For example, the sensors you carry around with you on a daily basis in your smart phone and tablet are collecting data. This data can be used to learn an awful lot about your immediate surroundings and enhance your awareness, to help you make better-informed decisions.

This should come as no surprise to anyone with the ability to access lots of data, but, of course, data by itself is not the important thing. Data, when interpreted as information, can provide insight. Insight, when applied, can create impetus for action.

So, in essence, by creating a conduit to our surroundings via a device that can provide the data, the use of applications or services that interpret this data to give the user insight can lead to better and more successful actions. Fewer mistakes, better outcomes, more productivity, and more safety can be provided by virtue of successful use of the data gathered by the devices we carry with us everywhere.

I Sense Something, a Presence
I've Not Felt Since. . . .

It could seem like we've gone a bit off the ranch here, but smart mobile devices are essentially the current-day equivalent of what has been represented in the Star Trek universe as the Tricorder (per Wikipedia: "a multifunction hand-held device used for sensor scanning, data analysis, and recording data").

The sensors I've discussed in other chapters—cameras and GPS, and others—are now pretty much universal. That is, all the devices we would consider smart phones or tablets have them on board, although many other sensors out there might be a little more on the fringe of most people's experience. It's clear we are just at the beginning of the sensor age on these ubiquitous devices. A few non-typical sensors that we've spotted in the wild include:

- Light sensors
- Barometers
- Pressure sensors
- Thermometers
- Altimeters
- Humidity sensors
- Magnetometers
- Breathalyzers

The Android world seems to be leading the way in this era of adding "extra" sensors to your devices. For example, if you want a thermometer-enabled device in the Android world, simply pick up a Samsung Galaxy S4, but if you want the same feature on your iPhone, you're going to need to buy a Thermodo. Certainly doable, but considering the built-in sensors in the Android devices likely only cost a few dollars, you can see why adding sensors to your non-enabled devices can become unnecessarily costly.

We're Just Warming Up

This is really just the tip of the iceberg. Where these sensors are now a luxury item or a hit-and-miss proposition, we're going to see an influx of them across the buying spectrum as this technology becomes cheaper and smaller. With these additional sensors, we'll see the growth of a software segment call "appcessories." Of course, if you have sensors, you need the apps to provide information and insight to the new data you're gathering, right?

With the next-next generation of devices, the third-party adapters and add-ons for them, we could see things like air quality sensors, motion detection, EKG/pulse and blood pressure monitors, and PH/alkalinity sensors in the not too distant future. Touch-free gestural inputs and the connected nature of wearable computing all fit right in here. Your entire body and the environment around you become the just-in-time information gatherer and delivery mechanism.

Although it may be a little frivolous, want to see something available today that is certainly a sign of things to come? Check out the brainwave sensing cat ears from Necomimi.com that you can buy right now to let everyone know just what you are feeling. Goofy? Definitely! When similar technology can be used to provide brain scans or MRI data in real time as a consumer technology, we will have reached a breakthrough in health, science, and human augmentation.

What sorts of things can you do with these sensors? Of course, there are the immediate applications where sensors directly add to your user experience, such as being able to measure light level, temperature, and more. The immediate uses obviously give your audience more inputs about the world around them and can allow them to make more accurate decisions on a one-on-one basis.

But what if your "appcessories" that use these apps are gathering the data in an aggregate form? The creation of big data on your workers' surroundings could change a lot about how we do business today.

Are your workers always in high-humidity situations? What are the temperature readings like for your workers at a jobsite? Are your corridors adequately lit to perform the maintenance you want? Are your workers using the devices when they are driving, even though they shouldn't be?

You can see where this quickly moves beyond the typical view of what learning is. Maybe the role of the learner is flipped here. The users are the creators of content, and their managers are the learners.

What's Next, and How Do I Start?

What is going to drive the addition of sensors to mobile devices? As an answer, I recommend reading up on how a thermometer made it into the Samsung Galaxy S4 (OpenSignal, 2013). It's going to require openness by the platform providers to include some of the required hooks in their operating systems, and sensor manufacturers may also want to write their own driver code to get the hardware manufacturers to put the sensors in their phones. It's going to start slowly at first, but competition will heat up (pun intended).

Another interesting way to approach this topic is by creating the sensor device you need and then applying for acceptance from initiatives like Apple's MFi program, in which you can create AirPlay or Lightning connector-enabled add-on devices for iOS. There are lots of requirements for such a program, so be sure to check whether you qualify first.

It's clear there are many areas of potential growth for mobile sensors. The best thing you can do is to keep your ears and eyes open right now. Take a look at your target platforms and devices if there is a chance you want to access something in the users' immediate surrounding and help them do their jobs better.

You may be pleasantly surprised to find out that you can assist them in ways that seemed like science fiction only a few months ago.

Reference

OpenSignal. (2013, June 12). The story of how temperature and humidity sensors made it into the Samsung Galaxy S4. OpenSignal. http://opensignal.com/blog/2013/06/12/the-story-of-how-temperature-and-humidity-sensors-made-it-into-the-samsung-galaxy-s4.

CHAPTER 21

Alternative Reality Games as Mobile Learning

John Feser

Sometimes, learning can take place by participating in activities in the real world, where mobile devices are used to supplement information or give direction to learners who only occasionally look at their screens. This is the case for many alternate reality games or ARGs for short (pronounced by saying the letters A-R-G, not by sounding like a pirate), interactive narratives that use the real world as a stage for telling a story, acting out a scenario, playing a live game, or creating a learning experience. ARGs make use of diverse media and game elements to help tell and impact the outcome of the story. In an ARG, participants are presented with clues in an effort to solve puzzles and make informed decisions in the game's unfolding narrative. These clues can be located in different places from physical locations (such as a library, school, office building, or grocery store) to media (such as websites, recorded telephone messages, videos, or images).

In many ARGs. the story evolves as the organizers stay one step ahead of the participants, changing the direction of the game based on the responses and reactions of those playing. Because ARGs link a fictional story to real-world objects and places, mobile devices are a natural medium to involve in the gameplay. Often, mobile-specific technologies are employed to enrich the experience and further blur the lines between the game environment and the real world, such as QR codes, geolocation data, and using the device's camera to acquire evidence. The emergent technology of near field communications (NFC) will likely also have great potential for ARGs in the future.

Examples

ARGs have been used in many areas for a number of different purposes. From a marketing perspective, a number of very successful ARGs have been written as a way to build product awareness. A very popular ARG called I Love Bees was produced to market the 2004 video game Halo 2. In 2007, Nine Inch Nails released an ARG called Year Zero as a way to market their upcoming album by the same name. The game was well received and won a couple of Webby awards as evidence of its overall success and well-constructed world, depicting a crumbling society that echoed the state of the music industry. In perhaps one of the best known ARGs to date, fans of the TV show LOST could participate in an ARG called The LOST Experience. The following description comes from The LOST Experience website:

> The LOST Experience takes LOST fans on an expansive, international Easter egg hunt through websites, commercials, emails, phone numbers, and more, in search of pieces to a larger puzzle, a puzzle which, when solved, will enlighten LOST fans to some of the show's deepest mysteries!

ARGs have also been used to solve real-world problems. An ARG called World Without Oil was created to obtain collective input from players about dealing with the world's dependency on oil. World Without Oil simulates the first thirty-two days of a global oil crisis and establishes a "citizen nerve center" to track events and share ideas. In October 2008 the British Red Cross created a serious ARG called Traces of Hope to promote their campaign about civilians caught up in conflict.

The more serious ARGs, such as World Without Oil and Traces of Hope, are just the tip of the iceberg when it comes to using "serious games" to enforce learning objectives and help drive key takeaways home for the learners/gamers participating in them. These collective problem-solving efforts promote teamwork, creative problem solving, and responding and communicating effectively in a fluid and continuously evolving situation. Strong stuff, indeed!

The Applicability of ARGs in Organizational Learning

ARGs are an excellent way to enhance or supplement an organization's learning program for many reasons. Let's examine a few of them here.

ARGs Are Immersive: The gaming nature of ARGs naturally has the ability to involve people, require them to collaborate and solve problems, and can be written to tap into people's competitive spirit. If a game is written properly, all of this can be done in a way that ensures learning is occurring and incented.

ARGs Can Ensure Baseline Knowledge: Often, organizations struggle with developing training that meets the needs of people with different levels of expertise and experience with a particular topic. ARGs can be used to help people build prerequisite knowledge necessary for the next level of learning. Those who have the background and experience can quickly solve the puzzles and challenges presented, and be rewarded accordingly, while those who need more background can spend the time and use available resources to build their knowledge base. This helps level the playing field going forward and reduces remediation.

ARGs Help Spice Up Dry Content: ARGs can be used as a part of employee on-boarding programs, where much of the information presented is less than exciting, but nonetheless important, and in some cases required by law. By sharing this information through a story and in a game format, the elements of a game, keeping score, competition, problem solving, and so forth, can be used to enhance content that otherwise may be presented in a presentation or written format. Envision an office park scavenger hunt and you may be onto something here.

ARGs Are Helpful in Assessing Knowledge: Well-designed and scripted ARGs can be a powerful way to assess learner knowledge and retention. Because of the problem-solving nature of ARGs, observing how players react to various situations provides great insight to what they really know. In addition, those running the ARG can control events as gameplay occurs, allowing them to adjust the difficulty level in real time. Countless metrics could be occurring behind the scenes, from execution time to accuracy and much, much more.

ARGs Are Cost-Effective: ARGs offer a significant amount of flexibility when it comes to their design and complexity. The writing and story are the basis for a good ARG, not the specific technology. Very elaborate ARGs can be written with the only tool needed to play a mobile phone with text messaging. A simple bridge between an SMS gateway and an LMS or CMS is all you would need for tallying and record-keeping.

Getting Started

ARGs may seem daunting from a design perspective. As with any form of learning development, success comes from first creating a good plan. First consider the audience, the message to be conveyed, and the resulting behavior. Use these discoveries to inform your game framework, the writing, the media asset creation, and the ongoing gameplay and measurement.

Audience: The audience will have a big impact on the design of an ARG. Is the audience tech-savvy? Do they know each other well? Are they located where they can physically work together or will collaboration mean working remotely? Understanding the users' personas will go a long way toward ensuring a solid design that works well for the players.

Messages: Determine the key messages to be communicated as a result of the game. Is the information to be presented high-level or subtle details of a situation? Is the subject matter easy to understand or complex? Approach these messages much like you would in creating the learning objectives for your courseware or crafting the use cases for your mobile applications.

Behaviors: What behavioral outcomes should result from this experience? Maybe the purpose is motivational or team building, or maybe it is to emphasize a point or raise awareness. Whatever your desired conversion point, ensure you have created the interaction points to drive these concepts home and you have placed measurement tools at these critical junctures in order to measure effectiveness. Considering these elements up front is critical to making sure the storyline and the gameplay achieve the desired results.

Environmental Considerations: The next step in developing an ARG design doc is to plan for the setting and timeframe. Will the game space be limited to a specific venue, or will it encompass a wider area? The answer to this question can impact the technology that can and should be used. Will the game occur over a couple of hours or days, or will it happen over a period of months? Finally, how will the ARG integrate with other aspects of the training or learning environment? ARGs are most effective when they are integrated with a larger plan and not just something that is "piled on" as an extra. For example, if an ARG is being used to introduce and excite people about an upcoming conference, then the ARG should have a direct tie-in to the themes and events of the conference. An ARG used at the corporate headquarters as part of the on-boarding process is going to be doomed to failure unless it is given consideration in the new employees' schedules. Plan accordingly.

Writing the Story: The story surrounding the ARG should be written to match the audience and environment, as well as meet the goals and objectives that have been established. However, there are a couple of other considerations to take into account. The first is the game lifespan and refresh cycle. Will the ARG be played once by a group of people with a specific end date, or is the game intended to be ongoing with people starting at different times over a longer period? Will there be a reset at intermittent times in order to start again? Another important consideration is monitoring and controlling of the gameplay. Is the outcome fixed and the same for each participant, or will the game be allowed to evolve with no specific outcome identified ahead of time? These decisions will greatly influence how the story is written and how the clues are developed.

Developing Your ARG: Obviously, playing a few ARGs is an important first step to being able to develop a successful game. A number of online resources are available to help you start. Giant Mice has a nice resource page with many links on various ARG development topics. There are also resources on how to design and organize your ARG. There are so many ways to design and develop your ARG that explaining them all in this chapter would easily double or triple its size. But many resources on the web provide excellent information and numerous ideas. Tandem Learning has a number of great resources at their website, as well. From a mobile development perspective, there are many easily available tools and services, such as SMS (text messaging) and open source, and other free tools that can be adapted to serve as a framework for building your game.

Key Components of a Successful Learning ARG

Some other qualities you should keep in mind as you craft your masterpiece include:

Verisimilitude: The story supporting the ARG, while often fictional in nature, still should have an element of reality and truthfulness. Because gameplay takes place in the real world in physical locations, the storyline should be informative, engaging, and believable.

Easy to Use: In many cases, the players will not be deeply familiar with ARGs and, in some cases, will not even know what an ARG is. The technology used to play the ARG should not be the focus; the story should be the focus. Therefore, successful ARGs use technology to enhance the experience by being easy to use. If players have to spend all their time trying to figure out the technology, they will be distracted from the real intent of the game. In other words, Know Thy Audience.

Importance: Consider the importance of the ARG to the overall learning experience. Again, thinking about the audience and their receptiveness to this type of experience, many ARGs are designed to be an optional supplement to the real training. In these cases, people should be able to enter and leave the game at any time without real-life consequences. As an example, The LOST Experience, written for the TV series LOST, was not required in order to understand the TV show or to follow the plot. But for those who were interested in increasing their engagement with the show, the ARG served to provide additional insights to the overall story and enhance the viewing experience. Likewise, other ARGs we have played at conferences and events add to the experience of the event, but were not required in order to have a baseline experience at the event.

Conclusion

Mobile devices, combined with a good story and an educational game, can be a powerful way to increase engagement and the activity level of your learners. ARGs offer an interesting way to bring your mobile technology along for the ride. ARGs are being successfully used in marketing and entertainment, as well as to train and solve real-world problems. Organizations that are looking for creative ways to engage in mobile learning should consider the benefits ARGs have to offer. By crafting a realistic, enjoyable experience, you'll be reinforcing behaviors that most companies are actively seeking in their employees: critical problem solving, inquisitiveness, and creativity.

CHAPTER 22

Using Mobile Games for Sales Training and Assessment

Chad Udell

Most of us would agree that salespeople are competitive by nature. This is obvious and necessary for performing well in the job. After all, these are the people we put on the front lines to win the day and bring back revenue-producing opportunities for the company. They are assessed on their sales performance via metrics and measurements, and they're incentivized with compensation and perks. Many organizations even have annual sales drives or competitions to quantify the level of performance and measure who is the best.

This driving force is often left out of the learning and development world, and we see the effects of this all the time. In my experience, salespeople have often been some of the most disinterested in training in the entire organization. They want to be out there on the road performing, not in a classroom or behind a desk taking some coursework.

Some of the most effective sales training materials I have helped create have included gaming experiences. A competitive approach to testing product knowledge or soft skills can liven up interest among your sales audience and bring them back to the fold in order to make sure they are equipped with the most up-to-date information on company products, policies, and best practices.

Surveying conferences and the bookshelves, it's clear that gaming and gamification are emerging as powerful learning tools. Gaming may be a bit over-hyped in some circles, but you can tell just by how successful public sites, products, and services, such as Fitocracy, Foursquare, Nike FuelBand, and others, are in appealing to people's competitive nature, that there is something worth looking into in your learning practice areas.

We live in a world of badges, mayorships, awards, and mobile social networks that reward contributors for doing everything from checking into a coffee shop to trying a new beer at Untappd. com. When applying gaming and gamification to your learning, it is important to know that simply adding badges to course completions and high assessment scores is not enough and is really counterproductive, in many cases.

Well-designed game experiences are a careful blend of dynamics (featuring emergent gameplay styles and progression) and mechanics (the construct for the game and reward/penalty cycle). The successful game is bounded by rules and constraints whereby a player achieves some amount of progression or success by leveraging these to his benefit. Adding badges to a training curriculum does nothing of this sort and will not be noticed by the competitive sales team.

A balanced approach is needed, and balance is achieved through a careful design process. For a great overview on the game design process and how to apply it to your learning experiences, I recommend you read *A Theory of Fun for Game Design* by Raph Koster (2004) and *The Gamification of Learning and Instruction* by Karl Kapp (2012). After delving into these titles, you'll have a solid grounding in game design principles and, if you so choose, a base to start designing your own experiences. Raph's book is a great survey of what makes games good, and Karl's book is a study of the elements of games that can be applied to instruction.

After you have the principles in your quiver, it may be time to look around to see what tools you have available to help you. If your sales team uses Salesforce as their customer relationship management (CRM) program, you may be able to turn it into a game itself. A few companies have created gamification layers to add to Salesforce: Compete, Bunchball, and a few other bigger players. Keep in mind that the technology is only a part of the equation. It's up to you to craft the experience that works for your team and the content you are delivering.

Prefab frameworks are a good place to start, but I think that custom-designed experiences offer the best chance for success—when implemented correctly. Some key tips to help you in this process follow:

- Keep the desired outcomes in mind throughout the design process.
- Excess ornamentation or needless hoops to jump through impede the learning process. Don't build lengthy tutorials or instructions into your experiences; your learners will "get it."
- Make the game easy enough to offer some level of success, but not so easy that people lose interest. You want them to keep plunking their quarters in!
- Use the gaming mechanics and dynamics to reinforce the behavior you want to shape and enhance the knowledge transfer. The game isn't fluff added to the learning; the game *is* the learning.
- The gamification methods and tools you use must lend themselves to the content you are delivering.

Sticking with these tips is harder than it may sound. The most successful projects I have been involved in that used gaming had a few things in common:

- Using a public scoreboard can be an effective motivator.
- Using true mobile design conventions puts your experience on equal footing with other gaming experiences on their devices.
- Don't neglect proper time for quality control (QC) and testing. Games can be easy to break and have notoriously tricky bugs to locate and fix.
- Hire a proper game designer if you are not confident you can deliver. Designing a proper game for learning is not like designing straightforward learning content based on your previous experience. It's okay to ask for help.

Jack Welch is credited as saying, "An organization's ability to learn, and translate that learning into action rapidly, is the ultimate competitive advantage" (quoted in Slater, 1999). It's up to you to take that competitive nature and use it to feed that flywheel.

References

Kapp, K. (2012). *The gamification of learning and instruction.* San Francisco, CA: Pfeiffer.

Koster, R. (2004). *A theory of fun for game design.* Phoenix, AZ: Paraglyph Press.

Slater, R. (1999). *Jack Welch and the GE Way: Management insights and leadership secrets of the legendary CEO.* New York: McGraw-Hill.

CHAPTER 23

Voice and Messaging for Mobile Learning

Chad Udell

With all the really cool things mobile devices can do, it's very easy to overlook their original function—communication. More specifically, mobile devices were originally created primarily for voice communication. The first cell phones in the early 1970s didn't have LED screens, QWERTY keyboards, or touchscreens. They were created to make voice calls. When Martin Cooper unveiled the Motorola cell phone in 1973, he made a voice call to rival Joel Engel at Bell Labs (Ziegler, 2012). No text message, no email. These phones didn't have cameras on them or any sort of extra features we all take for granted now.

After all, in the evolution of long distance communication, bidirectional voice would be considered superior to other methods such as the telegraph or two-way radios, where only one person can speak at a time. Voice is synchronous, requires no typing or transcription, and can take place anywhere. Now, as cell phones have progressed and gained Internet connectivity and various forms of messaging and media capture, there are many other channels to communicate with others while on the go.

Voice can still be a very powerful way to learn something. No one can forget the *Who Wants to Be a Millionaire* "Phone a Friend" lifeline rule. When you are stuck, why not call someone? Of course, that someone could be a co-worker, mentor, or other person in your learning network, but with the use of interactive voice response (IVR), it could just as easily be calling a computerized switchboard that can provide you an answer.

My favorite example of IVR might just be Kramer's Moviefone service from *Seinfeld* (www.youtube.com/watch?v=qM79_itR0Nc), but while that was comically bad and confusing for the users of the service, many new IVR systems are quite powerful and economical to set up. If the problem you are trying to solve can be fixed via troubleshooting, a defined process, or other sorts of defined steps, an IVR system might just be a valuable performance support tool for your workforce. Via HTML telephone tags and data detectors in your web pages and apps, it's very easy to trigger the telephone function on your phone. With VoIP apps and options like Google Voice and Skype, you can even make phone calls from your tablet devices.

IVR is great for simple applications, but if you want to unlock the power of voice, examine the "speech to text" (STT) and "text to speech" (TTS) world of software available to you on mobile devices. Apple made a splash when it introduced Siri with iOS 6, but while it was certainly a big step toward creating a personal digital assistant, the actual functionality of text to speech and speech to text has been available in Apple's mobile operating system for some time.

Dictation had been available for messages and other application text fields since iOS 5 via technology from Nuance, the makers of Dragon Naturally Speaking voice recognition software for desktop computers.

Google has since followed suit, adding voice dictation and TTS/STT features to its Android platform over time. The Google Now feature set and Android Voice Actions allow you to do a lot of great things with your device using only your voice. As of early 2014, here's a list of things you can do with Android Voice Actions:

1. Make a phone call
2. View a map of places around you
3. Start navigation (voice guided) to a location
4. Send a text message
5. Write and send an email
6. Play some music
7. Send a written "note to self" message

8. Find a website online
9. Look up a definition

Simple, but useful. The functionality in this area is only going to expand as the operating system makers add functions that are voice controllable. The features will expand more dramatically when the application programming interfaces (APIs) for interfacing with voice controls are made more open. Siri on iOS is pretty much a black box at this time. Google Now is a bit more open. Some things you can query Google Now for using voice and the required APIs, according to Programmableweb.com, are

- Ask how long your commute will take, with an option for alternate routes (Google Directions API)
- Find next arrivals when commuting by train or bus (Google Directions API)
- When traveling, see nearby places and find local recommendations (Google Places API, Zagat)
- See your next appointment and see when to leave (Google Calendar API, Google Directions API)
- For an upcoming flight, see the terminal, gate, and status (likely an external source, such as Flight Stats API)
- Updates on favorite sports teams in real time with the score (likely one of the three sports data APIs)
- While traveling, automatically get a translation, currency conversion and the time back home (Google Translate API, Unofficial Google Currency Converter)

A number of third-party software development kits (SDKs) are emerging to add voice control to your apps as well. For example, Nuance now has industry-specific voice libraries available for use in your mobile applications, allowing people in engineering or medical professions to add field-specific jargon to their apps in order to facilitate voice control and increase utility. Their NDEV mobile developer program offers application starter kits and more to jump-start your mobile development efforts.

The rest of the technology world is quickly ramping up their support of speech control in their products. People want easy access to technology, and voice definitely lowers the bar in terms of ease of use, when done well. It keeps your hands free and allows you to maintain your focus on the task at hand. Vehicle makers are all over this, with announcements galore featuring vehicle and voice integration, data, search, and much more at the 2014 Consumer Electronic Show in Las Vegas.

Google Glass is nearly completely navigable via voice when you get the hang of it. The smart watch market is also on board, with Samsung's Gear offering the S Voice feature set, allowing you to interface with smart phones and websites seamlessly using simple voice commands.

I recently picked up an Xbox One game console for my home and almost never need to touch it. I can power it on and off, watch a movie, start a game or video chat, and much more, with just my voice. It has some minor wrinkles and bugs for sure, but overall it works pretty well, and I have to say, it all seems very futuristic to me when I use it. After all, who didn't watch Star Trek and have some bit of wonder and awe at how they asked their computers to do tasks for them—make them Earl Grey tea, and much more, simply by talking to them.

So what are you waiting for? There are a lot of options to start using voice in your mobile learning projects. Time to talk with your team about how you can talk to your learning systems.

Reference

Ziegler, C. (2012, February 20). The Verge interview: Marty Cooper, father of the cell phone. The Verge. www.theverge.com/2012/2 /20/2811861/marty-cooper-interview.

CHAPTER 24

Using Mobile Devices as Research Tools

Gary Woodill

Because traditional e-learning has mostly been about presentations and activities designed by expert instructors, distributed to learners via desktop and laptop screens, we tend to forget the power of the multidirectional capabilities of mobile devices.

Mobile phones are not just for phone calls, and tablets are not just for viewing materials; both can also be used to collect data in several different formats and send them to a central server or to other people. With a server and appropriate software, the data can be aggregated and analyzed, with tables and visualizations automatically generated, creating new knowledge that can be distributed to many others via electronic networks. Gathering research using mobile devices is an active and valid learning activity because learners must engage in the real world in which they are immersed, using their mobile phones or tablets to record and send back interesting information about the context in which they are located.

The use of mobile devices dramatically increases the sheer number of observation points that are potentially available to researchers, as well as opening up the possibilities of automatic data collection through programs that track user location and activities. With more than six billion mobile phones in use worldwide, including one billion smart phones, the mobile phone network is emerging as part of a "global brain" with sensors everywhere. Companies such as Fourier Systems provide inexpensive purpose-built mobile devices that are specifically designed for data logging for both school science projects and industrial settings.

We are only now starting to grasp the immense potential of mobile devices for research. Let's look at some examples of how mobile devices are being used as research tools.

Research on Mobile Phone Use

One obvious area of developing research is on the use of mobile phones themselves. For example, Nokia hired U.K. company GfK to monitor their whole portfolio of digital channels, including both standard and mobile websites or online shopping. This posed a number of challenges in developing an online survey that would work on both a mobile phone as well as a PC, across all possible brands and models of mobile phones, on the various different mobile operating systems, as well as in all the languages for the countries in which Nokia operates. Nevertheless, GfK achieved over 100,000 completed interviews in less than a year.

Because they are data collection devices, mobile phones can be used to track users' behaviors while they are using their phones to see who, how, and why they use specific apps or websites.

UserZoom has developed a user experience (UX) research tool that collects this data for iOS and Android devices. Researchers are able to conduct studies on persona definition, satisfaction surveys, usability testing, exit opinions, and more. Actual behavioral data is collected, as well as the results of surveys.

Mobile Devices for Market Research

With the proliferation of channels communicating brand messages to consumers in today's world, there is a growing need to help businesses understand which messages are the most effective and how they resonate with consumers. "Mobile Moments of Truth" is a research tool being developed by GfK that uses the mobile phone to capture and collect the full range of brand experiences. Rather than waiting to ask consumers to recall all brand exposures during a given time frame, selected consumers are able to take an image using their mobile phone every time they see or experience a brand and give a short report on where, why, and how they felt. This is all achieved through a simple online survey tool that not only gives time-sensitive, granular feedback, but also consumer-created images that give a real-life context for each experience.

In another example, Qustodian, a Spanish start-up, connects people with brands they like via their mobile phones. Members choose the companies they'd like to hear from, then earn cash by downloading apps or checking for the latest news and offers from their favorite companies, and answering surveys. Qustodian already has more than 50,000 members and has worked with brands such as Pepsi, Adidas, and Ford.

Hewlett-Packard conducted a qualitative research project that followed the purchasing paths of incoming college students by allowing them to use their mobile phones to document their behaviors. The methodology included the use of mobile cameras and screen tracking to follow the students' movements and experiences throughout the day. This kind of data is invaluable to market researchers.

Mobile Research in the Human Sciences

Because most people carry them around, mobile phones seem particularly useful for research in the human sciences. Surveys, questionnaires, videos, audio recordings, and polls can be produced using mobile phones, tablets, and notebook computers.

But what if you want to go beyond surveys and questionnaires and obtain more in-depth descriptive information from people via their mobile phones? There's an app for that, as well.

For example, in 2011, Stephane Dufau and his colleagues in France collected data in cognitive science experiments from thousands of subjects from all over the world. The team reported that "this mass coordinated use of smart phones creates a novel and powerful scientific 'instrument' that yields the data necessary to test universal theories of cognition. This increase in power represents a potential revolution in cognitive science."

In a different approach to mobile research, a team at the London School of Economics has launched an iPhone app to discover how people's feelings are affected by their surroundings. The Mappiness app asks people a few times a day to say how they are feeling, what they are doing, and where they are. It can also use GPS to pinpoint the user's location. More than 45,000 participants have already signed up, generating more than three million geolocated responses.

Not just the behavior of individuals is being researched using mobile devices. These devices are also being used to make sense of social networks and the connections among large groups of people. Harris Interactive is using GPS data from mobile phones to track respondents' locations as they combine the use of social media and other data with survey results. GPS can be used to observe behavior patterns, look at how people use the mobile web when they're out and about, and send relevant surveys to participants based on their locations. Their Research Lifestreaming service has already tracked more than twenty million Facebook posts from twenty thousand participants in the United States.

Monitoring subtle social signals is now possible thanks to mobile devices. Professor Alex (Sandy) Pentland and his colleagues at MIT have invented a "sociometer," a specially designed digital sensor worn like an ID badge that monitors and analyzes social interactions among groups of people. In his book, *Honest Signals*, Pentland suggests that by "reading" our social networks with these devices, "we can become more successful at pitching an idea, getting a job, or closing a deal." These devices are also being used to research how people interact with one another.

Mobile Field Research in Agriculture

The term "field research" takes on new meaning when we look at all the possible uses of mobile devices in agricultural research. Of course, making sense of a large amount of data needs a place where the data can be collected and analyzed. The U.S. Department of Agriculture, the U.S. Geological Survey, and researchers at Colorado State University have developed an object modeling system (OMS) that allows data collected in the field to be analyzed against the OMS model. Jason Smith (2011), writing in the *Compute in Motion* blog, talks about how this works:

> [A]n agricultural researcher might look at a field and try to glean clues about erosion and rainfall to better map conservation directions. With the help of a mobile phone's GPS, the coordinates of the

researcher's location are sent to a modeling service hosted in the cloud to calculate soil erosion and other agricultural elements based on any number of given conditions. Within that remote resource, the coordinates will be matched to stored information about the nature of the area in question. Furthermore, as more is known about particular areas on the map, more information will be added to the cloud service's well of geological, agricultural, hydrological, and other data.

As more and more farmers use mobile devices to document and manage their farms, or the food distribution chain tracks the location and condition of food from field to table, the mass of data collected will be mined by agricultural researchers in the near future. Whether we like it or not, we are all crowdsourcing for someone's research as our movements and actions are tracked and documented.

Mobile Research in Healthcare

The potential of using mobile devices and networks to track diseases and therefore do research on how and where they spread is now well recognized. The SARS outbreak of 2003 resulted in hundreds of deaths and billions of dollars in economic losses. There was evidence of this disease on the Internet as early as November 2002.

Since that time, the tracking of diseases and disasters through mobile technologies has improved greatly. A mobile phone–based health program called Alerta DISAMAR allows Peruvian military doctors to report disease outbreaks and ask for help with treatment. Laboratories that test for diseases, traditionally isolated from each other, are now being connected by computer networks in order to share results and to integrate the inflow of data about diseases. This ability is invaluable to epidemiologists.

Many other examples of mobile research in healthcare are available. Health information is changing the ways drug makers develop medicines and communicate with doctors, insurers, and patients. Information from patient records is helping companies design more cost-effective clinical trials and tailor marketing materials to the people who most need them. For example, mobile phone software can help patients find clinical trials for cancer or track blood sugar levels.

Mobile Research and Citizen Science

A 2005 project with school students in the U.K. called Mudlarking in Deptford (FutureLab, 2005) showed how mobile devices can involve *anyone* in the collection and transmission of data as part of personal research or crowdsourcing. Mobile computing is one of the technologies that have fueled the rise of "citizen science" in which any person with an interest can become a dedicated researcher.

"Citizen science" is already happening in a big way, aided by the widespread distribution of smart phones and, more recently, the explosive growth of adoption of tablet computers. For example, the What's Invasive? Project uses community data collection with mobile phones to locate and track invasive weeds that are threatening native plants and animals in several different locations in the world. Other citizens are gathering information on pollution sources, identifying birds, or plotting bicycle use, and feeding their data into applications that analyze patterns from this information. Researchers in the SixthSense project at MIT are building prototypes for wearable devices that will automatically collect data as the wearers move around their environments.

We are just beginning to scratch the surface for the use of mobile computing in research. Mobile learning has become a two-way activity.

References

Dufau, S., Duñabeitia, J.A., Moret-Tatay, C., McGonigal, A., Peeters, D., et al. (2011). Smart phone, smart science: How the use of smart phones can revolutionize research in cognitive science. *PLoS ONE, 6*(9).

FutureLab. (2005). Mudlarking in Deptford: Mini report. http://archive.futurelab.org.uk/resources/documents/project_reports/mini_reports/mudlarking_mini_report.pdf.

Pentland, A. (2008). *Honest signals: How they shape our world.* Cambridge, MA: MIT Press.

Smith, J. (2011, February 20). Mobile modeling tends to needs of agricultural researchers in the field. *Compute in Motion.* http://computeinmotion.com/2011/02/mobile-modeling-tends-to-needs-of-agricultural-researchers-in-the-field.

CHAPTER 25

Performance Support as a Form of Mobile Learning

Gary Woodill

One of the most frequent themes in discussions of mobile learning in the conference sessions and workshops that I give is a debate about whether or not "performance support" is a form of mobile learning. People who argue that it is not seem to think that learning is something that only happens as a result of instruction or study, and not something that can happen on the job or through a search by a learner. But learning is something that takes place at any time and in any location where a person has discovered something new, no matter what the source or circumstances. Therefore, we need to consider performance support that is delivered through mobile devices as a form of mobile learning.

The vision of mobile learning being used as a form of performance support goes back to some of the first publications on mobile learning. Diane Gayeski, in her 2003 book *Learning Unplugged: Using Mobile Technologies for Organizational Training and Performance Improvement*, certainly advances the case for mobile learning as performance support. Performance support can be delivered using mobile devices in a number of ways; the two most common approaches are the provision of "job aids" and the availability of mentors via mobile devices.

Making job aids available on mobile phones and tablets. Given that most of us have mobile phones, and more and more of us have a tablet computer, it is not surprising that some analysts see giving just-in-time assistance to employees as they need it as a service that will become common in the near future. Job aids are especially appropriate for a mobile workforce. On the road, there is often a need to find out a specific answer to a question, look up a set of directions, or refresh one's memory about a certain process. Sometimes, in emergency situations, we are called upon to carry out procedures for which we have no training. A mobile device can be very useful if it contains a set of instructions that we need or if we can contact an expert at another location who can guide us through the emergency situation. Already, there are examples of this in the medical field where a doctor who was not trained in a particular procedure was able to perform it by receiving text messages from a colleague who was familiar with the operation.

Setting up mentoring, support, and cognitive apprenticeships. As we move away from the classroom model of training, learners often need mentoring, psychological support, and direction in terms of what they need to know in the workplace. Instead of being removed from the real job situation where knowledge is needed, mobile communications allow expertise to be available to the learners as they are performing a task. There are many examples of the use of mobile communications for just-in-time performance support and coaching, especially in the field of healthcare and medicine. The United Nations Foundation reports that the National Leadership and Innovation Agency for Healthcare introduced a radical approach to mentoring using social networking with guided learning principles. The University of Southampton's MPLAT Project supported healthcare students in clinical placements with a mobile learning toolkit that included practice-based learning, mentoring, and assessment using mobile devices.

In New Zealand, Chan and Ford (2007) describe how apprentice bakers are supported in the workplace with mobile learning. The program uses text messaging to disseminate the results of both summative and formative assessments. The apprentice bakers use their mobile phones to take photos, videos, audio, and text evidence of their workplace skills, and assemble an e-portfolio for later assessment by faculty. The whole system is tracked and reported using Moodle, an open-source learning management system. Similarly, workers in the oil sands industry in Canada can take courses from Keyano College through a mobile electrical apprenticeship program. This allows the students to continue working through their apprenticeship with no increase in their living expenses. The employers have the benefit of a steady workforce of highly skilled workers.

At the ICEL conference in New York in 2007, a team from Denmark (Bertelsen, Kanstrupand, & Christiansen, 2007) presented a checklist for evaluating personal digital assistants (PDAs) as performance support to medical professionals. They said:

> The checklist facilitates the communication between designers and innovators throughout the development of . . . a prototype, dubbed "e-pocket" [that] is supposed to replace and expand the support which inexperienced but professional physicians normally get from carrying books, paper slips, and personal notes in their pockets, when on duty. The checklist addresses the key issue in developing professional competence: how to integrate formal rules of procedural and declarative knowledge with personal experience of problem-based learning.

There are other examples of mobile learning being used for performance support, but this concept is just in its infancy. Watch it grow as our ideas of learning and support change in the next few years.

References

Bertelsen, P., Kanstrupand, A., & Christiansen, E. (2007). Problem-based learning in medicine: Performance support with mlearning. In D. Remenyi (Ed.), *Proceedings of ICEL Second International Conference on e-Learning*, Columbia University, New York.

Chan, S., & Ford, N. (2007, February). mLearning and the workplace learner: Integrating mlearning eportfolios with Moodle. *Proceedings of the MoLTA Conference*, Auckland, NZ.

Gayeski, D. (2003). *Learning unplugged: Using mobile technologies for organizational training and performance improvement.* New York: AMACOM.

CHAPTER 26

Mobile Learning in "Third Spaces"
The Move to Alternative Workspaces

Gary Woodill

Mobile computing has had a major impact on the lives of many workers, who now work at home as independent contractors or as telecommuting employees, hardly ever showing up at a traditional office to do a 9 to 5 job. As a consultant, I often work online with colleagues and clients from all over North America, and occasionally from other parts of the world, and also find myself working on the move, using my mobile devices to work and stay connected with clients and colleagues, who also may be anywhere in the world.

There are advantages and disadvantages to this shift in the location of work, but there is no denying that this is a growing trend. One of the major downsides to working at home or by yourself in a hotel is the sense of isolation from other workers. And many independent knowledge workers don't have the space or privacy to effectively work at home, especially if other family members (or noisy pets) are also in the house during the day. With a home office, there is no real work-related socializing, except perhaps with a spouse or other family member. There's usually no sitting back and saying, "What do you think of this?" or "Can I bounce this idea off you?" Often, there's no one asking for your advice. No creative side trips. No impromptu informal learning.

One solution is the use of "third spaces," alternatives to home or a traditional workplace, such as cafes, libraries, and community centers, where you can use mobile tools to connect to others. I can sometimes be found working at the train station in Toronto, using a laptop connected to the free wireless Internet connection available from the railway company. Or I can sometimes be found working at a coffee shop using a USB stick to connect to the mobile phone network for online service. Yet, there is something missing in these nomadic sanctuaries. It is the contact with others, the everyday banter, exchange of gossip, and assistance from interested colleagues that occur in the traditional office environment.

Co-working is a solution that has been developed to address this problem. You still can work for yourself (or remotely, away from a central office), but not always *by* yourself. Co-working is about building a community of people who work together. It's not about finding "office space" and renting out spaces.

Co-working is redefining the way we work. The idea is simple: independent professionals and those with workplace flexibility work better *together* than they do alone. Co-working answers the question that so many face when working from home or on the road: "Why isn't this as much fun as I thought it would be?" Beyond just creating better places to work, co-working spaces are built around the idea of community-building and sustainability. Co-working centers agree to uphold the values set forth by those who developed the concept in the first place: collaboration, community, sustainability, openness, and accessibility.

There are many benefits of co-working. When working by oneself, there is a tendency to continue working without taking breaks, because there is no one else to talk with. Co-working re-humanizes work, while allowing workers to maintain their independent status and/or entrepreneurial spirit. Bringing a group of people together makes collaboration easier, builds social ties that extend into the community, and allows the sharing of resources that are often too expensive for an independent worker to buy and maintain.

This arrangement seems ideal for knowledge workers, mobile workers, and creative people who are trying to earn a living from what they produce. There is value, too, in a "many jobs loosely joined" setup, where it is easier to meet the needs of a large client organization that no one person could easily handle. But co-working is not just for the self-employed; people working as full-time or part-time employees, contractors, and entrepreneurs can all enjoy co-working.

Camaraderie, a Toronto co-working location, has this message on its website:

> Welcome to Camaraderie! We are a shared office space for entrepreneurs, freelancers, independents, and any form of digital nomad that is looking for a vibrant community and a space for collaboration. We have combined the best elements of café culture with a productive, functional work environment that is affordable for startups to gain ground and succeed. Camaraderie is the spirit of friendly good-fellowship, an apt name for an open, shared facility where being a lonely freelancer is yesterday's news and today's entrepreneurs usher in the future.

Co-working is a global movement. There is even a Co-Working Visa Project, where you can use office space in a city that you are visiting, in the spirit of sharing and reciprocity. Essentially, it is an exchange program where, if you are a member of a participating co-working center, you can work for up to three days at another participating co-working center without having to pay additional fees. There are now participating co-working centers in thirty-eight states of the United States and in an additional sixty-two countries. An online co-working directory lists more than twenty co-working sites in Canada, from Victoria to Halifax. The list is growing each month.

While the initial co-working movement is mainly about sharing *physical* spaces, one can apply the principles of co-working to the mobile world and reap many of the same benefits. I have colleagues in Georgia, Illinois, New Jersey, and New York City—my "virtual cubicle mates," who show up to chat on Skype or Yammer on a regular basis. It really doesn't matter whether my interactions are on my desktop computer or my BlackBerry, it is still contact. Many people form small groups on Facebook, just to chat on a daily basis. These groups often share skills sets (design, research, teaching, graphics, authoring, etc.), conversation, and support—the essence of co-working in a virtual space. There's a great deal of informal learning taking place in both physical and virtual co-working environments. This is why co-working should be of interest to the learning and development community.

More and more workers work from non-traditional sites, usually from their homes. This is good for the environment, reduces time wasted in commuting, and often increases flexibility to better balance childcare, work, and social activities. At the same time, we all need to learn from each other and to be connected in a satisfying way to other people who understand and are willing to talk with us about what we do. Co-working is a growing trend that makes a new world of mobile work and mobile learning possible.

CHAPTER 27

The Impact of Mobile Learning on Assessment and Evaluation

Gary Woodill and Chad Udell

There are many, many ways to assess and evaluate learning. But, for most people, assessment and evaluation are all about testing—answering questions in multiple-choice format or essay style that are then marked, usually by the same person who created the questions. What is often being assessed in typical paper-and-pencil tests is the memorization and recall of specific content that has been "taught" as part of a standard curriculum.

Because many instructional designers see mobile learning as a spinoff of e-learning, which, in turn, is based on a classroom model, they are inclined to develop the same traditional assessment techniques, but on a smaller screen. So it is not a surprise that we can find examples of mobile quizzes, mobile grade books, and mobile polls and surveys. While there is nothing particularly wrong with this, it is a quite limited view of the potential of using mobile devices for assessment and evaluation.

If you are skilled and diligent, there are ways of using written test questions to assess learning objectives other than memorization—especially higher order cognitive domain objectives, such as those identified in Bloom's Taxonomy (Bloom, Engelhart, Furst, Hill, & Krathwohl, 1956)—comprehension, application, analysis, synthesis, and evaluation. But tests are not a good way to assess affective and psychomotor domain objectives—those that include values, organizational skills, perception, and creativity. Assessment of these areas usually includes the need for human observation and recording of what a learner does. Often, assessing and evaluating complex emotions and skills requires that the learners be in a specific context, interacting with the environment that elicits these behaviors. Sometimes, that context is a group of learners, where the requirement that is being assessed is based on group behaviors or collaboration processes.

Two forms of assessment are generally recognized: formative and summative. *Formative assessment* evaluates people's knowledge or performance while they are learning and provides feedback so that they can improve as they learn. Formative assessment can be used in adaptive teaching, varying the learning activities or materials available to the learner. *Summative assessment* generally comes at the end of a period of learning and summarizes learners' progress to date in a particular area.

Advantages of Mobile Assessment

Mobile technologies are particularly useful for going beyond the assessment of memorization and other "lower order" cognitive skills. As Clark Quinn explains in his 2012 book, *The Mobile Academy*, with mobile assessments learners can capture their own performance, whether directly or by measuring or recording it. He adds:

> These can be brought back for self-evaluations and comment or instructor feedback. These stored performances can also serve as components of a portfolio to be coupled with other work products. Having learners perform or create and then annotate a version with their reflections and underlying thought processes involved in the creation or performance provides a valuable tool for evaluation of their thinking and begins to develop literacies beyond text, an important 21st century skill. (Quinn, 2012, p. 72)

There are further benefits in using mobile technologies for assessment. In a 1999 study in Germany of over nine thousand psychometric tests, Rose, Hess, Hörhold, Brähler, and Klapp showed that "in comparison with paper-and-pencil versions . . . usage of mobile computer-assisted assessment reduced the time by two-thirds spent on documentation, because data organization and accessibility for clinical, scientific, and educational needs were significantly improved. Moreover, no differences in stability coefficients and data distribution were seen between the two methods." In New Zealand, Parsons and Ryu (2006) identified ubiquity, convenience, localization, and personalization as additional benefits of using mobile assessments.

Mobile assessment represents a shift from old methods of summative assessment based on testing and grading, with its focus on individual achievement, to a new approach based on assessment information that has formative uses and is adaptive and learner-centric. The results of assessment become much more complex and are based on the accumulation of evidence from many sources, using many different methods (Pellegrino, 2013). What is being assessed is now more dependent on the learners' needs, context, and organizational requirements, rather than a standardized set of facts that need to be memorized and retained, although some level of memorization will likely continue to be required. Pellegrino (2013) argues for an "evidence-centered design process" and says that "a new generation of innovative assessments is pushing the frontiers of measuring complex forms of learning."

The process starts by defining as precisely as possible the claims that one wants to be able to make about student knowledge and the ways in which students are supposed to know and understand some particular aspect of a content domain. While the claims one wishes to make or verify are about the student, they are linked to the forms of evidence that would provide support for those claims—the warrants in support of each claim. The evidence statements associated with given sets of claims capture the features of work products or performances that would give substance to the claims.

Mobile devices are ideal for capturing student input and collecting evidence of processes such as problem-solving sequences or use of strategy in a game, for example. Leonard Low (2006) documents some of the many ways that mobile devices can be used to gather evidence for workplace assessments, such as:

- Capturing images of evidence of competency using a digital camera,
- Recording sound productions or interviews,
- Note-taking by observers in the form of completion of checklists or observational rubrics,

- Self-evaluation against competencies,
- Maintenance of a journal of reflections on learning, and
- Completion of quizzes or tests.

As Chad Udell documents in another chapter of this book, the number of different metrics available to measure behavior with a mobile phone is well beyond what can be provided by paper-and-pencil tests and includes such new data types as location, movement, and biometrics. The increase in the amount of data allows for new algorithms that can measure a student's level of achievement, as well as predict what concepts he or she needs to learn next, based on performance. An adaptive teaching approach can then be used based on the large amount of data that is collected on each student. As devices become faster and more powerful, the possibility of real-time feedback as someone learns is close at hand.

Because of mobile devices, assessment and evaluation can now move directly into the workplace, and occur while the learner is actually doing his or her job (Coulby, Hennessey, Davies, & Fuller, 2011). This is particularly useful in that an assessor can check whether, in fact, a learner is applying the concepts learned in a real-life situation. To quote Clark Quinn (2012) again: "The core of meaningful practice is application," because ". . . the only summative assessment to care about is whether learners can ultimately perform to the desired level" (pp. 63–64).

Because the person who is doing the assessment and evaluation now has rich sources of data from multiple directions, a much more nuanced and complex picture of a person's learning achievements and potential can be compiled. A recent study by Taylor, Dearnley, Laxton, Nkosana-Nyawata, and Rinomhota (2012) using mobile 360-degree performance feedback tools with over nine hundred users in health and social care practice placement settings in the U.K. showed that mobile assessment produces a much more useful picture of each person and his or her interactions within a group, than previous methods of standardized testing could ever do.

The Near Future of Mobile Assessment

New developments in mobile technologies foreshadow even more changes in the use of mobile assessments in the near future.

Computerized adaptive testing (and most smart phones and tablets are powerful computers) is a special case of computer-based testing, where each learner takes an individualized and unique test tailored to his or her ability level. The process starts with the software giving the learner an item of moderate difficulty in order to assess his or her level. If it is answered correctly, the next item is harder. If the answer is incorrect, then an easier item is presented. Using this method, the knowledge level of a learner can be assessed very quickly. This approach has several other advantages, including allowing testing on demand using a mobile device, which means that a learner can take a test whenever he or she is ready. A variety of item types using multiple innovative forms of media can be used (Triantafillou, Georgiadou, & Economides, 2008).

Another recent innovation in mobile assessment mixes QR codes in with printed materials. The QR codes allow students to take a test regularly and receive immediate, constructive feedback as well as suggestions for review materials or additional resources (Lan, 2013). Two other recent innovations are assessment methods using automatic sensors (Trinder, 2012), and the use of the new Experience API (xAPI) and the concept of a learning records store (LRS) for recording and sharing of informal learning achievements.

Mobile devices are having an impact on assessment and evaluation of learning, and further developments are on the way.

References

Bloom, B.S., Engelhart, M.D., Furst, E.J., Hill, W.H., & Krathwohl, D.R. (1956). *Taxonomy of educational objectives: The classification of educational goals; Handbook I: Cognitive domain.* New York: Longmans, Green.

Coulby, C., Hennessey, S., Davies, N., & Fuller, R. (2011, March). The use of mobile technology for work-based assessment: The student experience. *British Journal of Educational Technology, 42*(2), 251–265.

Lan, Y. (2013). Integrating smart phone with QR code technology into adaptive learning activities. Unpublished paper at http://nfuplus .nfu.edu.tw/nfuplus/sites/default/files/result.pdf

Low, L. (2006, May 31). Workplace assessment with mobile devices. *Mobile Learning: An Online Reflective Journal on Mobile Learning Practice.*

Parsons, D., & Ryu, H. (2006). A framework for assessing the quality of mobile learning. *Proceedings of the 11th International Conference for Process Improvement, Research and Education (INSPIRE)* (pp. 17–27). Southampton Solent University.

Pellegrino, J. (2013). Measuring what matters in a digital age: Technology in the design of assessments for multisource comprehension. In D. Sampson, P. Isaias, D. Ifenthaler, & J.M. Spector (Eds.), *Ubiquitous and mobile learning in the digital age* (pp. 259–286). New York: Springer.

Quinn, C. (2012). *The mobile academy: mLearning for higher education.* San Francisco, CA: Jossey-Bass,

Rose, M., Hess, V., Hörhold, M., Brähler, E., & Klapp, B.F. (1999, June). Mobile computer-assisted psychometric diagnosis: Economic advantages and results on test stability. *Psychotherapy and Psychosomatic Medicine Psychology, 49*(6), 202–207. [Translated from German]

Taylor, J., Dearnley, C., Laxton, J., Nkosana-Nyawata, I., & Rinomhota, S. (2012). The perceptions of health and social care students of using mobile 360-degree performance feedback tools in practice placement settings. *International Journal of Mobile and Blended Learning, 4*(1).

Triantafillou, E., Georgiadou, E., & Economides, A. (2008, May). The design and evaluation of a computerized adaptive test on mobile devices. *Computers and Education, 50*(4), 1319–1330.

Trinder, J. (2012). *Mobile learning evaluation: The development of tools and techniques for the evaluation of learning exploiting mobile devices through the analysis of automatically collected usage logs—an iterative approach.* Doctoral dissertation, University of Glasgow.

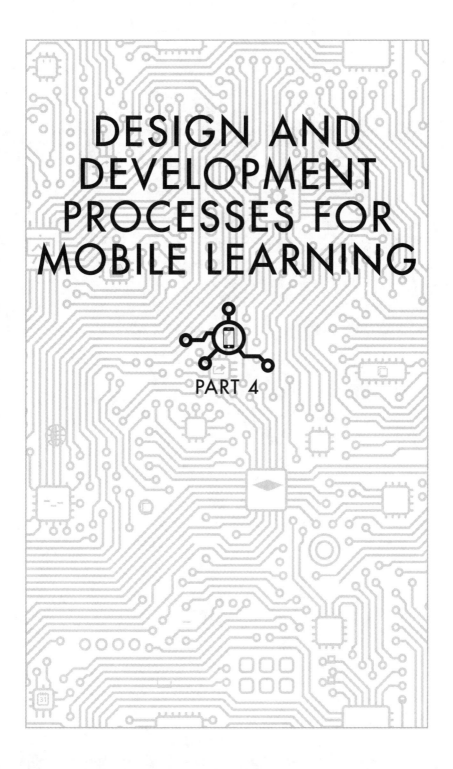

DESIGN AND DEVELOPMENT PROCESSES FOR MOBILE LEARNING

PART 4

CHAPTER 28

Mysteries, Heuristics, and Algorithms
Design Thinking for Mobile Learning

Gary Woodill

Designing for mobile learning is somewhat of a jungle. That is, there are no easy answers to the question: "How do I design for mobile learning?" In our discussions with clients, we are often asked whether, in the training and development world, there is a learning theory or pedagogical system specifically developed for mobile learning, such as ADDIE or Dick and Carey. Unfortunately, for those who want quick answers and easy-to-follow formulas, the answer is "no." At least not yet.

Instead, as learning and development specialists, we need to approach the problem as true designers—ready to work to identify the actual problem and come up with creative solutions that don't just alleviate the symptoms. We live in a world of rapid change where many of the issues that arise in enterprise learning and development have never been seen before. With the development of mobile computing, we have a new toolset to develop solutions that we have never thought of before.

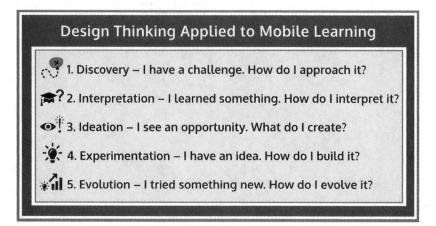

But it is not logical to start with tools before defining the dimensions of a project. What are the challenges and problems that a company is facing? Are these known issues with standard solutions that have worked in the past? Is mobile learning, in one of its forms, the obvious solution? Then apply these solutions and get on with solving the problems.

What if this is a unique problem a company is facing, for which there is no obvious solution? Then there has to be a more creative approach to problem solving, a process known as "design thinking." Design thinking is a structured process to generating and developing new ideas. It has been articulated by IDEO, the well-known product design company headquartered in Palo Alto, California. The steps for design thinking advocated by IDEO are listed below:

1. *Discovery*—I have a challenge. How do I approach it?
2. *Interpretation*—I learned something. How do I interpret it?
3. *Ideation*—I see an opportunity. What do I create?
4. *Experimentation*—I have an idea. How do I build it?
5. *Evolution*—I tried something new. How do I evolve it?

The dean of the Rotman School of Business at the University of Toronto, Roger Martin, says that in order to innovate and win, companies need design thinking in addition to the quantitative management approaches that they traditionally have used. In his

2009 book, *The Design of Business: Why Design Thinking Is the Next Competitive Advantage*, Martin says that knowledge advances from one stage to another—from mystery (something we can't explain) to heuristic (a rule of thumb that guides us toward solution) to algorithm (a predictable formula for producing an answer). In a 2010 talk in Australia (http://vimeo.com/10452582), Martin elaborated on these three stages of knowledge.

In the Mystery stage, we are faced with questions and problem statements about which we do not have answers. This is the stage that many companies find themselves at today in regard to mobile computing in general. What can we do with these iPods we just bought? How can I use mobile learning for competitive advantage? What new things can we do with the current state of technology that we couldn't before? What policies make sense in terms of employees' use of their own mobile devices? There are no standardized answers here, just the possibility of creative answers if one wants to move forward. Early adopters and innovators set the stage here and plot new courses for others to follow.

In the Heuristic stage, those in charge of training and development understand the possibilities of mobile learning, but still don't have a strategy or understand how to put a comprehensive system together. Based on what they already know about learning technologies and the advice of newly minted mobile learning experts in the field, they are ready to try something and make it work. At this stage of mobile learning, much of what is going on is strategy development, experimentation, and pilot studies. The important thing is to find something that works, whether it is an elegant solution or not. By doing this, the company advances as key managers and trainers gain experience and learn the possibilities of mobile learning. Mimicry or replication of previously successful cases can serve as a way to test whether a recipe may work for your organization.

In the Algorithmic stage, standard procedures and policies for mobile learning are in place for a specific company. Almost no one is there yet in the mobile learning arena. There are just too many things to try out and to learn in order to make mobile learning standard operating procedure. Yet, this is where many people want to start—and expect that consultants and vendors have the skills and information that will make this easily possible. Virtually no one's current situation is enough like someone else's to make a "mobile learning in a box" approach successful. They don't want to go through the hard work of examining strategic business problems, technology choices, and innovations in pedagogy or to undertake iterative trials of mobile learning within their own companies. But, without these early stages, implementing mobile learning may very well be a failure that impacts a company's bottom line. No reputable consulting company should suggest that it has solutions that don't require going through the mystery and heuristic stages of knowledge development before settling into a comprehensive system.

As Roger Martin pointed out, the benefits of going through these three stages can be huge. The results are often a massive efficiency gain, and if your company is out there first, it can be rewarded by being a market leader. However, in this day and age things change rapidly, as new mysteries arise. So the process has to be started over again, if companies are not to lose their competitive advantage. As Clayton Christiansen (1997) has shown in *The Innovator's Dilemma*, most companies that have a winning product are "one-hit wonders." Rarely do they have multiple winning products or innovations that make them leaders in the next innovation cycle.

Right now, the field of mobile learning is moving from the mystery to the heuristic stage in that we are trying to figure out what problems it can solve and put together crude systems and single-purpose apps to solve those problems. There are some successful recipes, and even more unsuccessful ones, out there for you to review, learn from, and choose to replicate or avoid. Considering this further, mobile learning has not reached an algorithmic stage in that there are no standard procedures or methods that have been shown to get reliable results. That will come, but not before a lot more innovation and experimentation.

References

Christensen, C. (1997). *The innovator's dilemma: When new technologies cause great firms to fail.* Boston, MA: Harvard Business School Press.

Martin, R. (2009). *The design of business: Why design thinking is the next competitive advantage.* Boston, MA: Harvard Business School Press.

CHAPTER 29

Ubiquity and Mobility as Design Considerations for Mobile Learning

Chad Udell

It should be abundantly clear by now that mobile devices are like no other technology we have ever created learning content for or placed in the hands of our employees. They are fundamentally different because they are always on, always near us, and always connected. How has this changed how you access information and interact with others? Try this quick statement on for size. You've probably said, "I'll look that up the next time I'm online" once or twice if you have been an Internet user since the late 1990s or even early 2000s. Think about the last time you said that. It might be hard to remember when you struck that from your vocabulary. It likely corresponds to one of two primary events:

1. You installed reliable, easy-to-use wireless Internet access in your home.
2. You acquired a smart phone with a data plan.

With the first event, you still need to deliberately open up a laptop, boot it up, sign in, and then browse to find the information you seek. But with smart phones being an arm's length away, always on, and always connected to the web and other services, information that you need can arrive even before you request it.

The very concept of "the next time I'm online" is anachronistic. It's a bit like saying you will "tape a show" with your digital video recorder (DVR).

This shift is transformational. Are you taking full advantage of this change in your mobile learning efforts? If not, read on to find some ideas on how you can leverage this powerful new affordance of mobile devices.

Going from read-only access via a learning management system at a prescribed location and time (at work, during business hours) to this new deliver information anywhere, any time mindset takes a bit of rethinking of learning and development's role and approach to implementation for you, your team, and your organization. To start, consider how you can use these devices in the always on, always with you, always connected fashion already described.

Always On

I don't know about you, but I almost never turn my mobile device off. I may restart it to apply an update or fix an issue that is occurring, but the times I turn the device off are few and far between (and even more so, now that the FAA allows devices to remain on during takeoffs and landings). Even when I'm not actively using the device, it's usually in standby or sleep mode, not fully turned off.

Contrast that with how I use a laptop. If I know I won't need it for some time, I'm inclined to turn it off to prevent extra battery drain or fan/heating issues in its storage bag. Granted, I rarely turn my laptop off, but I know many people who turn their machines off every night and reboot every day, even though it's not really needed anymore, with solid state drives and locking heads on hard disks (old habits die hard).

What do you gain when you have a device that is never turned off? Well, here are a few things that spring to mind:

1. *Instant availability:* You never have to wait to reboot and log in.
2. *Information currency:* You know that you will be able to receive updates as they happen.

3. *Replacing other devices and functions:* Need a watch? An alarm clock? A calculator? A level? A camera? No need to hunt for one and turn it on when you have a multifunction device that is always powered up.

4. *Dependability and familiarity:* When you have something like this in your life, the tool becomes a vital part of the way you get things done and your daily routine.

How can you apply this design framework to your workplace information and learning content distribution? You can start by changing how you design access points to your content. Virtually any information on the web is two or three clicks away via a search in a browser on a smart phone or tablet (or a voice search away via Siri or Google Now). If accessing vital company content takes much more effort than that, you have some obstacles to remove. In the words of Conrad Gottfredson and Bob Mosher (2012), make your content no more than "two clicks or ten seconds" away. Anything much more than that, and not only are you not taking advantage of the always on nature of these devices, but you are driving your learners to other information sources that are easier to use and quicker to access.

Always with You

Most people check their mobile devices dozens of times a day—according to Nokia, upward of 150 times a day. Mobile analyst Tomi Ahonen (2013) dissected this number in great detail on his blog, illustrating just how glued we are to these things. He added, "the mobile is the last thing we see before we fall asleep and the first thing we see when we wake up." For many of my friends and family, myself included, I know this is true. I use my mobile phone as my primary alarm clock for waking when at home or on the road, and I usually check any social feeds right before I nod off for the night. In the morning, with my coffee, I use it to read the news and find the weather for the day. It is my informant, my assistant, my planner, and news source all in one. How can it do all of this so well, and why can I depend on it so deeply? It's because of the trust I place in it. Besides the spectacles on my face and the wedding ring on my finger, no other object gets as close to me or spends as much time with me as my smart phone.

It's personalized. I've tricked it out, customized it. Added text tones and wallpapers. I have a connection to it, just as it is connected to the network. Because of this, I can be more informed and smarter than I ever could have been without it.

Are you leveraging this closeness and personalization in your mobile learning? If not, you're missing out on a powerful way to connect your audience to your content. Make it theirs, and they are more likely to want what you have to offer. Hand out the same thing on a big screen and see them walk right by it.

This isn't about content being in the form of courses or non-courses. It's not even about performance support, job aids, or whatever you want to pin it on. This is about humanizing your content and making it fit the lives of users, not your needs as a designer or developer.

This is a fundamental shift in how we create our content. This requires research into topics like human computer interaction (HCI), user-centered design (UCD), design thinking, and user acceptance testing (UAT). It also requires abandoning some of our ego. Our users will show us the path, if we give them the ability to make choices and contextualize the experience to meet their own needs.

The depth to which these devices have already penetrated our lives is profound. People like them. You have a strong advantage here in your content-creation process. Create something employees like and deploy it on devices they like to use and always have with them, and you will succeed.

Always Connected

With 3G and now 4G/LTE networks, our mobile devices have constant connection to the same web you use on your desktop or laptop computers. The same news, social content, games, and more are just a tap away. No longer confined to a computer in the den or a cubicle, information is always available. This is a boon for us in the information-delivery business. We don't need our learners to come to us in a classroom or via a clumsy intranet site that only works on a specific outdated browser. No way. We can go straight to them via push notifications, email, messaging, and many more emerging channels like near field communication (NFC) and Bluetooth low energy (BLE).

This changes the game in a lot of ways, but it does a few things especially well:

1. It meets the point of application of learning in a much more meaningful and powerful way.
2. It gives the learner a tremendous tool to use to find solutions when things go wrong.
3. It provides wayfinding and guides for when processes or tools have changed.

Beyond these three moments of need, the always-connected nature of these devices accommodate, for most of us and in most situations, the fact that most learning is simply unplanned. We simply don't know when we may need to know something. As learning designers, we can take advantage of this. We don't need to wait for the next time users access our content; we can send it to them based on contextual clues such as time, setting, or intent. With digital agents and AI, we can interact with employees and colleagues to help them before they even know they need it. Is staff fumbling about in a new application? Perhaps we can alert them to some contextual help available. Have managers just traveled to a new company facility they haven't visited before? Maybe you can offer to show them a map or check-in procedures based on their current location.

Without the always-connected nature of these devices, those sorts of performance support use cases seemed like sci-fi. Now they are almost second-nature for application designers and developers producing consumer products. In the training world, we must harness that type of thinking and bring it to our audience as well.

Entering the World of the "Three Always"

To assume the role of mobile learning master and leverage the always on, always with me, always connected power of these devices, consider the following:

• You should expect your users to be able to access information they need and not have to go somewhere else, stop what they are doing, or change their focus to receive help.

- You should expect your learners to use the company-provided mobile learning tools as their first line of defense.

- You should consider your mobile learning content and applications as a backstop that never fails.

- You must acknowledge that turning to and using mobile learning is not an admission of failure of training/learning, but rather the success of your designing great mobile tools.

- Mobile learning isn't about performance support in simple terms; it's actually much more about augmenting every employee to make him or her the absolute best he or she can be.

- Ponder this. Does Yelp look at the frequent use or access of its resources as a failure? Are return visitors to Wikipedia bad learners? If I need to check weather.com more than once a day, is this really all that bad?

To design learning with the "three always" in mind, start with these tips:

- Simple read-only, lecture-style content delivery doesn't cover this sort of access by itself, but can be augmented to do it by adding hooks for searching and smart indexes, tags, and other metadata.

- This style of learning needs some user experience design—not just instructional design.

- You must understand how, where, when, and why this content will be used. What are the use cases?

- You must empathize with the learners. Understand how they access and why they access information.

- Survey the users' locations. Get in their shoes—literally travel with them during the definition phase of your projects if you can.

- Put your content directly in their line of activity. Don't require them to come to you.

- Provide content to them before they need it and become their most trusted source of information.

"Always available" is one of the most powerful aspects of mobile learning technology. Understanding how to put it to work for you will undoubtedly take some work, but when you do, your learners will be empowered, no matter where they are.

References

Ahonen, T. (2013, July 22). An attempt to validate the 150x per day number based on "typical user." Communities dominate brands (Blog). http://communities-dominate.blogs.com/brands/2013/01/an-attempt-to-validate-the-150x-per-day-number-based-on-typical-user.html.

Gottfredson, C., & Mosher, B. (2012, July 9). Ten seconds: Performance support in two clicks. *Learning Solutions* magazine. www.learningsolutionsmag.com/articles/964.

CHAPTER 30

Design Considerations in Converting e-Learning to mLearning

Chad Udell

Converting content and moving from one type of learning technology to another are core requests we receive from visitors to our website, people who come to hear us speak, and clients who want us to do work for them. Upon initial consideration, it makes sense that people are very interested in this. After all, there is likely a wealth of content already in existence at your workplace that has been designed and approved for use in training your employees. Companies want to leverage existing resources and investment in the content they have produced.

In *Learning Everywhere* (2012), I wrote extensively about this type of mlearning content: "content converted from other sources." I praised it for its ease of transitioning your company into a mobile learning–enabled organization. I also cautioned against wholesale content conversion or approaching this as an exercise in miniaturization of content. It's not just a simple exercise in shrinking the elements in your course to meet screen real estate requirements. You can't really just move things around to make them smaller and expect that to work. In short, there is no big red easy button to make your move to mobile a simple, automated process.

A Plan for Transitioning Content

In making the move to the small screen with existing content, I recommend using these four main steps. Establishing a plan will help ensure success and reduce wasted efforts:

- Assess your existing content for opportunities to go mobile.
- Redesign your experiences to provide optimal learning solutions.
- Be mindful of key considerations as you port content to mobile.
- Remember what not to do when converting your content.

Each of these points will provide guidance and assist you in reaching your goal—a mobile learning–enabled workforce using the best content to help them do their jobs.

Assess Your Existing Content

We find that many people want to jump in and convert entire libraries of courses and job aids to mobile. In some cases, this could even be hundreds of modules built over a long period of time. This would, of course, be thousands of hours of labor if done correctly.

The thing I caution against, though, is that, without an understanding of the content you are converting and the ways in which it would be used when mobile, there could be a significant amount of wasted effort.

Before attempting to produce a replicated version of your library in a smart phone or tablet–accessible format, consider this. Will this content be made more useful when brought over to a mobile use case? If the information would rarely be accessed when the learner is on the go, you may be able to skip it. If the information is best suited to ahead-of-time delivery and not really ready to move to a just-in-time process, perhaps you should leave it where it is or assign a lower priority for redesigning it.

You can gain insight into these issues by reviewing how your learners do their jobs and are accessing resources to help them. Do they have commonly printed out materials, Post-it Notes, or other reminders in their job area? Do they access intranet resources or other company web assets frequently?

Use clues like this to point you to the content in your library that should be brought over to mobile and made available to your workers while they are on the go.

Redesign Your Experiences

Another key aspect of the content conversion process to remember is that simply making the course or content compatible with your audience's mobile device platforms is not likely to lead to successful uptake and ongoing usage.

You must redesign the user experience to match expectations of how mobile-optimized sites and services function. Up to this point, if you have come from an e-learning background, you have mostly designed linear experiences that heavily depend on the use of the Next and Back buttons for moving around and experiencing the content in modules you have created.

This works for new content and for experiences related to learning something for the first time. But what about for refreshers or digging deeper to find an answer when you need it or when you are on the go?

Consider this example. If you were at home planning a trip and wanted to find a place for lodging and also some restaurants before you traveled, you might be happy to browse a website, clicking around and viewing things casually. However, if you were already on the road and needed to find a hotel and a place to eat before turning in for the evening, you would likely have a much different browsing strategy. You would depend more heavily on search, and you would also want answers to be arranged in a format that gave you the highest rated and closest items first.

Not only would you expect the user experience to change from your home or desktop computer use, but you would expect the interface to change, too. You would desire less focus on exploration, more focus on directed content. You would demand more accessible searching and filtering. If the menu were inaccessible and you had to navigate the site completely linearly, you would likely abandon the site altogether. Take cues from the most helpful mobile sites you use when you convert your desktop content to mobile.

You must also adjust your user interface to be more "finger friendly." The cursor on a computer is a far more precise interface tool than your finger. While it's not uncommon to have buttons and other interactive elements that are no bigger than 7 to 12 pixels tall on a computer experience, an interactive hotspot of that size on a touchscreen would be cumbersome to use. You must consider that a human finger has a touch point area of roughly 1 cm in diameter and position elements accordingly.

This includes considering not just the space the items occupy, but also the negative space around the items. You must give your menu items and buttons room to breathe in order to prevent "fat fingering" the elements and allowing for easy interaction around potentially crowded areas on-screen.

Another area of user interface that will require adjustment is understanding that, with touchscreen input, there is an expectation that some things will change to make navigation easier for fingers. Keep in mind that smart phone apps are often navigated with one hand, while users hold the device and navigate experiences with their thumbs. Also, swipe gestures and pinch and zoom style interface features are expected to advance through image galleries and navigate detail views, respectively.

User expectations also shift when you move to a mobile design paradigm. What would have been an acceptable mouse hover interaction to add engagement is not only annoying when people want information quickly, but also impossible on mobile devices because there is no hover state for interactions with elements.

Last, every screen or state in a mobile experience should be designed with a key interaction point or conversion point in mind. If the screen doesn't basically scream, "Do this and don't do this" from the elements you have chosen to put on-screen and the prompts or cues you have given the user, than you are probably not designing an effective user interface (UI). It should be virtually impossible to look at a mobile interface and be confused as to what you are supposed to do.

Be Mindful of Key Design Considerations

Mobile users are not only impatient, but they are also busy. Keep your content to the bare minimum needed to aid them, and offer more information only as an adjunct or for further reading. Don't place obstacles in their paths that require users to listen to a complete audio clip or pass through every screen in order to reach their final choices.

The objective, after all, is to provide the most useful content to them to solve an issue they may be having or to offer a refresher. Offering the supporting materials as an option or footer for a page is a great idea. Burying the content behind twelve "Next" buttons is not.

To help you do this, break up content and tag it for easier searching and browsing. Give your pages and areas descriptive, easy-to-decipher titles. Something like "How to Lay Floor Tiles" is far better than "Home Construction 12: Flooring."

What Not to Do

We've focused on some adjustments you'll want to make as you bring your content over to mobile. Here are some things you definitely don't want to do.

Include Everything: When we produce classroom instruction or e-learning, there is often a habit to include an exhaustive inventory of the content and all of the related information. This is often due to the fact that we expect that we will only have one chance to interact with the user. Mobile is almost always a repeat use case, so there is no need to take the kitchen sink approach so prevalent in other instructional design delivery methods.

Listen to Everyone: Here's a joke for you: How many stakeholders does it take to kill your mobile learning project's productivity and delay your planned launch date? The answer: One less than you currently have on your project. It sounds farcical, but it's true. Add too many people to the approval chain on a new technology like mobile delivery, and you are bound to have hiccups. Keep your project teams small and only include must-have team members who add value to your efforts.

Force Artificial Deep Exploration: Requiring users to explore graphics, participate in every interaction you designed for a module, or visit every screen in a course before it can be marked as complete can be seen as an engagement strategy on the desktop. Don't bring this sort of interactive design over to mobile. Not only is this contrived form of engagement not effective in many cases on a computer, but it can seem downright hostile to a user who is looking for a vital piece of information when on the go via a mobile device. If your content is good and your experience is easy to use, you will have no issues engaging your users with your app or website.

Reinvent the Wheel: It is an unfortunate thing that we inter-activity designers ignore tried-and-true methods for success and attempt to design completely new types of interaction models and design patterns. In the desktop world this can lead to poor usability, testing issues, and more. In the mobile world, it leads to those things, and, ultimately, user abandonment. We should strive to follow accepted user interface conventions and only stray when a specific use case is not supported adequately by existing user interface controls and design patterns.

The Last Word

I hope these tips have been helpful to you in your pursuit to bring existing content over to mobile.

Really, it seems to boil down to one key concept: Designing for mobile isn't rocket science. Keep the user in mind, and you'll do just fine.

CHAPTER 31

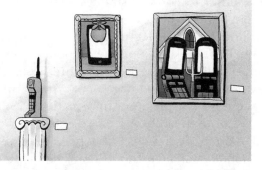

The Importance of Curation for Successful Mobile Experiences

Chad Udell

It's easy to see that web-connected smart phones (basically, the post-iPhone market) signaled the end of an individual being unable to answer the trivia question at the pub with a friend. Virtually any piece of information is available to an inquisitive user, no matter where he or she is located. In many ways, it also signaled the end of the "less is more" approach in terms of content curation for mobile learning that characterized the wireless application protocol (WAP) days, due to low-speed connections and low-powered feature phones with limited input options. There is no question our phones have become faster, and our connections to the mobile web have, too. Why, then, is information retrieval time on task for mobile web content still lagging steadily behind the PC? The simple answer: We're enamored with the power. The easy access to deep content anywhere, any time is making us drunk on information and makes it take far too long to access our end goals. A carefully crafted content strategy that includes curation as a core concept is crucial in helping the user find the right information.

Consider Your Focus

Curation in relation to content strategy is the process of selection and presentation of the content that will be used by a mobile learner. How does a mobile learning strategy that includes content curation help? Think for a moment about the worst-case scenario, the proverbial "drinking from the fire hose." A real-world example: envision a content management system with more than 200,000 unique nodes or pieces of information with all of it laid out for every visitor to the website, regardless of whether that user is using a PC or a mobile device. This type of content strategy or, rather, lack of strategy, creates the endless category tree user interface (UI) design pattern and requires ceaseless querying to return the newly filtered result-set as the user traverses the information on a mobile device. This is a poor mobile user experience and should be avoided in order to make the user experience friendlier and more intuitive. The primary alternative to a browsing experience, the search, can be hit-or-miss, depending on your content indexing and the search capabilities of the platform being used. Relying on this as a key use case to overcome the flood of content is not wise.

Even on a smaller scale, this sort of content dump approach can be deadly for an optimal user experience. Consider the possibility of putting a 200-slide PowerPoint deck used as a sales tool or performance support onto a mobile device. It's a lot of content, sure, but is it the right content? You've probably had to endure a two-hour unedited and unsegmented video with no index, chapter points, or searchability. You may have seen a technology project executed that focused on providing unfettered access to a cavernous SharePoint server, with the producers of the content expecting a positive experience for users. The content dump approach can be an inexpensive way to go mobile, certainly, but the consequences are dire.

What is wrong with any of these scenarios? It should be obvious that, without having a clear concept of users' goals, the unique context of their situations, a guide for their decisions, or use of curation to assist the content to bubble up in the right spots, it is going to be very difficult to achieve a successful user experience. Simply forcing an overabundance of content into a small screen is an untenable solution. Remember, a content strategy that doesn't cull the content to meet the needs of the mobile user is ineffectual. Not having curated content that allows a focused, directed experience is not economical from a total cost of ownership or lifecycle perspective due to lost productivity or sales, perceived failure, and damage to your brand. The bad, or even unsatisfying, user experience will cost users and lead to a possible redesign or, worse, killing of the project.

Research Paper Equivalents

So what should be done to make content usable and to make the user experience as pleasant as possible? The first step is to acknowledge the problem. You must recognize that the context for the mobile user changes the user's content needs and desires dramatically. Often, PC-based access to content is to prepare for later requirements, and it is performed under less restrictive technical and physical constraints. The bandwidth is higher, the processor is faster, the screen is bigger, and the user input is often more precise.

Mobile access, on the other hand, is done under a "micro-tasking" mindset: "Get in, get out, get on with your life." You must understand and design for the fact that accessing a wealth of uncurated data on a device is difficult. Input constraints, data throughput, and connectivity issues necessitate that you design and think differently about your content. In the non-digital parallel, think about how these types of information and performance support tools work. At-a-glance reference cards, laminated phone directories, cross-tabulated mileage charts, and so on—these typical learning and development documents share a common thread. They are designed for easy, quick use on the go, and they contain only the information needed for the task at hand.

Some of the more advanced examples of these mobile references you may have in your possession have index tabs, spinning discs with revealing die cuts, or other intelligently designed information-revealing tools that allow the user to quickly filter a curated list of data or options. They may reveal deeper layers of information, but only as needed and only by careful design. Consider how you can emulate not the physical design via some contrived skeuomorphic metaphor, but rather, capture the essence of the piece and translate it to a mobile user experience.

Cull the Content

How do we get past this content access issue and provide better, more relevant user interfaces and experiences to our mobile learners? Even though we have rich service-oriented architectures (SOA) with deep data, a successful user interaction is as much about the irrelevant content we leave out as it is about the information that is accessed. Content curation is vital to the mobile user experience because it provides focus and reduces time on task.

You must aim to augment, attempt to support, or intend to provoke a thought in providing your content. Assist the user in speed, accuracy, and safety in retrieval. The key is to cut the content until you have the minimum you need to provide true utility and timeliness. Consider this: Are you providing only actionable information to your users, or is there a lot of fluff along for the ride? What is the least amount of information you can provide and still be useful, providing real value to your audience? If you have more information available than this self-imposed limit, or if you are considering supplying more content or are getting pressure to display chart junk or useless metadata along with the real focused information, you must resist the urge to throw in the kitchen sink. Go back to the personas you have crafted, reread the use cases you wrote, and make sure that you haven't over-served the content needs simply because you could or were receiving pressure from sources not close enough to the real user goals.

In your next project try this: Resist the urge to "get it all out there." Don't let ubiquity in access cloud your judgment in shaping the available information for your users.

Finally, get support! Mobile still needs curators. Don't count them out just because you are no longer chained to a desk. Craft a curated experience and you'll find engaged users able to locate the important information you want them to have.

CHAPTER 32

Selecting Tools for Mobile Learning Development

Chad Udell

One of the first questions I am asked when approached by learning professionals is: "What software should I learn to make mobile learning websites and apps?" My answer is usually greeted with some confusion. "All of them, none of them, any of them," I say. It's okay. I'm purposefully being coy.

The real answer is that a single software solution won't save you. There is no magic program that creates the ideal mobile learning experience for your users. The latest version of whatever you use to produce e-learning may be able to output content for mobile. I am not disputing marketing claims by software makers here, nor is that my intention in this chapter.

We need to learn less about the tools we use to output our content and more about the processes, practices, and the purpose behind the design and development of the content. We are moving, in some ways, to a model more akin to web design, web development, and information design. Bob Mosher and Conrad Gottfredson's (2012) mantra of "Two Clicks and Ten Seconds" rings true in mobile design, just as it does in desktop-focused electronic performance support systems. We are designing experiences for the enablement and information augmentation of the learners. We are creating experiences that provide the information they need to know at a specific moment, as well as directing the users to the deeper content that leads to knowledge transfer and retention.

For this reason, software and tools alone will not save you. You will now have a lot in common with the designers of news sites, travel sites, restaurant guides, and the rest of the World Wide Web community. With this bag of tricks, you need to prepare for changes. As new technologies, processes, and platforms are needed for mobile learning creation, it's clear that we need to reexamine the roles and skills we have represented on our teams and find where we may have gaps.

Instead of sending your teammates to a two-day boot camp on software products, I recommend a more comprehensive approach to growing your skills. Some areas I think that you may want to look into are explained below.

Information Architecture (IA): Information architecture is a discipline that has been in place on the web and in the interactive design world for some time. It is the art and science of organizing and labeling websites, intranets, online communities, and software to support usability. This is a new area of practice for most learning professionals, but one that many instructional designers can adapt to with some study and preparation. I know that it's a few years old, but I still love *Information Architecture for the World Wide Web* (2006) by Rosenfeld and Morville on this topic.

User Interface/User Experience (UI/UX): More than graphic design, user interface design and user experience design are core skills needed for effective development and building of mobile apps and websites. An instructional designer, who in the past was often tasked with creating user interfaces for e-learning, will definitely be tested here. The role of a UI designer for mobile experiences is less about creating interfaces to explore and more about creating interfaces to facilitate information retrieval and task completion. For further reading on this, I recommend picking up Steven Hoober and Eric Berkman's excellent resource, *Designing Mobile Interfaces* (2011), or Josh Clark's slightly older, yet indispensible text, *Tapworthy* (2010).

Curation and Content Strategy: With social media playing such a crucial role in mobile learning and informal learning's growing importance, it's clear that much more content will be available to learners than is truly useful. You must learn to cull the wasteful content and curate the very best information to make mobile experiences focused and beneficial for your audiences. The book *Curation Nation* (2010) by Steven Rosenbaum may help you see where you need to beef up your skills.

Software Development: Mobile development tools and practices are distinctly different from the practices with which you are likely familiar. While rapid tool vendors are making strides here, you would be well served to train your development staff on the HTML5 specification and how to author using native code (primarily Objective-C and Java due to their prevalence in iOS and Android development, respectively), instead of waiting for the rapid software tools to play catch-up. The real takeaway from this, in my opinion, is that you, as a learning designer and developer, may be better served finding a partner in your organization's technology group or a trusted vendor to help you with the final development of your products. You, after all, are likely a learning technologist, not a computer scientist.

These are all vastly different skills than you are likely to possess. What do you think? Have your thoughts shifted on what it takes to produce true mlearning?

References

Clark, J. (2010). *Tapworthy: Designing great iPhone apps.* Sebastopol, CA: O'Reilly.

Gottfredson, C., & Mosher, B. (2012, July 9). Ten seconds: Performance support in two clicks. *Learning Solutions.* www.learningsolutionsmag.com/articles/964.

Hoober, S., & Berkman, E. (2011). *Designing mobile interfaces.* Sebastopol, CA: O'Reilly.

Rosenbaum, S. (2010). *Curation nation.* New York: McGraw-Hill.

Rosenfeld, L., & Morville, P. (2006). *Information architecture for the world wide web* (3rd ed.). Sebastopol, CA: O'Reilly.

CHAPTER 33

Instructional Design Patterns for Mobile Learning

Gary Woodill

The use of mobile learning tools, processes, and procedures is not a guarantee of effective learning, because, like all tools, they can be used either well or ineffectively. At the present time, there is no coherent instructional design theory to guide the creation of mobile learning content. At the same time, pragmatic executives in large organizations demand proof that mobile learning can effectively and efficiently produce desired outcomes. It is clear that traditional training methods such as ADDIE or Dick and Carey were not designed for the realities of mobile learning. In fact, ADDIE's adequacy has recently come under fire (Bichelmeyer, 2004; Gram, 2009; Wagner, 2009), and many alternatives, such as the successive approximation model (SAM) and others, have been proposed (see Kapp, 2006, for a list), but none address mobile learning.

One alternative approach that should be considered is the adaptation of instructional "design patterns" in mobile learning, identified by reverse engineering successful case studies. An instinctive tendency of most designers when approaching a new project is to ask: What's worked in the past? What are others doing right? How can I leverage existing best practices? Finding and analyzing relevant case studies is a worthwhile endeavour, as it serves to determine which companies are using mobile learning, their success rates, and how they are using it, in order to gauge what might work in similar settings and circumstances.

Already, several articles and at least three books have been published on the design pattern approach. *Technology-Enhanced Learning: Design Patterns and Pattern Languages* (Goodyear & Retalis, 2010) contains eighteen chapters on this new approach to instructional design. Diana Laurillard's 2012 book, *Teaching as a Design Science: Building Pedagogical Patterns for Learning and Technology*, discusses a variety of learning and teaching patterns. Also, the Pedagogical Patterns Project (2012) has recently put out a book of readings for educators. But none of these books specifically discusses design patterns for mobile learning.

Background

The idea of design patterns comes from the field of architecture, when Alexander, Ishikawa, and Silverstein (1977) defined them as a technique that "describes a problem which occurs over and over again in our environment, and then describes the core of the solution to that problem, in such a way that you can use this solution a million times over, without ever doing it the same way twice." The related concept of "pattern languages" refers to a set of design patterns that work together to generate more complex interrelated solutions. Design patterns have their roots and strong precedents in the software development and web design fields as well.

The fact is that no one method of instruction exists for teaching all concepts or for facilitating learning. Laurillard (2012), for example, identifies five broad types of learning, all of which can be supported by mobile learning:

- Learning through acquisition
- Learning through inquiry
- Learning through discussion
- Learning through practice
- Learning through collaboration

The appropriate design pattern to be used depends on the type of learning that is needed, which points to the best design approaches to be taken. At the same time, an instructional designer must take into account the various strengths and weaknesses of available learning technologies, choosing those that are the most likely to support the successful delivery of desired learning outcomes. Mobile learning technologies have many strengths, but they are not the most effective or cost-efficient solution for every learning situation.

In Table 33.1, I have adapted and expanded Laurillard's list by matching learning outcomes with specific design approaches that

Table 33.1.   Matching Desired Learning Outcomes with Specific Design Approaches and Sample Mobile Applications

Desired Learning Outcome	Suggested Design Approach	Sample Mobile Applications
Memorization of material	Direct instruction, drill, and practice	Flashcards, quiz games
Carry out a physical skill	Repeated practice of desired skills	Simulations and immersive experiences, checklists and productivity tools
Imitation of behaviors	Model performance	Watch a video, use scenarios and artificial intelligence or wizards
Understand thinking of others	Hold discussion groups	Mobile video conference, voice or text chat
Experience a complex sequence of events	Provide real or simulated experiences	Follow a geofenced trail through a setting, use other device sensors to help a user learn more about his or her environment
Discovery of new information	Guided inquiry	Search agents and/or augmented reality, suggest new material based on past activity or intent
Build social relationships	Provide social networking opportunities	Social network platforms, company contact lists, and mentoring apps
Learn to work with others	Provide collaboration opportunities	Collaboration apps, push notifications, and messaging
Create something new	Encourage and support innovation	Note-taking or diagramming apps, photo, video, and audio acquisition, and manipulation tools

make sense. This listing is not meant to be exhaustive, but rather to show that instructional design is about deciding on the best ways to help a learner or a group of learners achieve a specific set of learning outcomes. One size definitely does not fit all.

When looking for the ideal learning approach for a group of learners in a specific environment, design patterns can be useful for suggesting a set of instructional design ideas, which can then be modified to suit the circumstances and the characteristics of the learners. This is especially useful when a learning development team does not have an in-house designer to develop custom instructional designs, or when efficiency of development is paramount.

To develop or identify a design pattern, it is helpful to find successful case studies that have similar outcomes to those that you are trying to achieve. Then, ask a set of questions to draw out the design pattern in such a way that you can use it again or easily modify it according to changing circumstances. The list below is an adaptation of questions that Laurillard (2012) asks in her book, offered here as a template that can help to analyze a case study involving the use of learning technologies.

Technology-Enhanced Learning Design Patterns Template

1. What is the basic design pattern? (Give it a name based on the broad learning outcomes and technology being used, and describe it in a couple of sentences.)
2. What features of the learning technology are useful for learning? (I refer to these features as the "affordances" of the technology. What problems can the use of this technology solve?)
3. What are the "human factors" for deciding why and how this particular learning technology should be used? (Describe the purpose of the learning program, the experience level, and physical, cognitive, and emotional characteristics of the learners.)
4. What equipment or settings do you need to use this technology? (Describe the learning site and equipment needed.)
5. What are the limitations or problems with using this technology for learning? (All technology has limitations.)

6. What external influences can affect learning while using this technology?

7. What does the learner do while using this technology?

8. What is the role of the instructor/designer in using this technology for learning? (What is needed to prepare materials and what does the instructor/designer do while the technology is being used?)

9. What is the nature of the educational content used with this technology?

10. How can this case study be extended to other circumstances and learners?

Adapted and expanded from Laurillard, 2012.

In order to make this real, let me work through a mobile learning example, a case study of the use of podcasting, taken from my book *The Mobile Learning Edge* (2011). In Chapter 4, I describe how Cognizant, an e-learning company in India, supplied its employees with iPods as a gift in order to provide instruction in English using a mix of podcasts and classroom training. Employees loaded a set of "learning nuggets" on speaking English onto iPods for their personal use. The employees were also supplied with additional reading materials, were required to attend a five-day classroom session that provided an overview of mobile learning as well as some English instruction, attended an online follow-up session for reinforcement, and took an online audio-based assessment consisting of listening and comprehension tests. This blended program was highly successful, making this case study a good candidate for analyzing its design patterns. There was a significant rise in learner satisfaction, program completion rose from 50 percent to 80 percent, and the time spent in learning activities increased from eleven hours to twenty-seven hours per month. The number of employees passing the final assessment for the program jumped from 70 percent to 83 percent, and the ROI was a cost saving of about $26,000 per month.

Analyzing a Mobile Learning Case Study

The Cognizant learning and development department used several different approaches to reach their objective, which was "to improve the conversational skills of associates through the use of a non-traditional, informal learning medium." The training provided by Cognizant was a blended approach, but for the purpose of illustrating the analysis of design patterns, we will focus on the use of iPods for teaching English.

Let's use the questions above as a template to look at how the mobile learning design pattern worked.

1. What is the basic design pattern?
    *   Podcasting—Listen to iPods or MP3 players in order to learn new information. The approach is based on the design pattern of lectures, but adapted to work with new technology, allowing information to be presented differently.
2. What features of this learning technology are useful for learning?
    *   It is mobile, can be used to push content, play rich media, and learn through listening and/or viewing.
    *   Podcasts can be listened to on mobile devices or laptop computers, allowing learners to move around while learning, as well as learn in a greater variety of locations.
    *   It is scalable—the number of learners in the class is not limited by the use of the podcast.
    *   The ability to pause the podcast allows learners to take the course at their own pace, thus encouraging them to work on it when they are motivated and focused.
    *   Instructors creating the podcasts must try to make them engaging and clear in order to engage learners' interest.
3. What are the "human factors" for deciding why and how this particular learning technology should be used?
    *   The company wanted all their employees to improve their English verbal skills.
    *   Employees spoke many native languages. For many, English needed to be improved in order to work in a global market.
    *   Many employees wanted this new technology, and the fact that the company gave each employee an iPod as a gift increased motivation and positive feelings toward the project.

- Podcasts can be used while the learner is walking, running, or traveling in a vehicle. Learning using the iPods could take place anywhere, any time.

4. What equipment or settings do you need to use this technology?

- To produce a podcast, you need a digital voice recorder.
- In order to play it, you simply need an iPod, an MP3 player, or a computer with sound capabilities. Smart phones are also an option.
- The physical setting can be anywhere, at any time.

5. What are the limitations or problems with using this technology for learning?

- Podcasts do not allow for interaction and feedback between the instructor and learners.
- Learners may lose focus if the instructor's voice is not interesting. There is no guarantee that a learner will listen to and understand the information the podcast provides.
- There are also difficulties when trying to present concepts that are best explained with visuals. Vodcasts (video podcasts) were created to fill this void.
- Other aspects of the course would need to provide an avenue for communication with the instructor.
- Finally, it is difficult to search and find specific items in a podcast.

6. What external influences can affect learning while using this technology?

- The learning will be unsuccessful if the learner is distracted, unmotivated, or uninterested.
- Lacking the proper background information would also make it difficult to understand and benefit from the podcast.

7. What does the learner do while using this technology?

- Learners must listen to the podcasts and absorb the information or take notes.
- The learners can imitate and repeat what they hear on the podcast.

8. What is the role of the instructor/designer in using this technology for learning?

- Instructors prepared the podcast for the class and were available to answer questions in person or through conferencing software.
- The podcast was used to supplement classroom instruction.

9. What is the nature of the educational content used with this technology?

- Small audio files ("learning nuggets").
- The content is dependent on the course being taught.

10. How can this case study be extended to other circumstances and learners?

- Although ideal for learning languages, different types of organizational learning content and company information can be delivered using the iPod.
- With available Wi-Fi plans, instructors/designers could push updated and additional content out to learners in the field, if using smart phone technology.
- Podcasting for learning can be used by employees in almost any industry, especially when employees have non-productive time such as commuting or waiting.

Conclusion

As Ellen Wagner (2009) noted, "*ADDIE isn't a learning model* [Wagner's italics]. Nothing about it says 'learning model.' It's a process model. It tells you what to do, in broad heuristic terms. It provides a systematic framework, a linear workflow."

An instructional designer must still choose specific activities and tactics to encourage and facilitate a learner's engagement in the completion of a specific set of learning objectives. Given that there are literally thousands of possible combinations of activities and approaches to this task, it seems a good idea that instructional designers develop their own catalog of learning design patterns that work. Once they have established a set of tried-and-true methods of instructional design, these can be shared, combined, and improved upon with others in a peer-based community approach. It is time to get to work developing mobile learning design patterns in order to produce a set of recommended methods for this emerging field.

References

Alexander, C., Ishikawa, S., & Silverstein, M. (1977). *A pattern language: Towns, buildings, construction.* New York: Oxford University Press.

Bichelmeyer, B. (2004). *The ADDIE model–A metaphor for the lack of clarity in the field of IDT.* Paper presented at the 2004 AECT Conference, Chicago, Illinois.

Dimitriadis, Y., Goodyear, P., & Retalis, S. (2009). Using e-learning design patterns to augment learners' experiences. *Computers in Human Behavior, 25*(5), 997–998.

Goodyear, P., & Retalis, S. (Eds.). (2010). *Technology-enhanced learning: Design patterns and pattern languages.* Rotterdam: Sense Publishing.

Goodyear, P. (2005). Educational design and networked learning: Patterns, pattern languages, and design practice. *Australasian Journal of Educational Technology, 21*(1), 82–101.

Gram, T. (2009, September 9). ADDIE is dead! Long live ADDIE! *Gram Consulting: Performance by Design.*

Kapp, K. (2006, December 4). Definitions: Alternatives to the ADDIE instructional design model. *Kapp Notes.* www.uleduneering.com/kappnotes/index.php/2006/12/definitions-alternatives-to-addie.

Laurillard, D. (2012). *Teaching as a design science: Building pedagogical patterns for learning and technology.* New York: Routledge.

Mor, Y., & Winters, N. (2007). Design approaches in technology-enhanced learning. *Interactive Learning Environments, 15*(1), 61–75.

Pedagogical Patterns Project. (2012). *Pedagogical patterns: Advice for educators.* New York: Joseph Bergin Software Tools.

Sharp, H., Manns, M.L., & Eckstein, J. (2003). Evolving pedagogical patterns: The work of the pedagogical patterns project. *Computer Science Education, 13*(4), 315–330.

Wagner, E. (2009, August 28). What is it about ADDIE that makes people so cranky? *eLearning Roadtrip.* http://elearningroadtrip.typepad.com/elearning_roadtrip/2009/08/what-is-it-about-addie-that-makes-people-so-cranky.html.

Woodill, G. (2011). *The mobile learning edge.* New York: McGraw-Hill.

CHAPTER 34

Creating Digital Publications for Mobile Learning

Heather Ford

It's important to understand how to best publish learning materials for your organization's employees. When creating a publication, you must understand the differences between the various output formats and tools you can use. What tools are best to create different types of publications? What are the differences among an EPUB, PDFs, and digital publishing?

With so many options out there, it could take a while to discover what the differences are for each competing standard. Here are some tips that will put you ahead of the learning curve as you assess your workflow and create your first publications.

When setting out to create any digital publication, there are some important differences to consider, such as what platforms the publication will be viewed on, the focus of the content, the appropriate design to reinforce your message, and other factors related to content and business strategy.

Only when this decision-making process is complete will you truly be able to determine the best tool to create the publication and whether any additional features or development efforts outside of the design should be included in the project plan.

Let's begin by defining EPUB, PDF, and digital publications:

EPUB

The electronic publication format (EPUB) is one of the most popular file formats for e-books. An EPUB is similar in some ways to a web page, in that it is based on HTML markup at its core. It is an open and freely available standard that can be used by anyone. An EPUB e-book is simply an archive containing several other files stored together using the common.zip format (and then changing the file suffix to.epub). The files in an EPUB archive can include your words, images, tables of contents, style sheets, fonts, and details or metadata about a book, such as author or title.

EPUB's standard format means your publication can be read on many e-readers or converted easily to other e-readers that don't use EPUB directly. EPUB is a layout-agnostic format that allows the content to be read even on small screens. EPUBs can be created for and sold on iBooks and/or Amazon for the Kindle, among other monetization paths and digital publishing stores.

The EPUB specification continues to evolve. The current version of the specification, 3.0, was approved in 2011.

PDF

A portable document format (PDF) is an open-specification file format maintained by Adobe that allows documents to be easily shared while retaining the same visual formatting. It is page-oriented and has a static layout, compared with an EPUB, which is display-oriented and allows content to be dynamic. Although PDF files are read easily on computer screens, they are not compatible or very usable with many mobile devices that have smaller screens.

Digital Publications

Beyond standards like EPUB and PDF, a number of emerging "digital publication" formats are competing for adoption. These publications often focus around increased interactivity and a rich media display, eschewing flexibility in display for immersive and engaging design.

When creating a marketing publication, interactive elements that enrich the user's experience, such as video, audio, slideshows, and animation, are beneficial. Coupled with attractive navigation design options, the layouts and structures possible are virtually limitless. These formats are becoming familiar to users, since they are more and more popular in the publishing marketplace, with major publishers like Condé Nast getting on-board.

Authoring Tools

There are many different types of authoring tools to choose from when creating electronic publications. Some of the more popular tools out there are Sigil, Adobe Digital Publishing Suite, iBooks Author, and Adobe InDesign.

Sigil is a free tool that can be used to create EPUBs. The software was designed to allow designers to easily create great e-books using the EPUB format, since the core of an EPUB is XHTML, SVG, and CSS.

Sigil has the following features:

- Multi-platform authoring
- Complete control over directly editing code
- Table of contents generator
- User interface translated into many languages
- Supports import of HTML files, images, and style sheets
- Documents can be validated

Adobe's Digital Publishing Suite (DPS), Adobe InDesign, and Apple iBooks Author are examples of the tools you can use when creating a digital publication. These types of publications are great for magazines, catalogs, or immersive interactive publishing experiences. Using a cloud service called Adobe Site Catalyst, you can perform marketing analysis on each publication's usage, which you can use for custom HTML tracking, determining the number of issues downloaded and purchased. The Wikipedia article on EPUB contains a table listing popular electronic publication editing software, with tools available for Mac and/or Windows platforms.

Content and Best Practices

No single set of best practices exists for creating all types of digital publications across the various platforms and delivery systems. It's up to you to consider the different types of content you might have available or want to display when creating a publication. For example, a magazine, catalog, document, brochure, and book each has its own different set of best practices.

EPUBs are generally great for books, while PDFs are best for documents and brochures. If the content requires enriched interaction or is appropriate as a magazine or immersive interactive experience, then a digital publication is what you want. Greg Albers, an admitted critic of digital publishing methods, provides these useful tips:

- Don't add in fancy multimedia features just because you can.
- Avoid giving written directions.
- Consider limiting the scope of the content.
- Consider making a secondary version to give your book/app a life and purpose beyond a single screen.

Tying It All Together

So what type of digital publishing end-product should you create? I hope, with the information you now have about the platforms and tools available, you'll be able to answer that for yourself.

The correct platform choice depends greatly on the content you are designing for, the user experience you're trying to create, and what type of market you are trying to reach. Once you determine these, you just need to choose the correct tool and delivery mechanism that can be used to develop the solution.

The information provided here will help steer you in the right direction and clear up any confusion on the differences among different publication methods.

Still a bit confused? Here is a summary table of the differences among EPUB, PDFs, and digital publications.

Table 34.1 Summary of Differences

Category	EPUB	PDF	Digital Publication
Multi-Platform			
Viewable on Various Platforms	●	●	●
Popular Authoring Tool			

Category	EPUB	PDF	Digital Publication
Adobe Acrobat	○	●	○
Adobe InDesign	●	●	●
Custom XHTML, CSS, and JavaScript	●	○	○
iBooks	○	●	●
Sigil	●	○	○
eCub	●	○	●
Appropriate Content Types			
Magazine	○	○	●
Catalog	○	○	●
Document	●	●	○
Brochure	○	●	●
Book	●	○	○
Features			
Video	●	●	●
Audio	●	●	●
Interactivity	○	●	●
Animation	○	●	●
Image Sequences	○	●	●
Panoramas	○	○	●
Pan and Zoom Images	○	○	●
Slideshows	○	●	●
Buttons	●	●	●
Scrollable Frames	○	●	●
Embedded HTML	●	○	●
Immersive Experiences	○	○	●
Marketing Analytic Capabilities	●	○	●

CHAPTER 35

Designing for Multiple Screens in iOS

Daniel Pfeiffer

Devices running iOS now come in a pretty wide variety of flavors. Five different screen resolutions are available across four different screen sizes. Together, these account for the three different aspect ratios iOS developers have to take into account when creating an app.

The different aspect ratios generally don't affect the core functionality of an app, but it does directly affect how the user experiences the functionality through the interface. With only three different aspect ratios, trying to handle the differences on your own requires a pile of hard-to-maintain conditional statements. Even the smallest of changes will become a time-consuming task.

Apple gives iOS developers a number of different tools to efficiently handle the various screen sizes and screen resolutions without writing a lot of extra code. Less code always translates to fewer bugs and time saved.

Let's focus on one tool iOS developers have for efficiently designing layouts for multiple screens: autoresizing behaviors. The autoresizing behaviors have been around since iOS 2.0 but can be tricky to master, and it's not always apparent how valuable they are.

iOS 6 introduced a brand-new interface tool for iOS developers called autolayout. Autolayout goes far beyond simply resizing views based on their superview and gives developers a layout engine that can intelligently position views based on relationships

229

with siblings and the content of their siblings. Since autolayout is only available on iOS 6 and later, apps hoping to keep support for iOS 5 and earlier won't be able to take advantage of the powerful new layout tool. Suffice it to say, it can do all that the autoresizing behaviors can do and much, much more.

Superviews and Subviews

When you think of the hierarchy of views in your application, each visible view always has a parent view or "superview." Each interface element (for example, a UIButton) is placed inside of a UIView, which may be placed within another UIView, which ultimately is inside a UIWindow. UIWindow is the only interface item that does not have a superview, as it should be your topmost view.

When a view changes size, by default it will attempt to resize its subviews (and those subviews will in turn attempt to resize their subviews and so on). A view may change size for a number of reasons: the device may have changed its orientation, the status bar or navigation bar may have just disappeared, or perhaps it was due to a custom animation. It also may change size due to the form factor of the device. In a universal application, you may design a view for the phone form factor with a width of 320px, but on the iPad, this view may display with a width of 768px or 1024px.

You can tune the behavior of the resizing action by setting the autoresizing properties of each interface element. This can be done in code by setting the value of the autoresizing Mask property, but I find it far easier to manage these properties in Interface Builder, as it is more visual.

View Autoresizing

Let's look at the Size Inspector in Interface Builder (View> Utilities>Show Size Inspector) to get our bearings with View Autoresizing.

Within the autoresizing options, you have six different toggle controls that control the autoresizing behavior. There are two groups of autoresizing options: the margin controls and the size controls. For both sets of controls, a dotted line indicates that the control is disabled, while a solid line indicates that it is enabled.

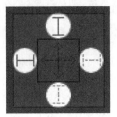

The controls around the outside modify the resizing behavior of the margins. "Margin" refers to the space around the top, left, right, and bottom of the selected view.

When any of these controls is enabled, it indicates to the OS that when the superview changes size, the selected view should reposition so that the view maintains a consistent margin from the edge of the superview. For example, if you place a label 10 pixels down from the top of the superview and you want the label to always be 10 pixels down from the top, regardless of the orientation or form factor of the device, you would enable the top margin autoresizing control.

When the control is disabled, it indicates to the OS that when the superview changes size, the selected view should move by the same ratio of the change in size. Let's take the same label as before—still 10px down from the top of the superview, but this time, the top margin control is disabled. The superview changes height from 400px to 480px, a 20 percent increase in height. The top margin will also increase by 20 percent from 10px to 12px.

What happens if you enable all the margin controls but leave the height and width controls disabled? You've created a mutually exclusive scenario; the system cannot both satisfy positioning a view 10 pixels from the left edge and at the same time 10 pixels from the right. The system gives precedence to the top and left. So in this scenario, it will honor the top and left setting, maintaining a consistent top and left margin, but ignore the right and bottom setting.

The two controls in the middle control the autoresizing behavior of the height and width of the selected view.

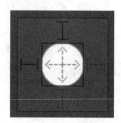

When one of these controls is enabled and the superview changes size, the selected view will also change size by the same ratio. A 20-percent increase in width of the superview will translate to a 20-percent increase of width in the selected view. When disabled and the superview changes size, the selected view will not change size.

By way of application, let's say you wanted a button to change its width with the superview so that it always has a 10px left and right margin. To achieve this, you would set the initial position of the button in Interface Builder, ensuring that there are 10 pixels both to the left and right of the button. Then, you would enable the width autoresizing control as well as the left and right margin controls. This indicates to the OS that you want the left and right margins to remain consistent and you're willing for the width of the view to change in order to make that happen.

Using Autoresizing to Design for Multiple Screens

Table view cells are a great place to see the value in view autoresizing and how it helps you create a design that works at a variety of sizes without having to write a single line of code. Table view cells frequently have to change height based on their content, but may also have elements that need to reposition when the cell changes size. Moreover, the cell may also need to resize based on the form factor of the device (phone or tablet) and the orientation of the device (portrait or landscape).

Let's take a look at Float's enterprise social network app for learning, Tappestry. One of the primary views in the app is the stream view where you can see posts (threads) created by yourself and other users. Each thread in the stream is a cell in a table view.

The thread cell has metadata about the thread at both the top and the bottom of the cell. The views at the top of the cell, the topic name, avatar, and name, all have the top and left margin controls enabled in the autoresizing options, because we always want them to be the same distance from the top left of the cell. The topic name and user name labels also have the width and right margin autoresizing control enabled, because when the cell is displayed on the iPad, we want the length of the labels to extend the full width of the cell, just as they do on the iPhone. The avatar's size should remain the same regardless of the size of the cell so it has the height and width autoresizing controls disabled.

The views at the bottom of the cell have to change position based on how tall the cell is. The height of the cell is dependent on a number of factors—not only the amount of content in the thread,

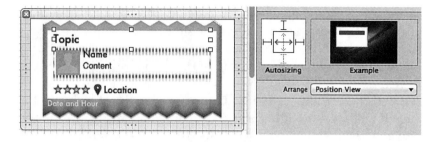

but also on the width of the cell. The wider the cell, the less height it needs, since more text will be able to fit on one line. Without writing a line of code, we're able to specify that the label containing the time the thread was posted should remain at the bottom of the superview (which is the cell). In this case, we have enabled the left and bottom margin controls. We have also enabled the width and right margin controls, since we want the label to extend the full width of the cell.

You can preview your autoresizing settings within Interface Builder by enabling Live Autoresizing (Editor>Canvas>Live Autoresizing). Now, when you resize a view in Interface Builder by dragging out one of the edges, Interface Builder will adhere to your autoresizing settings and resize the view's subviews.

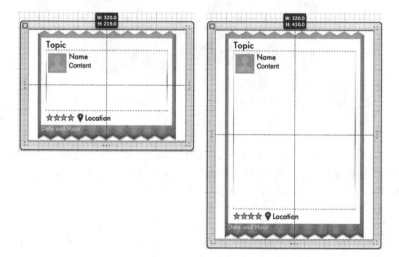

By mastering the autoresizing options, you can create interface designs that maintain consistent layouts, regardless of the size of screen they're displayed on. Mastering these tools will go a long way in efficiently supporting the various screen resolutions of iOS devices.

CHAPTER 36

Designing for Context

Chad Udell

In designing and developing any mobile application, it is critical to plan for the context for the use of the program being created. What is context in terms of mobile application terminology? Simply put, it is the combination of time, setting, and intent for which the device is being used. The context component "time" refers to time as a specific "clock" time, but also perhaps as a relative time unit, as the proximity of an event to another occurrence of the same type of event. For example, your needs from your company's intranet on or around a major holiday are different than they are on a typical Wednesday in August. Another example: when you access an airport's website on the day of your flight, you probably want different information than you want before you actually booked the flight weeks before.

The context component "setting" can refer to both social settings and geolocational settings. The people and places around you directly affect how you access information, why you want to access it, and therefore what information is actually important at that time. A search on Google placed at a local pub in Chicago with friends for a bar bet or trivia game about movies is certainly a different setting than searching for that same topic when you are touring Hollywood on your daytime "map of the stars" homes tour. Likewise, a search for "restrooms in Yosemite national park" obviously requires a different result ordering based on whether you are in the park or are merely browsing the site and considering visiting there. Let's hope the site's designers are considering this for you, or you may need to find an alternate solution for your situation, and quickly!

The final component of context, "intent," may be the most difficult to pin down and successfully design for at this time, largely because machines are, for the most part, dumb. Without explicit user input, your phone has no ability to understand why you are searching for a topic or browsing in a directory, even with its built-in sensors and indicators. There are algorithms that use combinations of mechanical indicators and sensors together to guess at your intent based on your past history, but it is still, at best, an educated guess. Software designers likely have one of their biggest challenges in trying to judge user intent. Artificial intelligence, smart agents, and expert systems all need to advance significantly before this can be accomplished.

How do you tackle these components in your mlearning design and development? Let's try to lay out a sample approach here.

Producing an up-front definition of the user(s) or personas for your system is a crucial first step. This will help guide the use cases that determine how the system can be deployed. This requires vision, business strategy, and polling of stakeholders and subject-matter experts who have direct experience in the roles that you have tentatively identified as end-users. Unlike a use case for traditional desktop software or even basic web-based rich Internet applications (where the context is either not required or perhaps impossible to determine), describing the context and potential users for a mobile application is crucial.

Next, you'll need to draft a requirements analysis or definition to create a list of key features that allow those use cases to be supported. This will require involvement by the developers creating low-level functional designs directly, with the user experience designer's high-level designs dealing primarily with information architecture. These designs absolutely must take into consideration the contexts that should have been written in the use cases.

After you have completed these steps, you have moved a long way toward designing a much more useful mlearning app for your users that supports their needs by being designed for their context.

CHAPTER 37

Using Mobile Devices to Leverage Social Media for Learning

Gary Woodill

Aristotle wrote that "Man is by nature a social animal." It's built into our genes, as documented by E.O. Wilson's new book, *The Social Conquest of Earth* (2013).

From birth, human beings experience themselves as individuals embedded in a social group. Children who are isolated at an early age tend not to thrive. If they do survive, they become "feral" or "wild" children, usually without language or the ability to connect with others. As Aristotle noted, we are all social.

Then why the recent concern on several websites, and in a number of keynote addresses, that social media and, by extension, social learning, "is dead"? Well, for one reason, using the word "dead" makes great attention-getting headlines. In this age of rapidly changing technologies, this idea is plausible simply because of the perception of the short shelf life of all technologies.

But this is a perception, based on vendors, writers, and consultants all chasing the "next big thing" in order to stay ahead on the change curve. What really happens is that new technologies are exciting for a while and then fade into the media background as they become commonplace, taken-for-granted, and replaced by a newer shiny object. It doesn't mean they are dead.

237

Also, we tend to confuse "social learning" with the concept of "learning with social media," which is what we are usually talking about.

What Is Social Learning?

Not surprisingly, the term "social learning" historically has several meanings, and the term has been reinvented with each new learning theory in psychology.

Behaviorist theories of social learning hold that people learn new behaviors via three methods: through overt reinforcement, through overt punishment, or through observational learning of social influences in their environments.

Early social learning theories incorporated behavioristic ideas that were current in the 1950s, but social learning has expanded beyond the focus of accounting only for observable individual behaviors to show how people learned by being embedded in a "social milieu."

In other words, to understand the behaviors of an individual, it is important to consider the social context in which he or she is operating. People learn from each other, an idea that almost no one disputes.

The problem with behaviorism was that it refused to examine or discuss what was happening in the mind of an individual who was learning. It also reduced the behaviors being studied to small units of analysis that ignored influences beyond the organism (rat or human) that was being studied.

This led to the rise of "cognitivism" in the 1960s in North America and to neurological research that tried to connect physical brain activities with indicators of learning. It also gave rise to new social learning theories, such as constructivism, that referenced both what was happening inside a person and the impact of the external social environment on learning.

Constructivist Theories of Social Learning

Although he is still not well known outside of school environments, the educational theory of Lev Vygotsky (1896–1934), a social psychologist who lived through the Russian Revolution, is very relevant for understanding social learning. Vygotsky's work has only become widely known in English since the publication of the translation of his major book, *Mind and Society: The Development of Higher Mental Processes,* in 1978.

Vygotsky's social development theory states that social interaction is the foundation of human development, consciousness, and cognition. His followers use the metaphor of "scaffolding" to illustrate how our skills are built one upon the other, with the help of people around us. He calls those who know more than we do "more knowledgeable others" (MKOs) and shows how they have an important role to play in our learning.

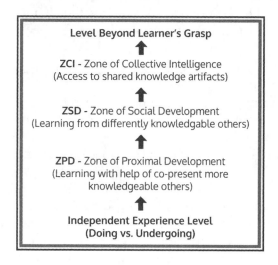

His concept of the "zone of proximal development" (ZPD) is also interesting. The ZPD is the distance between a learner's ability to perform a task under expert guidance, and/or with peer collaboration, and the learner's ability to solve the problem independently without assistance. According to Vygotsky, social learning occurs in this zone.

Good teachers know that effective teaching often involves assessing the current knowledge level of a learner and introducing materials related to the learner's current knowledge that move the learner to "the next step" of what he or she needs to know. This is similar to the idea of scaffolding as articulated by Vygotsky.

But being social is not just a matter of having other people, more experienced than we are, teaching us what we need to know.

The social aspect also occurs in the fact that we are embedded in a culture that we observe and where we act and share a common life with others. Language tools such as speech and writing are developed within a culture and carry meaning and concepts in their words. These words mediate the social environment through which each of us moves.

In contrast with the "instructionist" model of learning, where an instructor transmits information to students, Vygotsky believed that learners should play an active role in their own learning. In his view, a trainer should become more of a collaborator with his or her students as they individually construct their own meanings from their life experiences. Vygotsky's theory nicely aligns with the current constructivist theory of learning.

Learning Using Social Media

"Social learning" is also in vogue as a term for learning via "social media." Leading analysts of social media tend to use the term social learning in this sense. But this is a circular argument; that is, it assumes learning is social just because we use media that is called social.

We call media social when there is the potential for two or more people to interact online in some fashion. In other words, social media refers to Internet and mobile technologies that allow networked social interactions (because they are networked, social media were originally referred to as "social networking").

In particular, social media refers to new technologies that allow "many to many" relationships, rather than connections that are dominated by one person. Social media are part of what is referred to as Web 2.0, but Web 2.0 is a broader term that also refers to other aspects of information technologies such as access to "cloud"-based databases and distributed content.

Social media offers great new opportunities to connect with a wide range of people you might otherwise never meet. For those who take advantage of this opportunity, how does effective and useful learning take place?

Since the popularization of MySpace and Facebook within the past decade, social media has exploded onto the learning and development scene. Facilitated learning has broken away from the classroom model and can be found in many different places on the Internet and mobile networks.

Uses of social media for learning include retrieving information from anywhere at any time; gathering and sharing information by many people; networking, communicating, and interacting with learning applications, experts, and peers; and receiving information and alerts based on location and local conditions—what I call "learning in context."

Social Learning Is Not Dead

While traditional channels of information are in decline, social media is not dead. Print newspapers and magazines are rapidly migrating to an online format that almost always has a social component for commenting or contributing other user-generated content. People want to ask questions, state opinions, and support or challenge the argument, and, most of all, be involved. The traditional coffee shop discussion over the morning paper has been upgraded to a global cacophony of information exchange.

What does this mean for a corporation? It means that people are going to demand in the workplace what they are experiencing on the outside: efficient, effective, and participatory routes for learning. This is not against the corporation's best interests.

Lombardo and Eichinger (1996) have suggested that formal learning is a very secondary source of workplace knowledge. Their 70–20–10 model holds that 70 percent of learning applicable to the workplace is derived from practical experience, usually working with others; 20 percent is derived from just observing the examples of others; and 10 percent is derived from formal education.

According to this model, 90 percent of workplace learning is informal, and these days, much of that interaction is mediated by mobile technologies. If this figure is accurate, or even close to accurate, then this is where an organization should place its focus for optimizing training, learning, and development.

Long live social learning!

References

Lombardo, M., & Eichinger, R. (1996). *The career architect development planner.* Minneapolis, MN: Lominger.

Vygotsky, L. (1978). *Mind and society: The development of higher mental processes.* Cambridge, MA: Harvard University Press.

Wilson, E.O. (2013). *The social conquest of earth.* New York: Liveright.

CHAPTER 38

Responsive Design for Multiple Screen Formats

Chad Udell

If you have been following the web design community, you are likely very familiar with a term called "responsive web design," sometimes abbreviated as RWD.

The term "responsive web design" was coined in 2010 by *A List Apart* blogger Ethan Marcotte, in his landmark post, "Responsive Web Design" (of course). This is both a design technique and a development tactic aimed at streamlining content production, graphic design work, and overall web development workload.

This technique seems to have caught almost everybody in the e-learning industry off-guard. While we were largely concerned with the "When will Apple support Flash on iPad?" argument, someone moved the cheese. Surprise: our audience moved it. They decided that battles over plugins weren't anything they needed to be involved in and just started using content that worked on their devices. This meant working on all of them. We gnashed our teeth and really had a hard time with it. Now that the world has seemingly moved on, it's time for us in the learning industry to get over it and get back to creating for the audience, rather than complaining about their choices.

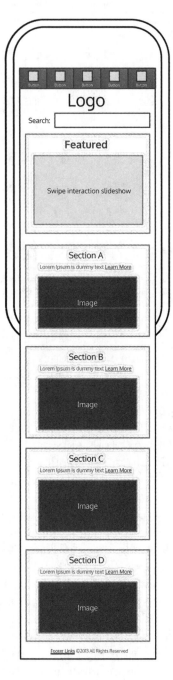

This chapter will help show you how to get started with responsive design, but more importantly, why we should be thinking about it and why learning the underlying technologies and standards behind any toolkit will take you far.

Diving Into Responsive Design

In his article Ethan Marcotte quoted John Allsopp (2000):

> The control which designers know in the print medium, and often desire in the web medium, is simply a function of the limitation of the printed page. We should embrace the fact that the web doesn't have the same constraints, and design for this flexibility. But first, we must "accept the ebb and flow of things.'

The mechanics of it are deceptively simple. It really hinges around a CSS3 technique (commonly lumped in with HTML5), "CSS media queries." These media queries look a bit like this (Pardon our CSS geekery here. It will be over soon, so don't go anywhere):

```
@media only screen and (max-device-width: 480px) {
div#wrapper {
width: 400px;
}
div#header {
background-image: url(media-queries-phone.jpg);
height: 93px;
position: relative;
}
div#header h1 {
font-size: 140%;
}
#content {
float: none;
width: 100%;
}
#navigation {
float:none;
width: auto;
}
}
```

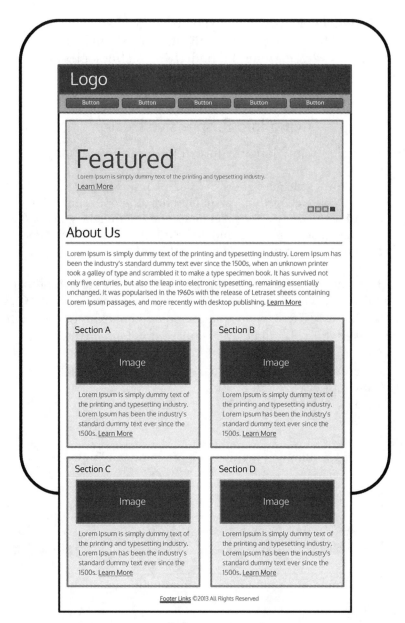

In the query depicted, devices with a maximum screen width of 480 pixels or less will have the styles following the declaration applied to the content in the browser viewport.

Pretty simple, really. The basic gist is that you create a "query" that, given a particular web browser's capabilities and specifications, renders the relevant style information to ensure the site looks and *hopefully* behaves properly.

Beyond the implementation of the technique, though, there are some things you should consider as you assess what it means for us in the learning industry.

1. The development of responsive web design is evidence of the fact that we need to be more cognizant of standards and specification of the broader industry—like it or not, we are web designers, developers, and development operations people, not just instructional designers, cognitive scientists, and trainers. We may be more focused on organizational performance than we are on getting people to like us on Facebook or sign up for a newsletter, but that doesn't mean we can't steal their tactics to help us achieve our goals.

2. Your tools are meaningless (or at least much less meaningful than they were). Throw them away and learn what makes the web work. Web standards aren't a new thing, and neither is the first draft of the SCORM standard (in fact, they nearly correlate chronologically in terms of acceptance), yet we have put up with tools that output substandard markup and junk for far too long in the name of a niche spec (SCORM). Moral of the story: Learn standards, not tools. If you must center around a tool, use one that outputs valid, sensible, standards-compliant markup and uses proper JavaScript and CSS in its output. Learning and understanding HTML5 is far more important than any specific authoring tool.

3. If a "little" wrinkle, such as not getting a plugin to be accepted on a new device or platform ends in a stalemate for an entire industry for more than two or three years, doesn't that signal the fact that we have been more than just a bit myopic in our view of what tools offer us? I mean, the web design world got on just fine after Flash flamed out. Why has it taken more than three years for major vendors in this space to give us alternatives? The likely answer: limited resources for over-stressed development teams and overdependence on a tool chain that required a proprietary plugin from all the vendors we depend on. You would have thought Authorware's demise would have taught us all a valuable lesson, but here it is—2014, and many of us have egg on our faces yet again.

4. Templates and starter kits are not adequate. The bottom line is that technology marches on. Get with the program and learn how technology advances, or face the consequences. Any vendor's starter kits or templates are likely to be behind where the rest of the web industry actually is. Learn the underlying technologies (HTML, CSS, JavaScript), and you can then use whatever tool you buy later.

5. Making standards-compliant markup compatible with LMS and LRS is much, much easier than taking learning tools output and trying to make it web standards–friendly. We've been getting it backward for years. Adding SCORM functionality or xAPI features to basic web content is not that difficult to do via some online tools or even manually typing out the manifests and other needed files. It's far more difficult to take a rapid tool's output and make it more mobile-friendly. Remember: mobile first!

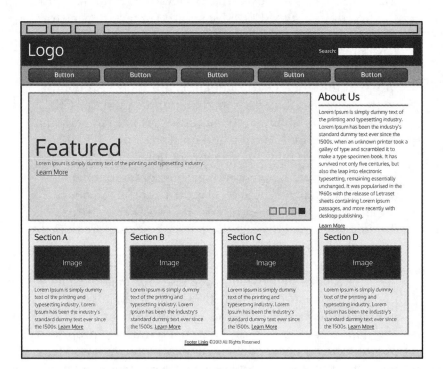

This missive isn't meant to be all doom and gloom. A number of people in the industry are starting to get it and do the right thing. At Float, we have been producing multi-screen and true mobile learning from our very beginning. However, a few others are also contributing. Producing valuable content isn't easy, regardless of what camp you fall in. In addition to private industry taking note, it's clear that the government is listening as well. Significant moves have been made to ensure that web properties are moving to responsive design. With the U.S. Departments of Defense, Energy, Education, and more being such huge consumers of training and proponents of web standards, won't that eventually require our learning information to be responsive as well?

Regardless of the initial uptake and response, it's clear that something has to change. No longer can we go on creating content for a proprietary or non-scalable plugin or renderer and consider it future-proof.

References

Allsopp, J. (2000, April 7). A Dao of web design. *A List Apart.*

Marcotte, E. (2010, May 25). Responsive web design. *A List Apart.*

CHAPTER 39

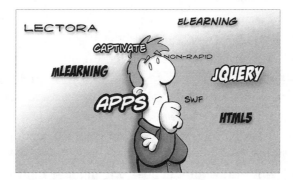

Design Choices for Mobile Learning Management Systems

Gary Woodill

Computer-based learning management systems have been available since the 1960s (for example, PLATO, on mainframe computers), but really took off in the late 1990s and early 2000s. With the speed of change that is happening in the world of education and training software, it is not surprising that some learning management systems are starting to look stale and worn. At the same time, many LMS companies recognize that their market is reaching a limit of saturation and are looking for new ways to sell their intellectual property. Just in time, along comes the mobile learning revolution, presenting new opportunities for learning management system companies to market their wares. How they have done that, however, varies greatly.

Some LMS companies have simply added the word "mobile" to their offerings without much change at all. Others have done cosmetic changes, redesigning their interfaces to fit on a small screen. A few companies have gone beyond this to have mobile learning management systems actually work on smart phones and tablets. Some have even developed stand-alone LMSs that do not need to be connected to a non-mobile LMS. And finally, a few LMS companies have dipped their toes into the waters of innovation and tried to create something new.

In reviewing mobile learning management systems, I have identified five levels:

- *Level 0*—LMSs not ready for mobile learning
- *Level I*—LMSs graphically redesigned for mobile devices
- *Level II*—mobile extensions ("plugins") for existing learning management systems; the extension only works in conjunction with a non-mobile LMS
- Level III—stand-alone, self-sufficient mobile learning management systems
- Level IV—innovative mobile learning management systems that use some of the new affordances of mobile devices, such as location detection or cloud computing

If we place some of the available mobile learning management systems on a continuum from Level I to Level IV it might look something like this (this is not a complete list of mobile LMSs, just examples).

Level 1	Level 2	Level 3	Level 4
LMS with a mobile-friendly design	Mobile LMS plugins	Stand-alone mobile LMSs with integration with a regular LMS	Mobile LMS fully integrated with a learner through cloud computing

	MLE-Moodle	Pushcast	mEKP
Moodle			
	MOMO	KMx	wearIT@work (formerly iTutor)
Sakai	Blackboard Mobile		CellCast

Spectrum of Mobile Learning Management Systems

The LMS Spectrum

As you can see, a few of the open-source learning management systems have been designed with mobile computing in mind. For example, the Moodle interface consists of a three-column layout that is very mobile-friendly. Sakai, another open-source learning management system, has a group of developers who have produced features that make this LMS mobile-ready. But these LMSs are not very different in their mobile and non-mobile versions.

Another approach is to design "plugins" or "extensions" for existing learning management systems (Level II). Moodle has several plugins designed for that purpose, including MLE-Moodle and MOMO (Mobile Moodle). Blackboard has an extension for their Learn 9.1 platform called Blackboard Mobile that lets users receive notifications of updates to their Blackboard courses, including new assignments, course content, study group updates, community discussions, and their grades/assessment results.

At Level III, there are stand-alone mobile learning systems that manage learning materials for users without needing to reference a non-mobile LMS. Examples are BlackBerry Pushcast (formerly Mobile Chalkboard), which runs only on the BlackBerry platform and is mostly used for delivering training to users (hence the emphasis on "push" in the name). It features text, graphics, video, and audio and will handle surveys, call requests, or email requests. It administers tests and tracks results and content usage. Similarly, KMx from Knowledge Management Solutions provides development and delivery of e-learning courseware, knowledge management, and collaboration tools for mobile devices with full conformance to the shareable content object reference model (SCORM).

Another contender in this category is CellCast from OnPoint Digital. This mobile learning program allows users to create, notify, deliver, and track audio and video learning content on a wide variety of smart phones, tablets, and netbook computers. It also allows for the delivery and tracking of mobile web content, web and PDF files, videos, animated narrated slide presentations, and spoken word and text-based assessments. CellCast is fully integrated with OnPoint Digital's learning management system, but can operate independently without reference to any LMS.

Unfortunately, there are no mobile learning management systems that I would classify as having reached Level IV. However, there are signs of innovative new solutions that will transform the world of mobile learning management systems, and not simply rehash the concepts of desktop LMSs. One example is the mEKP mobile learning management system from Net Dimensions that delivers a full-featured learning management system on a USB stick. This allows students to go off-line, do their work, and have it tracked without a connection to the Internet. They simply take their USB stick with them and plug it into an Internet-connected computer at the first opportunity.

The results of their work are then uploaded to a full Net Dimensions enterprise learning management system. This approach shows that Net Dimensions is moving toward the new definition of mobile learning—a definition that is about the needs of learners on the move, not about mobile technology, per se.

Finally, eXact Learning Solutions, headquartered in Italy, has been experimenting with a novel wearable learning management system called eXact iTutor. It is described on the company website as "the world's first wearable, wireless mobile learning platform." It is location-based and voice/gaze controlled for workplace delivery of crisis management instructions and just-in-time training materials. Unfortunately, in speaking with their North American representatives, I learned that this mobile LMS is just a prototype, not yet in production. However, it is definitely a step in the right direction in that its design is using some of the unique possibilities of mobile learning that have not been available before.

Examples of mobile learning management systems of any kind are few and far between. Of the several hundred LMSs on the market, only three or four actually have any features that support mobile learning. In the next year or two, watch for many more mobile LMSs to come on the market, as LMS companies jump on the mobile bandwagon. At the same time, pay attention to the market leaders described above. They will have the most experience in this new category of learning software.

CHAPTER 40

Maps 3.0
The New Route to Learning with Social Geospatial Data

Jim Ferolo

Portability, ubiquity, and connectivity—three affordances of mobile devices—have created a new learning platform that is distinct from all our other educational tools. But a fourth built-in feature of mobile devices—the generation of geospatial data—is transforming learning in ways we are just starting to imagine. In a 2012 interview, Jeff Jonas, IBM distinguished engineer and chief scientist, Entity Analytics, described geospatial data as "analytic superfood." "Geospatial data," he says, "is going to rip the lid off what's computable."

The creation of geolocation data is the tagging of a specific place with additional information or the addition of place data to existing information. Here is how it works. Your phone has a SIM card, your personal key that lets you operate on a cellular network. Inside the phone there is also a wireless Wi-Fi adapter that allows you to connect to Wi-Fi or WLAN networks, and that adapter is wired into an antenna to boost the signal. Finally, there is a GPS chip that pulls signals from satellites. The combination of these pieces allows for three or four different types of geolocation functionality: GPS geolocation, Wi-Fi geolocation, cell tower geolocation, and, for some phones, near field communication (NFC).

Near field communication is a set of standards for mobile devices that allows them to establish radio communication with other mobile devices that are in close proximity. NFC is an extension of earlier active or passive RFID technologies in that it now allows for two-way communications. Passive RFID tags are unpowered and can be as small as several millimeters and read at a distance of 5 meters. Powered or active RFID can be read at a longer range. The resolution of active RFID has proven to be trackable at the millimeter level in three dimensions, as well. However, while possible, most apps do not use this for their geolocation abilities.

Cellular geolocation triangulates the location of a mobile device using the cell network and can be accurate to around 2 or 3 kilometers, if the device is used over a sufficiently long period of time. Wi-Fi geolocation uses the unique SSIDs of several routers to provide location data and can be much more accurate. The most commonly known method of geolocation is public satellite–based GPS, which can accurately note your position within 40 meters, and often closer.

Understanding the Technology of Place

When my colleague Chad Udell proposed a new geolocation app called Wayfiler some time ago, he was clear that it was to be simple, it was to be an extension of functionality that could be found in some other apps, and that it was to be a tool that could be used for learning by individuals or by organizations. Wayfiler is an attempt to utilize a suite of services to provide unique geolocational mobile learning opportunities. The app consists of several different layers and is essentially a very sophisticated metadata app.

Two categories of services are within the application: the things that the app controls (Find Nearby) and the things that the user controls (Tag Now). This diagram shows the relationships within the app.

As a designer, I am extremely interested in the emerging vocabulary of the "technology of place." I want to consider these systems and the ways we can create engaging experiences that use not only the traditional x, y, and z positions within the geometry of our canvas, but also understand and use new methods for the visual representation of temporal and location information. Also, I was aware of the need to reflect actual behavioral patterns and possibly their magnitude as well. Yes, things are becoming

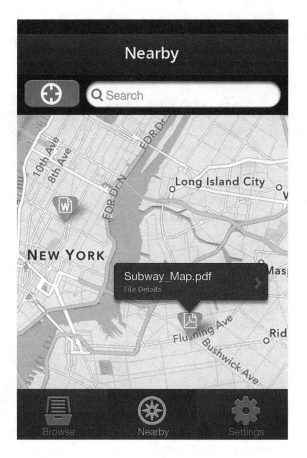

more complicated, and our job is to devise the simplest solution out of all of this. Simply, my job as a user experience (UX) designer is to author experiences that will facilitate desired learning outcomes.

But learning outcomes are dependent on what a person is trying to learn. A variety of "learning design patterns" are available to me as an instructional designer, depending on what I am trying to teach. There are formalized structures and frameworks within which we can develop that allow us to quickly apply patterns and create amazing new experiences to augment the "thickness" or impact of experiential learning.

As we began to investigate current design patterns that were present within geolocation apps of interest to me, we quickly learned that there was quite a bit of new information that would help me understand the underpinnings of how these devices work. Here are some of the possibilities that were considered in order to start the design of Wayfiler.

Geolocation Graphics

We graphically represent magnitude and location in iconic ways. Some are traditional. We see timelines and sparklines, and their derivatives, along with quadrant graphing and geometric scaling. Some of these translate well to the small screen, but the use of component sets within the frameworks of mobile is creating a synthesis of ideas when it comes to mapping, way-finding, and the construction of personal location-based points of view. It is clear we are all onto something new.

Map View

GoogleMaps came online in 2005, so we are approaching a decade of information and standards from that specific application. One of the first mashups on the web was HousingMaps.com, using a combination of Craigslist and GoogleMaps. At the end of the day, we end up dealing with two major design patterns within location. The first is the ever-powerful map view. We see markers in some type of cartographic system. When you take the map away, it devolves into a simple list view.

List View

A list view is a text-based representation of location, for example, places of interest that are a specific distance filtered on a radius from your current position. A lot of what we can do are derivatives of this technique, using various filters to help us answer such questions as: Where am I? How do I get to where I want to go? How am I progressing?

Where Am I?

There are different ways of showing current location, as evidenced by three major geolocation apps: Waze, Glympse, and Tom Tom.

Waze is a crowdsourced routing tool based on many users making their locations available to others in order to pluck traffic patterns out of the aggregated data generated by thousands of mobile phones. I am a fan of the Waze application due to its statefulness and approach to design that is responsive to the inputs of users, also known as "map contributors."

Users who drive with the app open on their phones passively contribute traffic and other road data to the system. They can also take a more active role by sharing road reports on accidents, police traps, or any other hazards along the way, helping to give other users in the area a "heads-up" about what's to come. This is clearly a social application that also has an active community of online map editors who ensure that the data for their areas are as up-to-date as possible and enhance the usefulness of this way-finding tool.

Glympse is a tracking tool that allows others, with your permission, to see your location on a map for a limited amount of time, and Tom Tom is a traditional GPS-based navigation device. All of them use geolocation and the same basic visual design patterns.

How Do I Get There?

The display of routing information is heavily dependent on the personality of the app iconography. It is important to have an understanding of where people are located at any given time and the overall "mood" of the route. Is it happy or is it sad? (That is, is it fast or slow?) At the same time, it is important to use algorithms that calculate the most efficient route in terms of speed of traffic or the location of barriers, not just the shortest distance.

How Am I Progressing?

Finally, we need to know how well we are getting along in our journey from point A to point B. These can be displayed as time saved or efficiency of travel. Essentially, the temporality of a journey is based on the hypothetical speed that you could traverse a route, given legal limitations and your mode of transport's capabilities. More importantly, it can be measured in context, given the inputs of travelers who are directly ahead or with an aggregation of travel progression data. The number of deviations from a mean can help determine travel trends and which delays can be predicted versus those that are random, such as accidents.

Mapping Your Personal Narrative

All of the geolocation affordances and other capabilities of mobile phones make it possible to map a personal narrative using a combination of these features. However, most current geolocation apps are very utilitarian and not designed with individualization in mind. But it is possible, as shown by the great work that Instagram has done with Photomaps. Instagram is widely known for its ability for users to take and filter mobile-based images in very artful ways and link them to users' social networks. The app also now allows for integration of geolocation data of images. While in map view, users see virtual "stacks" of photos with a single number on top of the stack that indicates the number of photos for that specific location. The granularity of the stacks changes as users zoom in and out of map view. It is simple, contains powerful and illustrative mapping patterns, and introduces the personal through photos and their associated magnitudes—brilliant simplicity.

Designing and Building the App

When Chad Udell originally scoped the application, it was developed through Float's own S3D process to ensure that a clear strategic approach was taken. A needs analysis was completed to identify a slice in the marketplace that had a very specific desire for such an application. The ability to locate content to help learners with their on-demand needs, the possibility of securing data with a security framework, the integration and leveraging of existing data types and application APIs, and a rapid development cycle were all taken into consideration. This led to several decisions— to initially only develop in Apple's iOS to limit the number of platform iterations that would be required by various devices, the integration of Dropbox as a widely accepted personal data repository, and the use of turnkey cloud-based application services that could easily scale given overall app usage levels. Given that the app is a very sophisticated metadata organizer, the database structure and build were extremely important.

For our database, we used the MongoDB to store all the content and coordinate data for everyone. We like using Mongo for its scalability and built-in support for specific activities. We are using its current support of latitudes and longitudes and the radial sorting method.

As mentioned, the app was built using the iOS operating system and currently only runs on Apple devices. As clients use the app, there are interactions with various Apple and Dropbox-based services. Here is how it all works:

1. Core Location is the part of iOS that tells you where you are and uses the geolocation methods described above.
2. Standard Location Service is what uses the constant GPS monitoring.
3. Significant Location service is actually a computation of differentials.
4. Region Monitoring checks to see whether you are in a bounded area and is commonly referred to as "geofencing."
5. This sensor data and positional information is then interpreted by MapKit, which does the related lookups of latitudes and longitudes.
6. Apple Map Services then translates these generic latitudes and longitudes into information that means something to the user.

Other Supporting Technology

A number of other technologies were used in constructing our geolocation app. Node JavaScript provided a way to encapsulate the information and handle the multiple connections from the client. This is a very important part of creating applications that require simultaneous connections to a cloud-based set of services.

We used Core Data for iOS as the interface for the database, extremely important, as it relates to the primacy and immediacy of the data we use the most through caching. So this is the place where information is stored on your device and is checked first before queries are made to cloud services.

Finally, we have Dropbox for file storage, which happens to be the system we used for our alpha version of the app, but could just as easily have been any other file server–based system that included its own authentication or security framework. Files are hosted in Dropbox and are related to the location metadata.

Use Cases for Wayfiler

The use cases for applications like Wayfiler are varied, and we offer the following as suggestions:

- For technical support related to plant locations or performance support documentation that is tied to specific pieces of equipment or processes
- For the agronomic organization that wants to place seed data and forecasting information based on its geographical positioning, slope, or GIS data
- For the sales or service professional who is looking for a visual distribution of specific services or machinery to ensure that routing and on-site calls are optimized and being informed by real-time traffic information
- For tourist bureaus who want to produce a virtual tour of their downtown, showing documents, images, and videos as a person visits a specific point of interest
- For geocaching mobile learning activities where files are collected rather than real objects. These could be clues in a learning game that promoted situated learning along with the benefits of physical activities.

There are many features we would like to consider adding in subsequent releases. We are extremely interested in the concept of geofencing and subsequent security frameworks. We would like to continue working to a user flow that would release files into the system based on proximity. So when users move closer to a specific region, a new set of files could be made available. There is also the opportunity to do time-locking along with this to add the component of temporal locks. Specific files would be available based on crossing a threshold during the day with availability opening and closing with the passing of seconds, minutes, hours, days, or years. Additional security frameworks could be added to tie it to associated services through a public API. Other developers would have the opportunity to use the metadata structures to tie their software into the geolocated caches of files.

Reference

Jonas, J. (2012, July 3). How big data is changing the world: Jeff Jonas IBM. [Online video]. www.youtube.com/watch?v=aopf7kZ9rcc.

CHAPTER 41

Using Push Notifications to Make Mobile Learning More Useful

Chad Udell

Let's set the scene.

You want to keep your mobile learners updated and engaged in the learning experiences you have created, and you need to maximize the effectiveness of the training by making users aware of changes to content and services that you have already deployed.

Working with mobile learners is a unique proposition for those of us coming from a traditional instructional background. No longer confined by space or time, the world is their classroom. Tasks are performed on demand, and immediate learning is often required in conjunction with the performance of those tasks.

They may not be in the office for days, or even weeks, at a time. In today's disconnected work environment, you can have remote or mobile workers who have no formal office space, per se. These workers all have to be reached in a uniform way that is tough to ignore and requires little or no user-initiated requests. While mobile learning is often a pull operation in that learners request data or help they need when they need it, it can also require a push intervention to make sure everyone is in sync with policy or procedural changes. This is where one of the unique affordances of mobile learning really shines. The "Push Notification" function has a large number of uses that are of value in getting a message to a mobile learner.

Think about your average day with your smart phone or tablet. You likely receive a variety of notifications on the device—everything from software updates to calendar notifications to messages and emails, all of which take advantage of the device's ability to notify you when there is content or information that requires your attention. People may trigger these notifications, but they may be automated system notifications as well. No matter the trigger, the user is looped into the message and the notification is stored in a message center or notifications area on the device for later review if the user is unable to react directly to the message as it comes in.

I personally use a number of apps that notify me about news, events, and other "need to know" information that didn't come with my device. Weather apps alert me when an emergency warning is broadcast, sports apps tell me when one of my teams is about to start to play, games apps let me know it's my turn to play the next round against a friend, and so on.

Without these notifications, I would have to keep checking the apps to see whether they required my attention. When using the notifications in the applications, I stay in the flow of my current activity on the device or in real life until I feel that familiar vibration and distinct tone from an app letting me know I have news to read or a sports team player trade to check out.

These notifications are powerful tools that can be used for your mobile learning apps as well. Consider the types of apps you may be deploying for your workforce, and then contextualize yourself in the settings and use cases in which your learners are interacting with your content.

What sorts of breaking news, just-in-time changes, or other information might make a difference to their tasks? How can you improve their performance by giving them a heads-up on what's going on in your company that they may not be aware of?

The possibilities could vary widely between industries and learning audiences, but try some of these examples on for size:

1. *Organization-wide safety bulletins:* Lockdowns, weather alerts, traffic issues, closures
2. *Geolocation-based targeted bulletins or alerts:* Useful tips about places you're in or nearby
3. *Application content updates:* Pushed from an application content management system

4. *Product bulletins or alerts:* Recalls, safety alerts, release information

5. *Sales alerts:* Major contract awarded, deadline for an RFP, process changes, pricing changes

6. *Application updates:* Bug fixes, optimizations, new features

7. *Team alerts:* Social network updates, goal/achievement messaging, assistance requests, daily tips or best practice reminders

8. *HR reminders:* Incomplete training events, overdue paperwork or goal completion, leadership development messaging

9. *Collaboration assistance:* "Phone a friend" scenarios, travel or destination coordination

10. *Serious games:* Scoreboard updates, leaderboards, play requests

These are just a few examples of how to use push notifications for mobile learning to get the juices flowing. Once you realize that mobile learning is neither a top-down, nor a bottom-up, learning proposition, but rather a combination of both, the sky is the limit.

Setting up notifications in your apps is easier than you may think. The major platforms all have good documentation on adding the feature to your applications. Each operating system is primarily focused either on local notifications (present only on your local device and requiring no network sync) or single-platform notifications (iOS or Android only, not cross-platform).

Generally, setting up push notifications with a server layer is a bit more difficult than a simple app deployment, requiring additional provisioning and certificates, but once you have the hang of it, you should be just fine.

You should be aware of a few other things when planning for an app with push services. You will need a server using SSL to broker notifications between your client apps and the content management system or custom web app you are using to populate the notifications.

Some vendors are emerging who help solve some of the cross-platform notification issues mentioned above. Pusher, Socket.io, Urban Airship, and others all have commercial services to help you get up and running with notifications that work across iOS, Android, and, in some cases, other platforms as well.

Many mobile application management (MAM) and mobile device management (MDM) platforms also offer features related to app notifications. Check with your vendors to see whether this is something they support.

One thing you want to keep in mind is that you should use these tools sparingly. Don't nag the user. These vital communications should never be used to "spam" your learner or advertise products or services. A constantly chattering application will soon find its notifications disabled. You should leverage these notifications to inform and educate, ultimately adding value to your application.

CHAPTER 42

Improving Performance for Mobile Web and HTML5-Based Apps

Daniel Pfeiffer

Mobile web apps are gaining a lot of momentum as developers are discovering how powerful web technologies can be and how mobile web apps can benefit from HTML/CSS/JavaScript. What we love about using web technologies to build our apps and wrapping them in PhoneGap is that it reuses a lot of knowledge that we've already mastered. Years had gone into developing our knowledge of HTML/CSS/JavaScript, and instead of tossing all that out the window for mobile, we're able to refine that knowledge even further. One thing we're finding, however, is that we can't build apps the same way we build websites—obviously from a design standpoint, but also from a development perspective.

The Reflow

The seemingly simple way a web page is displayed is actually a pretty complex process: the initial display of a page triggers what is known as a reflow. During the reflow process, the content is combined with rules defined in the style sheets and the measurements for the layout of the page are determined. After this process is complete, the actual pixel data is rendered and painted to the screen. Every node on a page impacts the time it takes to do a reflow. On a desktop browser, often the performance impact seems relatively unnoticeable. The user impact at a 10ms reflow time is rather negligible. However, reflows seem to be the cause of much of the performance loss on mobile devices. The same pages that take only 10ms to reflow on a desktop can take over 1000ms on a mobile device. Every single change to the document object model (DOM) further impacts reflow time (this is part of the reason why JavaScript-based animation looks so terrible on mobile devices).

Reducing the Cost of a Reflow

What does this mean for semantics (use of tags) in mobile apps? On the web, semantic-based HTML is critical for a website to be searchable by search engines like Google, as well as accessible to those using screen readers. HTML5 brings with it a whole host of new tags like <article> and <section> that help make the markup even more semantic and avoid the dreaded <div> soup that often plagued designs of any sort of complexity. However, we're finding that semantics often needs to take a backseat to making efficient use of our HTML. For example, to generate a tableview-like structure, we use an unordered list. Instead of wrapping the content of each list item in an <a> tag, we simply listen for user interaction directly on the <li> node and remove the <a> altogether. (Truth be told, we're finding that a lot of our <a> tags are extraneous.) We've also started applying some basic styling to the <html> tag to avoid wrapping the entire body in a <div> when our content needs a wrapper (we figured the <html> tag was already there, so might as well use it for something). Finally, we haven't been using the new tags offered with HTML5 (like <section> or <article>) very often, simply because <div> is shorter.

What we're working toward here is developing our apps so they spend less time in reflow. We've found that it is likely the reflow time that causes mobile web apps to "feel slow." First, we need to shorten the time it takes to perform a reflow. We take care of this by removing extraneous tags: removing <a> tags when we can just listen for tap events on an <img> or

<li>, cutting down on <div> wrappers, and so forth. Next, we need to limit the number of times a reflow is required. A reflow is triggered whenever the DOM is changed or the dimensions of an element change; this could be adding/removing an element or text or changing the margins or font size of an element.

Reducing the Number of Reflows

The developer tools provided with the desktop version of Safari provide a great way to determine how changes to a page affect the need for a reflow/repaint. While it doesn't give any sort of indication about how long a reflow/repaint will take on a mobile device, using the timeline tab in the developer tools in Safari does give a good indication of how many reflows will be required (because Mobile Safari renders pages similarly to the desktop version). Unfortunately, we have yet to find a suitable tool for monitoring Mobile Safari's processes.

Let's say you're adjusting the style of a node in your JavaScript:

This "simple" style adjustment triggered three reflow/repaints of the page. On a desktop, a reflow probably takes less than 15ms,

```
1  var node = document.getElementById('some_element');
2  node.style.border = '2px solid #0F0';
3  node.style.margin = '5px';
4  node.style.height = '30px';
```

```
1  node.style.cssText = 'border:2px solid #0F0;margin:5px;height:30px';
```

so it's not a big deal. However, on a mobile device, a reflow can easily seem to take over 500ms, which means that three reflows triggered in rapid succession could easily take a mobile device well over a second to finish processing. To avoid this, use classes to modify an element's style whenever possible. Style changes applied because of a change in classes only triggers one reflow. Alternatively, use the cssText property to affect all the styles at once (again, only triggering one reflow):

Beyond changing the dimensions of an element, there are times when you may need to make a lot of changes to the DOM (perhaps

```
1  var node = document.getElementById('some_element'),
2  new_node = node.cloneNode(true); // We want this to be a deep clone
3  // Apply changes to the cloned node
4  var a = document.createElement('span'),
5  var b = document.createTextNode('some content');
6  a.appendChild(b);
7  new_node.innerHTML = ''; // Empty all the children out of the node
8  new_node.appendChild(a);
9  // Out with the old, in with the new
10 node.parentNode.replaceChild(new_node, node);
```

when drastically updating a view). Unfortunately, every modification made to the DOM requires a reflow/repaint. The images below show the reflow/repaint cost of replacing the header on Float's mobile site with the word "hi" wrapped in a <div>. (See images on next page.)

To avoid a significant number of reflows being triggered, we need a way to modify the DOM without triggering reflows. The way to do that is to clone a node in the DOM, make changes to the clone, and then swap the old node with the new node.

This will only trigger one (or maybe two) reflow/repaints, whereas making the changes directly on the element would have

triggered four or five. The same principle applies when using a JavaScript framework like jQuery or Zepto.js. Clone the item you're modifying, make the modifications, and then swap it into the DOM. Here is the cost of the same modifications to the Float mobile site using a clone of the header. (See the following image.)

We also tested what the cost would be if we first hid the header (display:none), made the changes, and then made it visible again (display:block). A hidden element doesn't affect the layout of the page, so it shouldn't trigger a repaint/reflow, right? Well, sort of.

Below are the results of hiding the header, making the changes, and then making it visible again.

Seems like, while an element is hidden, Safari still recalculates style (although it doesn't attempt a reflow until we set display back to block). This seems to be an improvement over simply making changes directly to the DOM, but we're going to opt for the clone, modify, and swap method.

We tried using template files to help keep a project organized, but they are also very helpful toward performance optimization as well. Because the markup of a template is determined before being added to the DOM, it only triggers one reflow when adding an entire new view—making it rather inexpensive to manage a layout using templates. We used Safari to determine the cost of switching back and forth between two views from this demo from that post.

Despite the DOM of the page changing dramatically when I select a tweet and then click back, it only causes two reflows to occur.

Conclusion

We see a lot of comments that the mobile web browser needs a lot of work before its ready to handle complicated apps, and while that's true, web development skills also must be improved. The mobile device is simply not as lenient as a desktop device. Let's not forget, these devices have a fraction of the processing power, memory, and bandwidth of their PC counterparts. Every aspect of the mobile design and development process must be reexamined for efficiencies and places where you can improve your skills and know-how in order to provide better end-products for your users.

CHAPTER 43

Understanding the Experience API

Gary Woodill

After more than two decades of the development of learning management systems and the shareable content object reference model (SCORM), an interoperability standard for learning content, there is something new in the field of tracking online learning achievements. This is new software called the Experience API (xAPI), which for a period of time was also known as the Tin Can API.

One of the first applications to use the Experience API was Tappestry, an app launched by Float Mobile Learning at the DevLearn conference in 2012 (mLearnCon 2012 was its public beta release). In total, eleven companies had adopted the xAPI approach for their software by mLearnCon 2012, and by early 2014 more than seventy projects were using this new standard. In this chapter, I will try to explain xAPI in a nontechnical way and review its strengths and shortcomings. xAPI is an extension to the SCORM standard for e-learning courses (it's not a replacement for SCORM), a standard maintained and updated over the past fifteen years by the Advanced Distributed Learning (ADL) group within the U.S. Department of Defense.

One of the main purposes of SCORM is to make online learning content compatible with many different learning management systems (LMSs). The problem with SCORM that xAPI addresses is that communication is mostly one-directional between learners and learning management systems. Tracking with SCORM is carried out from the perspective of the system doing the tracking, rarely from the learner's point of view.

It is important to note that both SCORM applications and xAPI track "learning activities," not learning itself. Learning takes place in a person's brain (or within the networked storage facilities of "extended minds") and nervous system and does not automatically result from simply participating in an activity, whatever the intention of the activity's designer. That is true for all learning management systems and e-learning courses. We can only assume or infer that learning has taken place based on a person's participation in specified learning activities or the results of specialized activities called assessments. But learning occurs in many different ways, most of which are not prescribed in a formal way by an institution or training department and/or assessed by a learning management system.

We refer to this kind of learning as "informal." Informal learning events can range from accidents that happen to long discussions over a glass of wine. Any non-institutional experience that results in a relatively permanent change in the behavior or understanding of a person about any aspect of human existence can be viewed as an informal learning event.

Most informal learning is not tracked and reported. It just becomes part of our repertoire of knowledge and skills. But, in our society, organizations are generally run by managers who like to see reports, preferably with numbers, that describe the results of the activities of the organization. This data, in theory, can then be used to make decisions about the direction and activity level of the organization. Because of the desire for managerial control, many organizations want to track evidence of informal learning in addition to the data that is being collected about formal learning activities. This is one of the main goals of using xAPI.

Because informal learning can be so varied, there is currently only one efficient way to collect and track such data—the reporting of learning activities involving employees by learners themselves, by third-party observers, or by software agents connected to sensors. xAPI standardizes such reporting in several ways:

- Using standard statements that follow this form: Actor, verb, object: "I did this"
- Reporting outcomes after an activity has been completed

- Including content description only after an activity has been completed
- Using learning content stored anywhere on the Internet
- Designing a new learning record store (LRS), a much simpler idea than an LMS
- Allowing the LRS to store user-defined variables
- Tracking new types of data, such as those based on simulations or games
- Integrating real-world learning events with digital activities
- Allowing learners to start an activity on one platform and later continue the same activity on another platform
- Observing and commenting on the learning activity while it is taking place
- Tracking collaborative groups and teams as well as individuals
- Tagging or rating content for later retrieval

At first glance, it appears that xAPI does not take into account many of the unique affordances of mobile learning, such as the importance of location, orientation, time, and haptic feedback. But xAPI allows for levels of complexity in its statements that may cover this concern.

Its developers acknowledge that many aspects of learning experiences can happen outside an xAPI-based system. Standardized and comprehensive ways to make statements about learning outcomes are still needed. The xAPI website explains one approach to solving this problem:

> Statements can get as complex as you'd like them to be, and that's one way where the answer to a "more powerful" e-learning specification comes into play. . . . An example of a more complex statement would be:
> [Somebody] says that [I] [did] [this] in the context of [_____] with result [_____] on [date].

Of course, most LMSs do a lot more than this, launching courses, giving assessments, and plotting career paths for each employee. But from the perspective of what training managers want—good reliable data to use in their reports to senior management—xAPI will provide more comprehensive reports, without the massive architecture and cost of most enterprise LMSs. It is easily used with a mobile device such as a phone or a tablet. As shown in Tappestry, the API can be used as specified, but can also be extended with additional features that are not in xAPI.

There are other issues in the development of xAPI to date, but to the credit of the developers, they are listed on their website as weaknesses to be resolved through more discussion with the learning and development community. There is a call for suggestions and a recognition that more work needs to be done to get this initiative right.

CHAPTER 44

Implementing Mobile Learning Metrics

Chad Udell

Evaluating training effectiveness is a long-running challenge for our industry. How do we know what we are doing is having a real and lasting effect on our audience's behavior and, in turn, improving our company's performance?

An entire subset of the training industry is focused around this. Assessment tools and specialists, learning management systems, and many other products exist to make this easier or more effective. Vendors are doing what they can to help you determine whether your learners have achieved what you have set out to do. Common metrics used with these systems include whether the learners have attended class, completed courses, and achieved some level of mastery of the content you have designed and deployed for them to consume and internalize.

Does tracking all of these mean that learning has occurred? From a certain point of view, yes, it does. The industry benchmark, Kirkpatrick's levels of evaluation of training (Kirkpatrick & Kirkpatrick, 2006) (currently in a redesign process) devotes the first two levels of evaluation to "Did they like it?" and "Did they learn something?" This taxonomy is certainly not accepted by everyone to be the end-all, be-all of training effectiveness evaluation, but it definitely is widespread among its devotees. There is little in those first two levels to affirm success or even equate the training intervention with real-world performance. Just because they were there, they liked it, and they learned something doesn't mean that they will sell more or be more productive.

Measuring Results

We are a results-driven culture. What if Levels 1 and 2 were viewed as being a means to an end and not a valued form of measurement itself? How do we move past this view of measurement to get to the real questions: "Are our training materials affecting behavior?" and, most importantly, "Are our materials affecting organizational performances or results?" A key will be to reexamine the deliverables we are deploying to our learners and reframe their points of measurement to more closely align with the processes and tools in place to help them be successful.

With mobile being a new thing for many of us, it offers a place to do a "soft reset." We don't need to change everything, but have an opportunity to change the things that aren't working for us now. What and how will we measure, and how will we tie to real-world activities? Key components of mobile experiences that can be measured differ dramatically from traditional learning experiences. We are concerned with things like measuring competency or grasp of subject matter in our ahead-of time-learning materials. Just as usage data, goal/funnel conversion, time spent on task, and task success rates are more important for marketing activities, these same sorts of activities are useful for mobile and just-in-time learning content.

For example, directly correlating the delivery of training to specific shifts in data in the company customer relationship management (CRM) system, or other associated business process platforms, is a powerful tactic to explore as you evaluate your mobile learning strategy. By doing so, you might uncover a few things. For example:

- Do employees whose statistics have not improved need refresher training?
- Do high performers access training materials while doing their jobs?
- Are there ways to directly insert job aids or performance tools in problem spots in a particular employee's workflow?
- Do behavior patterns emerge between groups of learners? Product lines? Regions? Managers?

If your personnel need to update a CRM or application after a meeting, visit, or sales call, perhaps there is an opportunity to add fields to the support or ticketing screen that ask whether they used mobile help before or during a call. A follow-up field could ask what content they accessed or whether it was helpful.

Make these fields a required entry prior to logging the meeting notes and you instantly have data points to track to see whether your mobile learning is helping those you designed it for. Use this information to inform your revisions and additions, and continue to check in to see whether the overall evaluation of your software improves.

Covering Other Aspects of Learning

These are all tips for the formal learning process and content, but social and informal activity is also an area to explore.

When was the last time you reviewed your Salesforce Chatter or Yammer usage to correlate sharing with performance? Usage with closed sales? Are our best-performing employees active in Yammer or Chatter? Do they have their posts "favorited" or shared? The best chefs are on TV (a simplistic assumption, I know), but these chefs share their recipes with everyone to improve us all. I hope your best performers do the same.

Measuring event intervention access and assessing whether the spacing matches with product releases and other real-world events is also worth exploring. Do new product rollouts require more accesses of just-in-time information? Are job aids for older products available in a format that helps salespeople or customer service reps make quick decisions and easily find answers?

The lifecycle of your products and services may have some bearing on whether your salespeople remember things about them. Just because something is near the end of its life or not the newest offering should not mean that information tools are unavailable to help close the deal or answer questions.

Putting This into Action

Tying training intervention delivery to results is a bit of mythical beast in the training world. Mobile learning doesn't guarantee this, but it certainly brings us closer. This has been a point of disconnect previously, but it's testable now.

Pick one of your low-hanging fruit projects and insert real measurement into the process. Look at mlearning as a performance improvement tool, not a "have to have" for this test.

Because it's new and possibly not fully replacing your other methods yet, view mobile as an additional means to reach your audience instead of the only one. It's more content than you might have had before—an augmentation of sorts.

Take your learning and measurement hypotheses and do an A/B test. Give the new content to one group and not the other. Do the ones who receive the new tools do better? Make more sales? Move leads through their pipeline more quickly? Answer customer questions more quickly? These metrics shouldn't be vanity metrics (non-actionable, low-value numbers), but rather real-world indicators based on the results.

Once you know a bit of what works and what doesn't with this smaller effort, you can expand it. Pick larger projects, embed your content directly into the CRM, find new performance measurement tools for mobile, and start measuring metrics that matter.

Reference

Kirkpatrick, D., & Kirkpatrick, J. (2006). *Evaluating training programs: The four levels.* San Francisco, CA: Berrett-Koehler.

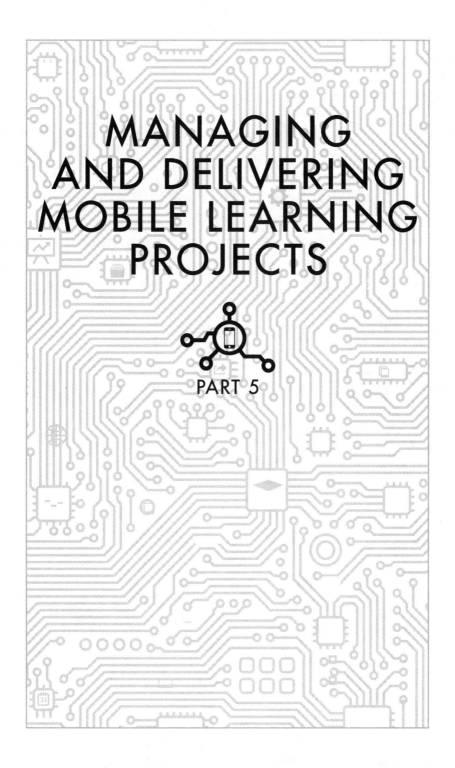

MANAGING AND DELIVERING MOBILE LEARNING PROJECTS

PART 5

CHAPTER 45

Managing a Mobile Learning Project Implementation

Gary Woodill and Chad Udell

What if you were tasked with leading the implementation of a large-scale mobile learning project? Where would you start? Do you have a good sense of all the steps that are required in order to be successful? Let's have a look at what it takes to bring an enterprise-level mobile learning project in on time and on budget.

Start with Business Strategy

At the enterprise level, the implementation of a mobile learning project needs to be a response or solution to a specific set of business problems. Without that, you are just riding a wave of adopting the newest technologies, without any real sense of what they can do for an organization. Don't make the mistake of buying mobile equipment first, and then trying to figure out what to do with it. Understanding the business issues that are driving a mobile learning project is especially important when it comes to selling the idea to, and obtaining a budget from, senior management. This understanding is usually stated in the form of a vision statement that identifies the overall impact that mobile learning will have on the organization.

Part of aligning a business strategy with the implementation of mobile learning is to identify stakeholders at all levels of the organization and gather and evaluate their requirements. Stakeholders can be used to develop "use cases" that help to define the needs of the organization and the impact of mobile learning on it.

There's no question that the introduction of powerful new technologies can have an impact on any organization. Therefore, it is necessary to create a change management plan, articulate and update policies that may be impacted by the project, and review ethical and privacy standards that this technology might require.

Early in the project, it is important to develop a mobile learning implementation plan that is dynamic and adaptable, anticipating additional decisions and information that may come later in the project. The plan should include a detailed specifications document, a preliminary budget, and a change management plan.

Decide on the Types of Mobile Learning Experiences

Any large-scale mobile learning project will likely include a range of learning experiences, so it is important that the project team know and evaluate the various options that they have in terms of types of content. Five types of content (or learning experiences) that are commonly used in mobile learning are listed below:

- Content that has already been created by someone either inside or outside the organization that can be converted from other formats or accessed through various data sources
- Content that is captured by mobile devices, often automatically, that can then be stored and/or distributed for later analysis and use
- Communications with others by voice or by text
- Computational functions such as calculators, databases, and apps made possible because of the fact that most mobile devices are quite powerful computers
- Contextual mobile learning content that uses the immediate environment to generate questions, requests for information, game-based learning, and/or informal learning activities

Once the mix of content types has been decided, the project plan should show how learning experiences and information are going to be created. Will it be commercial off-the-shelf (COTS) content, open-source content, content converted from e-learning or print materials, user-generated content, content designed and developed in-house, custom content developed by a third party, or some combination of these? The answers to these choices should then be reflected in the project budget, schedule, and activities list.

Make Decisions About Which Technologies to Use

Once the plan for content types and sources has been finalized, it is finally time to look at the technology side of the implementation plan. With mobile, you are faced with two basic choices—either supplying employees with company-owned devices ("company-liable approach") or allowing employees to bring their own devices ("BYOD approach") and use them at work. In either case, mobile learning software needed for carrying out the business of the company needs to be purchased (either off-the-shelf or custom-built), provisioned, and tested in order for employees to meet their goals.

This brings up the issue of who is going to manage the hardware and software to be used in the mobile learning project. Will it be the information technology (IT) department? You may have no choice in this matter, in that all technology used in the organization may have to be cleared through IT. Alternatively, a mobile learning system can be managed externally through a vendor that provides a hosting service or storage in "the cloud." Also, in some situations, a grassroots ad hoc system within a single department might already have been set up that is being used without any central control.

Whatever the management of technology situation is in your company, it is paramount that effective security procedures and policies be in place. Because mobile devices are controlled through carriers, and because they have built-in security features, it may be easier to provide security for mobile devices than it was for e-learning.

Prepare and Present a Business Case

By this time in the project, you should have a full draft of a mobile learning implementation plan, having gathered information from all stakeholders and finalized decisions about content and technology choices. In order to obtain funding for this project, you will need to do a number of things:

- Define the scope for the initial implementation: Will it be a pilot study, a staggered implementation, or a global rollout?
- Select metrics and assessment methods for the project.
- List estimates of all project costs and benefits in order to calculate a rough return on investment (ROI).
- Prepare a budget for whatever time period the project will run.

When ready, you will likely make a formal presentation to upper management, presenting the business case for mobile learning and obtaining budget approval.

Put Your Implementation Team in Place

In order to have a successful implementation of a mobile learning system, both the client and the vendor(s) must have strong project management procedures in place. While mobile learning project management is a relatively new field, there are already "best practices" that can be followed based on the experience of vendors and companies that have undertaken major mobile learning projects. The person in charge of day-to-day operations for the implementation effort should, ideally, have a background and training in project management, such as the Project Management Professional (PMP) designation from the Project Management Institute.

Right from the beginning, an executive steering group for the project must be formed to manage the entire initiative, including the development and guidance of the overall vision and strategy. This group should have an executive champion from the company's management team and, if a vendor is involved, from the vendor's management team. After that, a project management team for day-to-day management of the implementation must be put into place and meet at least weekly.

Follow Project Documents and Procedures

At this stage, the project management team has to start working with the project documents and set up working procedures to ensure a successful implementation. A detailed specifications document should be in place, along with a schedule to follow and a budget to track. Hardware may have to be ordered and installed, to be in place for later testing of content. A project communications operation must be launched, as all stakeholders have to be informed of the progress of the project in order to manage their expectations and to prepare them for changes that are coming.

The process of content design and development has to be tracked and managed, to keep the project on time and on budget. Once content has been produced, it should be uploaded to the actual system that it will run on and be thoroughly tested. At the same time, both print and online help and documentation for the mobile learning system must be prepared and made available.

Expect to make changes in your implementation plan as the project progresses. This is especially the case if the project is spread over a relatively long period of time, for example, several months or even a year or two. Although you can set a schedule, be prepared to adjust it as the project progresses, something quite common in any technology implementation. Because of the high stakes involved, it is important not to pull the plug on the old training system until the new mobile learning system is in place and shown to be working properly.

Transfer the Mobile Learning System to an Operations Group

Once the initial mobile learning system has been set up and thoroughly tested, it is time to turn it over to an operations team. This group will have to be trained in all aspects of mobile learning usage, management, and operations and in the procedures for the specific system just put in place, in order to be able to assist users going forward. New policies on the use of mobile devices, which should have been discussed and finalized by this point, should be put into place. Privacy and ethical standards will have to be monitored and enforced as the system is used. While maintaining ongoing operations, there must be regular evaluations and the collection of usage data for further analysis. Modifications will be made in the system as it is used and as content changes over time. Finally, content can become stale and technologies improved, making it important to keep the new mobile learning system up-to-date.

Planning for a full mobile learning project lifecycle is doable, but can be complex. Having a trained project management team and an experienced vendor who has done similar projects before can be important factors in implementing a successful mobile learning system in your organization.

CHAPTER 46

Security in a Mobile World

Chad Udell

As mobile devices become more powerful and more widely used, security has become the proverbial elephant in the room. Everybody knows that there is an entirely new set of security issues that come into play, but few people are quite sure what to do about them. The excitement to deploy mobile content can make companies and organizations compromise or even overlook the security implications.

The convenience of mobile devices is their downside as well. A portable item that can have access to your work and personal information is easy to misplace or be stolen. PIN security codes help to protect that information somewhat, but the only way to truly protect the information on a device is a mobile wipe. Of course, that task must be completed in a timely manner when needed to truly keep your information from falling into the wrong hands.

Custom applications for mobile devices are another problem area. Whether they are native code or mobile web apps, if they are accessing remote data, there is a risk. Researchers are finding that most mobile apps (over 50 percent, and nearly 90 percent of third-party apps) do not use secured connections for data access. Something as simple as requiring SSL connections can help protect important and confidential data.

Another concern as mobile devices are being more frequently used in the corporate world is that they add new vectors for potential threats. The devices are using new operating systems that don't fit with most security vendors' software offerings. Some companies, such as Symantec and F-Secure, have recently introduced security software for mobile devices, but they don't work with the integrated security systems that most IT departments already have in place. Some companies may be relying on their network security gateways to provide protection for mobile devices, until users switch to mobile connections and bypass those methods entirely. This adds the risk of a mobile user accessing a compromised file and bringing it into the network, bypassing security controls. Add in the already known issues of unsecured wireless networks and Bluetooth vulnerabilities when mobile users are outside of the office, and it is easy to see why some corporate IT departments are nervous about the proliferation of mobile devices on their networks.

After hearing all that, it might seem like mobile security is nearly impossible to achieve. It is easy to become paranoid about vulnerabilities when you start researching security issues. The good news is that there are some positive points to talk about as well. The new mobile operating systems run apps in separate memory spaces that make it more difficult for potential viruses to hijack a device. The review process for iOS apps and the new security requirements for Google Play should help keep apps more trustworthy. The mobile device makers are taking the issue seriously as well. They understand that people want their devices to be secure and are taking steps to improve security in the future.

So what's the answer? As with any evolving technology, use common sense and caution. Don't rush into content mobile delivery. Create a standard for best practices for your mobile users and then distribute the information through all of your regular channels, such as newsletters and your intranet site. You can also consider procedures, such as requiring PIN codes or passcodes, setting up a remote wipe method, and considering data encryption. The most important step is to find a comfortable middle ground between security and ease of use. This doesn't have to truly sacrifice security when done properly.

As mobile devices become cheaper, if your policies are too restrictive, users can easily buy and use their own phones or tablets and circumvent all of the protection that you put into place. Mobile devices should be used to make tasks more convenient. Keep them that way, and everyone will be happy.

CHAPTER 47

Education and Training for Mobile Development

Jim Ferolo

As an emerging media educator, I have had the opportunity and challenge of facilitating the teaching and training of students in higher education for the past ten years. The last two years have been spent developing a new curriculum and looking at the ways in which we introduce interactive theory and practice. We are faced with an interesting divergence and convergence of technology that I believe will help us form the ways in which we teach, and subsequently migrate students into the role of new media professionals.

No one can question the growth of mobile devices and the trending that shows it to be the most widely deployed computing device around the world. However, the very thing that makes the technology pervasive is also the thing that makes development so difficult. The wide array of host operating systems, service providers, protocols, and devices creates an environment that can be extremely daunting to deploy within an organization. Combining the technology hurdles with the limited amount of contact time that we have to teach a variety of development techniques provides two distinct paths that will allow students to get their product from the page to the screen.

I believe there is a clear demarcation in experience and approach for course content that splits after the second year of instruction. Lower-level students are typically highly skills-focused and working to ingest technology and history and find ways to process and apply the information to their specific aesthetic and evolving visual and technical styles. Upper-level students are often dealing with much higher levels of abstraction and conceptual work that forces them to engage in multiple associations and directed research.

Given this construct, I believe that mobile devices can provide clarity in the design process that is not always available in a less constrained environment of browser-based development. For example, if a student is engaged in developing an application for an iPhone, he or she will be limited to a specific screen size, a specific set of development environments, a specific set of gestural techniques, and many preexisting toolkits. This focus could create an environment in which more time is spent considering the implications of their interaction design and its associated usability than worrying about whether it should be developed in any variety of technologies. I have spent more time debating the relevance of devices than I care to recall, so I will put the caveat out there that I am device-agnostic and am not advocating for any specific platform.

Conversely, at the upper level, I believe that mobile computing will force us to more clearly consider the implications of how we teach interaction design and whether or not we are creating experiences that are standards-compliant and deployable across multiple platforms. I believe that we have the chance to begin to reinforce the importance of the information that we need to deploy and how it has to be available on a variety of devices.

I am fortunate enough to have a very interesting gaming app in the pipeline with a 300-level course that focuses primarily on the design document process for the first eight weeks of the semester and the production of the application during the second eight weeks. In the class, we have not been talking specifically about the capabilities of the iPhone or any other platform, but instead are discussing gameplay, UI, and usability. We only rarely touch on the capabilities of a mobile device, but I expect this to change quite a bit as we roll into production and barrel toward a final build.

CHAPTER 48

Integrating Mobile Learning with Social Media

Adam Bockler

The term "mobile social media" refers to social media used on a mobile device. Because of the new capabilities of smart phones and tablets, mobile social media is somewhat different from traditional social media, which, as Tom Standage (2013), in his book *Writing On the Wall: Social Media the First 2,000 Years*, has pointed out, has been around for at least two millennia. Mobile social media has depended on the development of smart phones in the late 1990s and the arrival of tablet computers starting in 2010. It differs from social learning on desktop computers in that it is available for use any time, anyplace, that is, at "the point of need."

Because most employees bring their mobile devices to work every day, the use of mobile social media has greatly increased in the past few years. Edwin Huertas (2012), writing for *Social Media Today*, lists multiple benefits of employees using social media while working:

1. Social networking tools help employees remain focused on and aligned with corporate objectives.

2. These tools flatten the corporate hierarchy, empower individual employees at all levels, and provide a direct path to decision-makers and executors.

3. Internal social networking encourages people to connect and communicate with each other, cross-pollinate ideas, and develop valuable insights.

4. The ability to communicate issues, insights, and solutions leads to generating new ideas.

5. News and information reach people more quickly.

6. People can share resources and information easily and effectively.

7. The company can more easily and effectively search for and consolidate employee skill sets to match specific project requirements.

8. Mobile devices allow employees to do all of these things and more, and, as a result, they expect that their organizations will provide efficient, effective, and collaborative routes for learning.

This chapter will discuss the importance of capitalizing on accessing social media via mobile devices at work.

The Informal Basis of Learning

The underlying and often quoted principle behind using social media for mobile learning is the 70–20–10 rule. Lombardo and Eichinger (1996) suggest that as much as 90 percent of workplace learning happens informally. The theory says most learning—70 percent—occurs as a result of practical experience, 20 percent comes as a result of observation, and just 10 percent happens from formal education and training. In other words, most of the activity of L&D departments goes to the least critical area for employee development.

Even though "social learning" is often associated with learning via social media, Jane Hart (2013), founder of the Centre for Learning & Performance Technologies (C4LPT), says there is a clear distinction between this term and learning with social media. She says, "Social learning is the latest buzzword in the learning industry, but let's be clear from the outset—social learning is not a new training trend; it's the way we have always learned from one another—whether it be at home with our family, at school with our friends, or at work with our colleagues."

Informal learning expert Jay Cross (2012) agrees. "Learning is social," he says. "We learn more from our co-workers, our bosses, our customers, our partners, and our friends than from our teachers and books. Improve the ease of free-flowing conversation and you improve the quality of learning across the 70, the 20, and the 10."

Social learning—whether it's associated with social media or not—and mobile learning are becoming inextricably linked. "I used to view mobile and social learning separately," writes Julian Stodd (2013), a learning consultant. "Together, they can support a full learning journey, from context through demonstration, exploration and reflections, assessment and footsteps back into real life. We are doing them an injustice if we just use mobile to deliver assessments to reluctant learners on the bus and just use social to push out messages from corporate [communications] departments."

Social Media and Learning in the Real World

You don't need to look hard to see the uptake in using mobile devices to access social media. According to the Adobe 2013 Mobile Consumer Survey (Pun, 2013), accessing social media is the number one mobile activity today. "People still predominantly use their mobile devices to gain information, including social. Of those surveyed, 71 percent reported using their mobile devices to access social media." The use of mobile devices in general is trending upward. More than one out of every three minutes (37 percent) in the use of ICT is now spent beyond the PC, according to comScore's U.S. Digital Future in Focus report (comScore, 2013).

Despite the number of people who are using social media, few organizations are adopting these technologies for learning. Jane Bozarth (2011) wrote in the eLearning Guild's *Social Media for Learning* report that, "as of July 2011, a little less than one-third of organizations are currently using social media tools for learning, with a stunning 83 percent of respondents feeling that social media for learning has value. Most respondents indicate feeling supported and encouraged to make use of social media for learning." The data also show that organizations intend to do more with social media for learning.

A key foundation of the deployment of social media for mobile learning is crafting a policy on its use within an organization's overall mobile policy. However, many organizations lack policy in this area, a barrier to the adoption of social media for mobile learning in large enterprises. According to the Society for Human Resource Management, only about 40 percent of organizations have a formal social media policy. What's more, 43 percent of respondents to its 2011 survey "reported that their organizations block access to social media sites on company-owned computers and hand-held electronic devices. The survey found that larger organizations (more than five hundred employees) are more likely to block access to social media sites and to track employee use." Ford Motor Company (2014) has one of the best-known policies, expressed on one page, with five brief principles highlighted at its center:

1. Honesty about who you are
2. Clarity that your opinions are your own
3. Respect and humility in all communication
4. Good judgment in sharing only public information—including financial data
5. Awareness that what you say is permanent

Putting It into Practice

The media theorist Marshall McLuhan (McLuhan & Fiore, 1967) foresaw the implications of digital computing in the 1960s. "Education must shift from instruction, from imposing of stencils, to discovery—to probing and exploration and to the recognition of the language of forms," he said. Social media follows in line with that thinking by allowing people to take control of what they want to learn at any time of the day, and from any location with mobile phone or Wi-Fi service. Here are some other ways that employees can use social media for mobile learning:

• Using social media for mobile learning helps curate information within a personal learning network or a community of practice. It does this in two ways: by allowing employees to be in touch with each other and in touch with employees in similar roles in other companies.

- Employees within the same company can share information within minutes. Jane Bozarth wrote for *Learning Solutions* about how an individual from one company shared a conference recap with his colleagues:

  - "Users, armed with phones equipped with video cameras, are increasingly comfortable with and adept at creating and sharing their own videos. Encourage them to be 'social' in the sense of contributing to course materials and organizational communication. When . . . Craig Taylor was the company's sole employee sent to Las Vegas for DevLearn, he ended each day by capturing about five minutes' worth of reflection about the experience: speakers he'd seen, an overview of key points, a few critical takeaways. In this way, he was able to document his day, reflect on new learning, and share it with those back at the office."

- Employees working for different companies but in similar roles can exchange ideas through social media in a variety of ways. They can engage in Twitter chats, for example, using a common hashtag. LinkedIn has discussion groups on different topics that workers can browse throughout the day, participating in the group discussions that appeal to them. Both methods have the potential for employees to expand their networks, ask questions, as well as be seen as an expert by providing answers.

- The combination of social media and mobile devices can give employees an idea of the whereabouts of a colleague. With many employees working from the road, social check-ins on enterprise social networks (and even on public ones) let colleagues know when someone may not be at his or her desk.

Columnist Clive Thompson (2013) writes about this last idea in his book, *Smarter Than You Think* (2013). He references the term "proprioception," which is the body's awareness of where its limbs are located, as a metaphor for our potential awareness of the status of our colleagues. Thompson relates this to the workplace: "When groups of people—friends, family, workmates—keep in lightweight online contact, it gives us social proprioception: a group's sense of self. Used correctly, social proprioception can make one's work life less frazzled by reducing the constant stream of interruptions. A group that's connected in an ambient fashion can—counterintuitively—spend less time on communication, particularly the writing and reading of endless email."

At the same time, the use of social media in the workplace has resulted in a major increase in the amount of information to which we need to pay attention. Social media and networks that feature the ability to organize and store information for later retrieval can be valuable tools for the enterprise in order to prevent the loss of institutional knowledge through employee attrition, changes in careers, and retirement. For instance, the National Archive and Retired Federal Employees Association calculates that 10,000 years' worth of American federal worker experience is lost every day, or forty-six days every second, according to *The Washington Post*. Enterprise social networks such as Jive, Yammer, and Tappestry all provide the ability to store and categorize information in their own ways if they are part of your overall strategy for preserving this knowledge.

Leveraging the Effects

In this era of "big data," the huge amount of information that social media generates can be used for all kinds of purposes. For example, Harris Interactive, a U.K.-based market research firm, revealed in 2011 (Bain, 2011) that they were "using GPS data from mobile phones to track respondents' whereabouts" because of GPS's ability to "observe behavioral patterns, look at how people use the mobile web when they're out and about, and send relevant surveys to participants based on their location." The service had tracked more than twenty million Facebook posts from twenty thousand participants in the United States.

Beyond location data, other social signals can now be measured in conversation, thanks to MIT professor Alex (Sandy) Pentland's (2008) "sociometer" device. "Using just this data, with no knowledge of what was said, Pentland could predict the outcome—whether a job offer, a second date, or investment in a business plan—more accurately than by using any other single factor." In his book, *Honest Signals* (2008), Pentland suggests that by "reading" our social networks with these devices, "we can become more successful at pitching an idea, getting a job, or closing a deal."

The use of social media for mobile learning is burgeoning in many different industries. For example, in finance and insurance firms, employees can quickly gather information, such as the latest stock or housing prices, when they need it in order to compete. Food producers and other agricultural professionals, who have up until recently worked in relative isolation, can now connect with others to share techniques and experiences, even when they're in the field. Retailers can train employees with mobile devices at the checkout lane or the customer service desk, and employees can refer to the devices when they need immediate performance support, even while interacting with customers.

The world of work is beginning to embrace the use of social media for mobile learning. To begin, develop your goals for using social media. Then find a network that works for you based on those goals, whether it's available publicly (like Twitter) or privately (choose an enterprise social network or an internal wiki). Next, find what others are talking about and contribute by answering questions or asking your own. Finally, keep evaluating to see whether you have to make adjustments to your social media strategy, whether it's for you as an individual or as a company.

No matter how you use social media for mobile learning, you're bound to make some discoveries.

References

Bain, R. (2011, February). Portable potential. *Research*. www. harrisinteractive.com/vault/HI_UK_Corp_News-Portable-potential.pdf.

Bozarth, J. (2011, September 27). Social media for learning. eLearning Guild report. www.elearningguild.com/research/archives/index. cfm?id=152&action=viewonly

Bozarth, J. (2013, November 5). Nuts and bolts: Making video more social. *Learning Solutions*. www.learningsolutionsmag.com/ articles/1299/nuts-and-bolts-making-video-more-social.

comScore. (2013, February 14). 2013 U.S. digital future in focus. Whitepaper. www.comscore.com/Insights/Presentations_and_ Whitepapers/2013/2013_US_Digital_Future_in_Focus.

Cross, J. (2012, August 3). The other 90% of learning. *Jay Cross Blog*. www.jaycross.com/wp/2012/08/the-other-90-of-learning.

Ford Motor Company. (2014). Ford Social Media Guidelines. www.scribd
.com/doc/36127480/Ford-Social-Media-Guidelines.

Hart, J. (2013). *A practical guide to the top 100 tools for learning.* Bath, UK:
Centre for Learning & Performance Technology.

Hicks, J. (2013, August 19). Retirement ticker tracks federal loss of institutional knowledge. *Washington Post.* www.washingtonpost.com
/politics/federal_government/union-retirement-ticker-tracks-
federal-loss-of-institutional-knowledge/2013/08/19/66249330–
08e7–11e3-b87c-476db8ac34cd_story.html.

Huertas, E. (2012, September 28). Internal social networks: The return
of new and improved intranets. *Social Media Today.*

Lombardo, M., & Eichinger, R. (1996). *The career architect development
planner.* Minneapolis, MN: Lominger.

McLuhan, M., & Fiore, Q. (1967). *The medium is the message: An inventory
of effects.* New York: Bantam Books.

Pentland, A. (2008). *Honest signals: How they shape our world.* Cambridge,
MA: MIT Press.

Pun, R. (2013, July 25). Adobe 2013 mobile consumer survey: 71% of
people use mobile to access social media. *Digital Marketing Blog.*
http://blogs.adobe.com/digitalmarketing/digital-marketing/
mobile/adobe-2013-mobile-consumer-survey-71-of-people-use-
mobile-to-access-social-media.

Society for Human Resource Management (SHRM). (2012). *Managing
and leveraging workplace use of social media.* www.shrm.org/
templatestools/toolkits/pages/managingsocialmedia.aspx.

Standage, T. (2013). *Writing on the wall: Social media the first 2,000 years.*
New York: Bloomsbury.

Stodd, J. (2013, January 22). The convergence of mobile and social
learning. *Julian Stodd's Learning Blog.* http://julianstodd.wordpress.
com/2013/01/22/the-convergence-of-mobile-and-social-learning.

Thompson, C. (2013). *Smarter than you think: How technology is changing
our minds for the better.* New York: Penguin.

CHAPTER 49

Budgeting for Social and Mobile Learning

Gary Woodill

Organizations face a choice in provisioning mobile devices for their employees. One choice is to have the corporation buy compatible devices for its workers and managers (often referred to as a "corporate-liable" solution). Another option is to allow employees to bring their own devices to work and use them for both work and personal uses, with the company supporting software that is important to its operation (also known as "bring your own device" or BYOD). A third option is to have employees supply both their own devices and any productivity software that is needed to do their work (known as "bring your own technology" or BYOT). Many companies use a combination of these approaches, depending on the position and work of an employee.

Don't overlook the costs of publishing mobile content that meets the needs of your company. While employees can choose and pay for apps in the BYOT model, for both corporate-liable and BYOD models, the company needs to invest in the software it wants its employees to use. Some of this content will be company-specific materials that can't just be bought off-the-shelf, so budgeting must include all costs for in-house planning, writing, graphics, editing, programming, testing, and maintenance (Udell, 2012). These costs can be higher for the BYOD model, because of the need to develop content for multiple platforms and screen sizes.

Finally, ongoing procedures will have different costs, depending on which deployment model you choose. If you are using a corporate-liable model, then the costs of maintaining and updating software will be the corporation's. If it is a BYOT model, then all the costs will be borne by employees. The BYOD model will have a mix of procedures and maintenance costs, depending on what software is being used.

BYOD represents both opportunities and problems for the employer. Employee-owned devices are often being utilized because the employees prefer them; they are convenient and help employees perform their daily routines in a comfortable and efficient manner. As they are the property of the employee, they can free the employer from having to negotiate and maintain mobile contracts. They are also alien to the workplace; they are not being introduced by a company decision, they are not standardized, and they may not be supported (or even condoned) by company policy or infrastructure. Despite this, they are interacting in various degrees with company information technology resources.

Many tout BYOD as unstoppable (MacLeod, 2012). In many cases, it is a powerful, work-enabling tool that is being pushed by employees, sometimes without any explicit company policy to do so. Trying to eliminate these devices may not be effective and could result in employees circumventing policy in droves; for some executives, this can be a frightening scenario (Kaneshige, 2012a).

If a company decides to support a BYOD policy, some of the traditional mechanisms of the company must change to account for the new technology, and some of the following questions are raised:

- How does IT handle access, security, and support?
- How does the executive decide on policy?
- As the device is used with company assets, who owns what?
- How does finance decide the costs in terms of allocated budgeting and employee reimbursement?
- What is the impact on overtime compensation if employees continue to do work for the company after hours?

Given the many variables involved in using a BYOD approach, this complex set of issues requires careful analysis for its impact on a company's budget.

A 2012 survey of business and learning professionals found three major issues identified as impediments to mobile learning (ASTD and the Institute for Corporate Productivity, in Sosbe, 2012):

1. *Security concerns:* 36 percent
2. *Integration with company assets:* 37 percent
3. *Budgetary concerns:* 46 percent

Despite all the noise in the literature regarding the first two issues, budgeting is the dominant issue for mobile learning.

To be effective in both social learning and mobile learning endeavors, an organization has to take an active role to promote, develop, police, and nurture the growth of a learning community that operates within the corporate cultural framework. This will demand planning, pilot programs, change management, implementation, and maintenance. As the existing IT infrastructure will account for most of the technology demands, the major budgetary concerns involve people to manage and support this initiative.

As indicated above, an organization can choose three basic approaches to deploying mobile:

1. *Corporate-Liable:* The organization selects, purchases, and supplies devices (with the software) to their employees.
2. *BYOD:* The organization supports employee-owned mobile devices and supplies software when necessary.
3. *BYOT:* The organization allows access to its systems through employee-owned devices. Software choice is left to the discretion, and responsibility, of the employee.

On first glance, it may seem that adopting corporate-liable devices is the most expensive route. Be careful! There are costs to deploying any new system within a corporation, and some of these costs are not immediately apparent.

Corporate-liable devices have some costs that are obviously higher than those of the alternative deployment strategies, namely hardware, software, and training. Obsolescence will also become a notable budgetary factor, as these devices are rapidly evolving and will probably need replacement long before they cease to function. This is not all downside. This approach does have cost advantages that come from the ability to negotiate bulk purchase discounts (particularly wireless fees), reduced employee expense reports that limit accounting costs, and reduced strain on IT due to standardized technology. Security and interoperability are also very strong with this strategy. This can reduce cost implications stemming from data security risks or business inefficiencies.

As an alternative, a company can choose to rely on the high-quality consumer devices that are already available, in most cases, through the employees. Ironically, BYOD can actually be rather expensive, more so than corporate-liable devices, despite the fact that the employees supply the hardware (Kaneshige, 2012a; Kaneshige, 2012b; MacLeod, 2012).

Understand that mobile devices are dependent on wireless service charges and that BYOD will alter these costs in three ways:

1. Compensating the employees for those portions of their bills that were accrued to the company's benefit. This is often handled through a stipend, but some additional charges may occur if the device is under heavy use or incurs justifiable roaming charges.
2. Handling additional expense reports.
3. Loss of negotiating power for bulk service provision.

Understand that IT will have to handle an additional workload to support these devices, especially because they will not be uniform brands or versions. This includes logging the devices into their systems, enabling access to company data, designing and implementing an appropriate security framework, providing support for devices and applications, and possibly developing new applications for a multiplatform mobile environment. Should IT fail to support these devices, a third party may have to become involved, and involving third parties to resolve mobile device issues may introduce an unacceptable element of risk and a major additional expense.

BYOT is the default strategy for many companies that fail to build a sound mobile device strategy and supporting policy. Employees start by using a myriad of mobile devices and software to access corporate assets. A company may actually choose this route because the cost advantages are clear, but serious disadvantages are also present. BYOT has all of the budgetary issues that are common to BYOD, but they tend to become magnified. Security and interoperability can become serious problems, with ballooning costs. Most importantly, BYOT introduces an element of chaos into your IT and accounting framework.

Mobile devices are a new workplace reality. They are going to be present in your company, and employees will be performing work-related tasks on them, regardless of management decisions. This means that your company has no choice but to try and gain some level of control over their use—or surrender to chaos. As BYOD is already a reality in virtually every company, a policy, support system, and budget must be put in place very quickly.

References

Kaneshige, T. (2012a, April). BYOD: If you think you're saving money, think again. *CIO*. www.cio.com/article/703511/ BYOD_If_You_Think_You_re_Saving_Money_Think_Again.

Kaneshige, T. (2012b, May). BYOD stirs up legal problems. *CIO*. www.cio .com/article/706086/BYOD_Stirs_Up_Legal_Problems.

Kaneshige, T. (2012c, August). When BYOD is a productivity killer. *CIO*. www.cio.com/article/714647/ When_BYOD_Is_a_Productivity_Killer.

MacLeod, J. (2012, July). Best practices for BYOD on a budget. *CIO Update*. www.cioupdate.com/technology-trends/best-practices-for-BYOD-on-a-budget.html.

Sosbe, T. (2012, June 6). Goin' mobile learning. TrainingIndustry. com. www.trainingindustry.com/blog/blog-entries/goin-mobile-learning.aspx.

Udell, C. (2012). *Learning everywhere: How mobile content strategies are transforming training.* Nashville, TN: Rockbench Publishing and Alexandria, VA: ASTD Press.

CHAPTER 50

Keeping Up with New Developments in Mobile Learning

Gary Woodill

In the *MIT Technology Review*, Michael DeGusta (2012) asked, "Are smart phones spreading faster than any technology in human history?" and answered, "Yes!" The article added, "mobile computers are on track to saturate markets in the U.S. and the developing world in record time." For learning and development professionals interested in mobile learning, one important question is how to keep up with technological changes, without being paralyzed with fear of information overload or getting out too far ahead of others in your organization because of euphoria over the latest gadget.

This concluding chapter outlines my techniques for coping with technological change in the mobile learning field. Using these techniques and sources, I have been able to build comprehensive "environmental scans" in such diverse verticals as health, pharmaceuticals, and agriculture. I also am able to predict the near future of mobile learning, based on the simple fact that every field of technology is based on a set of developmental curves for each new innovation. But the early stages of an emerging technology are often hidden, unless you really dig for them. This insight is the basis of the growing field of "predictive analytics."

Table 50.1 describes a dozen techniques that I use to keep up with developments in the field of mobile learning and to understand what is likely coming next.

Table 50.1. Sources of Information to Develop a Personal Radar System on Changes in Mobile Learning

Techniques	Examples	Benefits
1. Google Alerts	Enter a search string such as "Mobile Learning" in Google Alerts to receive a daily email on what is new each day in Google on this topic.	Daily alerts tell you what is new in a field. Click on all unfamiliar terms to check out what they mean. Look for trends as new ideas become more frequent.
2. Conference alerts	Register "mobile learning" and "mlearning" as topics on at least one conference alert site for a monthly list of all new conferences on your chosen topic. Scan the topics for new concepts and terminology.	Conferences are always looking for presenters with the latest ideas. The titles of keynotes and sessions will give you new ideas. The exhibitors list will show you new companies in the field.
3. Attend several large conferences a year.	ASTD's TechKnowledge and the eLearning Guild's mLearnCon and DevLearn conferences are very good for mobile learning.	Large conferences are a great source of business intelligence, both from sessions and from exhibitors.
4. Read websites that have a daily update on new information technologies in general.	Examples include TED. com, Mashable.com, ZDNet.com, Digital Trend. com, and Wired.com.	Most learning technologies are innovations that start in more general technology fields.
5. Subscribe to aggregators on your chosen topic(s).	See eLearningLearning. com, and cc. mlearnopedia.com as good examples for mobile learning.	These sites aggregate many blogs on a topic into one web page for easy scanning.
6. Once a month search for new theses and dissertations on your chosen topic(s).	Use academic databases to scan the titles of new theses and dissertations. Many are available in full text for downloading.	Graduate students need to be at the leading edge of their fields so their literature reviews are thorough and up-to-date.
7. Follow the blogs and tweets of futurists and consultants.	Relevant futurists and consultants include Ray Kurzweil, Thomas Frey, Ross Dawson, Clark Quinn, Judy Brown, and David Metcalf.	These people are dedicated to discussing new technologies and predicting the short- and long-term future of technology.

Techniques	Examples	Benefits
8. Read key popular technology magazines.	Examples are *Wired, Fast Company, New Scientist,* and *MIT's Technology Review.*	New ideas show up in magazines faster than in books or academic journals.
9. Scan the table of contents of all important academic journals in your field.	Examples include *Interactive Learning Technologies, British Journal of Educational Technology,* etc.	Academic articles are usually more in-depth on a topic than those in popular magazines.
10. Search social media for trending topics in your field.	Twitter, Facebook, and LinkedIn are examples of social media available on mobile devices.	Follow industry leaders to see what they are thinking. Use social search.
11. Review Google's patents site for new patents related to your topic of interest. Research the companies with the patents.	Go to Google.com/ patents to search for mobile learning and see what is new.	Patents show some of the latest ideas, especially those that have commercial potential.
12. Search for new books on mobile learning.	*Learning Everywhere* (Chad Udell), *Designing mLearning* (Clark Quinn), *The Mobile Learning Edge* (Gary Woodill)	While books may not contain the latest information on a topic, it is important to keep up with leading authors on mlearning.

Look for the Ripple Effects of Mobile Learning Technologies

Innovative technologies such as mobile computing can have a significant impact on existing business models, not just for the technology being replaced, but for all associated and dependent industries. For example, consider the impact of digital sound files on the music industry. The accessibility of high-quality, inexpensive (sometimes free) music files played on mobile devices such as iPods and MP3 players has largely displaced the formerly highly profitable compact disks. This has disrupted the business model of not only music publishers, but the artists, music distributors, CD manufacturers, and graphic album designers, to name a few.

As a second example, consider the impact of digital photography. Traditional film giants like Kodak and Polaroid were late in responding to digital files; many film development companies went out of business, and camera manufacturers like Nikon are now forced to compete with smart phones in the camera market!

This means that a late understanding of the ramifications of innovative technology not only results in a potential loss of competitive opportunities, but it can also mean that an organization's business model can be destroyed by an "innovative disruption" (Christensen, 1997). An innovative disruption is a product or service that effectively replaces not only the previous product or service, but the value chain that supports it. This was the case with the arrival of digital sound files and digital cameras. It is also the case that the developing mobile learning industry is disrupting the twenty-year-old e-learning industry.

Mobile learning shares many "affordances" of e-learning and, to that extent, developers have simply ported over models that seemed to be successful for desktop learning. But mobile learning has many unique possibilities that could not be carried out previously. Examples include:

- Learning while on the move or from any location
- Using location and surrounding environment as contextual variables in instructional design
- Learning at the time of need because your mobile device is always with you
- Collecting and sending out data while using your mobile device as a research tool
- Augmenting what a mobile camera is viewing with overlays of text or virtual objects
- Use of haptic technologies to recognize gestures and touch

These are only a few of the disruptive possibilities of mobile learning that will change the way traditional learning and development is carried out. Disruption does not mean that opportunity has been extinguished. New companies are starting up that capitalize on the new technologies by using novel value chains that work with the disruptive technology, not against it. Apple's success with iTunes and the iPod is one example. Digital photo-sharing companies like Instagram are another.

Tracking technological changes can alert an organization well in advance of potential innovative disruptions. This early warning information can be employed to evaluate the current business model and allow a company to consider options for change, such as developing a plan for business model innovation to complement the new technology (Osterwalder, 2008). Being prepared can help insulate the company from disruption; it may also allow the company to outcompete less well-prepared rivals.

In preparing for the new world of mobile learning, it is helpful to have partners who already know the landscape and have the skills and experience to anticipate and work through the unique issues that arise within your organization. We hope this compilation of tips and techniques for mastering mobile learning will help to move your projects to successful completion.

References

Christensen, C.M. (1997). *The innovator's dilemma.* New York: McGraw-Hill.

DeGusta, M. (2012, May 9). Are smart phones spreading faster than any technology in human history? *MIT Technology Review.* www .technologyreview.com/news/427787/are-smart-phones-spreading-faster-than-any-technology-in-human-history.

Osterwalder, A. (2008). Business model innovation matters! *SlideShare.* www.slideshare.net/Alex.Osterwalder/business-model-innovation-matter.

ABOUT THE AUTHORS

Chad Udell is the managing director of Float Mobile Learning. He works with industry-leading Fortune 500 companies on developing mobile learning strategies that are then implemented by Float. A recognized expert in design and development, Chad speaks regularly at national conferences on strategy, design, development, and mobile learning. Chad is the author of *Learning Everywhere: How Mobile Content Strategies Are Transforming Training*.

Gary Woodill is a senior analyst for Float Mobile Learning. Gary conducts research and market analyses, as well as assessments and forecasting for emerging technologies. Gary is the author of *The Mobile Learning Edge* and the co-author of *Training and Collaboration with Virtual Worlds*. He also presents at conferences and is the author of numerous articles and research reports on emerging learning technologies. Gary holds a doctor of education degree from the University of Toronto.

ABOUT THE CONTRIBUTORS

Adam Bockler is Float's communications manager. In that role, he develops and implements Float's communication strategy through event planning, writing, and editing Float's blog articles and research publications, engaging audiences through email and social media, and attracting and nurturing leads through inbound marketing. Adam also owns and operates Metamora Martial Arts.

Jim Ferolo is the director of user experience and user interface design at Float. Jim has more than twenty years of experience designing and developing interactive products and services and drives the design methodology and usability testing processes for Float. He is a full professor and chair of the Department of Interactive Media at Bradley University.

John Feser is the COO and a founding member of Float. Before helping to form Float, John worked for Andersen Consulting and Accenture, helping Fortune 500 clients to deliver value and change for their employees and customers. His focus has been on learning, with an emphasis on how the right learning improves employee performance.

Heather Ford is the lead designer at Float. She has worked with industry-leading companies to create customized mobile solutions. Heather designs mobile applications, along with marketing collateral for workshops and strategy sessions. She focuses on user experience and interface design and is the designer for many of Float's award-winning applications.

Scott McCormick is Float's director of client relations and a founding member of Float. Scott has more than three decades in training, e-learning and mlearning efforts for Fortune 500 companies. He regularly speaks on the critical strategies and the steps organizations must take when integrating mobile learning into their complete learning programs.

Daniel Pfeiffer is the lead developer at Float. He has a wealth of experience in developing mobile applications for a variety of platforms. He works with Float's clients to develop custom applications and security solutions to ensure these applications and their data are kept in the right hands. His expertise in data design has continued to allow him to build creative and robust solutions for client organizations globally.

About the Association for Talent Development

The Association for Talent Development (ATD), formerly the American Society for Training & Development (ASTD), is the world's largest professional association dedicated to the training and development field. In more than 100 countries, members work in organizations of all sizes, in the private and public sectors, as independent consultants, and as suppliers. Members connect locally in 130 U.S. chapters and with 30 international partners.

ASTD started in 1943 and in recent years has widened the profession's focus to align learning and performance to organizational results and is a sought-after voice on critical public policy issues. For more information, visit www.astd.org.

INDEX

Page references followed by *t* indicate a table.